ELLs IN TEXAS

WHAT **ADMINISTRATORS** NEED TO KNOW

John Seidlitz
Melinda Base
Mónica Lara

with contributions by
MARIELA RODRÍGUEZ

edited by Marguerite Hartill

Published by Seidlitz Education
56 Via Regalo
San Clemente, CA 92673
wwwseidlitzeducation.com

For related titles and support materials visit www.seidlitzeducation.com.

1.14

Table of Contents

Introduction

Why should administrators use this book?

Administrators come to positions of leadership from a myriad of backgrounds and experiences. Some may have extensive knowledge of second language learners and second language acquisition while others may not be well-versed at all in these topics. In any case, there are two truths about campus administrators: first, their time for processing information and learning is limited by the massive amount of email and phone/personal communications they handle every day (inter-campus, intra-campus, intra-district, from parents and community members); and second, there is a constant need to keep abreast of recent developments in education and the law. Working with these time constraints and with the need to know, administrators need a convenient and accessible resource that integrates the voluminous amounts of information in their binders, books, and manuals into one easy to read resource. *ELLs in Texas: What Administrators Need to Know* responds to this need with an understanding of the overwhelming tasks required of administrators on a daily basis.

★ This book IS...	★ This book is NOT...
• a comprehensible resource with explanations of current policy and law.	• offered as professional legal advice.
• a source for information and guidance related to Texas state law for ELLs.	• intended to replace current policy and law.
• a convenient and efficient resource for administrators at all levels of experience.	• a substitute for guidance documents produced by the Texas Education Agency (TEA). *
• a collection of current and relevant statutes, codes, and guidance for leading programs that support ELLs.	

**Note:* The authors of this book are not attorneys or legal scholars. They are ELL experts who saw a need for this resource and wrote it accordingly. If there is an error in the explanation of policy, law, or state guidance, it is accidental and not intended to undermine any existing policy, law, or state guidance.*

Who sets the education laws for ELLs in Texas?

Aside from federal statutes, the Texas Education Code (TEC) sets the state laws that govern public schools in Texas. The Texas Administrative Code (TAC) provides clarification and details regarding implementation of those laws. The language of the law can sometimes be complicated, and over the years, many questions about the laws have been asked by administrators. No matter the school district/campus, the same questions seem to surface time and again. In this book, *ELLs in Texas: What Administrators Need to Know*, there is a collection of questions asked by concerned administrators who want to interpret and apply Texas school laws accurately for their ELL students. The questions are answered in a straight-forward manner to help administrators comply with the laws set forth by the TEC.

What are the ELL statistics in the state of Texas?

The English language learner population in Texas is growing, and ELLs are increasingly represented in the state accountability system and system safeguards. According to the Public Education Information Management System (PEIMS) Snapshot data for Spring 2012 - Fall 2013, the ELL enrollment in Texas shows the following statistics:

- The total number of ELL students was 864,769. This is an increase of 27,000 ELL students when compared to figures from the previous school year.
- The total number of students in bilingual programs was 487,896. This is an increase of 10,500 students compared to figures from the previous school year.
- The total number of students in ESL programs was 328,879. This is an increase of 15,000 students compared to figures from the previous school year.

In addition, there are more than 120 languages represented in the state of Texas, and they include:

- Spanish • Vietnamese • Arabic • Urdu • Mandarin

As the ELL population in Texas continues to grow, Texas school laws for ELL education has increased and changed. This means that administrators are faced with interpreting the laws that regulate school operations for ELL students, and the laws can be difficult to understand. Consequently, administrators need to understand and interpret the law with confidence and assurance because no matter what, they cannot afford to be wrong.

Introduction, cont.

How do administrators use this book?

ELLs in Texas: What Administrators Need to Know was written to provide information and access to the statutes, guidance, and policies that set the legal climate for ELL education in Texas.

The book is divided into two sections. The first part is divided into chapters that identify key areas of information, e.g. Programs, Systems and Processes, Compliance, Curriculum and Instruction, Assessment, and Accountability. Each chapter is further divided into topics that relate to the chapter title. For example, in the chapter titled Assessments, the topics are STAAR/EOC (State of Texas Assessment of Academic Readiness/End-of-Course) and TELPAS (Texas English Language Proficiency Assessment System). For those topics, there is an overview that gives:

- a brief description of the topic.
- a list of the statutes and codes that are the law (Legal Lineage).
- a list titled Need to Know and a list titled Need to Do. (or…JEI – Just Enough Information).
- a list of the questions to be answered in the topic section.
- a list of resources with more information (or …FMI – For More Information).

The second part of the book is a collection of the actual statutes that govern ELL education in Texas. For instance, when reading about a topic and its Legal Lineage, references to the Texas Education Code, Texas Administrative Code, or Title III-Part A of the federal law will be made. The actual language of the law can be found at the back of the book. The reason it is made available is for convenience. Often, the local Board of Trustees or the superintendent will ask for an explanation about certain actions an administrator has taken, and he/she is expected to cite AND explain the relevant statute. This part of the book will assist campus/district administrators in meeting this expectation quickly and easily.

Are you going to create a new edition each year?

This book will be updated regularly to reflect changes in Texas law and guidance from TEA regarding bilingual/ESL program services.

A companion book, *ELLs in Texas – What Teachers Need to Know* will be published in the spring of 2014. It is our hope that administrators and teachers will be able to work together with these resources to transform the services provided to second language learners in Texas.

ELL PROGRAMS

Establishment of Programs

In Texas, two programs for English language learners have been defined and established: Bilingual and ESL. There are four bilingual and two ESL models.

LEGAL LINEAGE

- TEC, Title 2, Subtitle F, Chapter 4, Sec. 4.002
- TEC Title 2, Subtitle F, Chapter 29, Subchapter B, Sec. 29.051; Sec. 29.053
- TAC Title 19, Part II, Chapter 89, Subchapter BB, §89.1201

JUST ENOUGH INFORMATION

★ Need to Know

- The bilingual models: Transitional Bilingual Early Exit, Transitional Bilingual Late Exit, Dual Language Immersion One-Way, Dual Language Immersion Two-Way
- ESL models: Content-Based, Pull-Out
- When a bilingual program is required
- Local demographics of ELLs
- Program models currently in effect in the district/on the campus

★ Need to Do

- Select and implement a bilingual or ESL model
- Find appropriately certified teachers for ELLs
- Ensure the delivery of appropriate instruction based on program model selection

QUESTIONS

1. What do administrators need to know about bilingual and ESL programs?
2. How do administrators select an appropriate second language program model?

FOR MORE INFORMATION (FMI)

- Bilingual/ESL Programs in Texas – TEA Texas English Language Learners Portal
- Ong. F. (Ed.). (2010). *Improving education for English learners: Research-based approaches* (pp. 251-321). Sacramento, CA: Department of Education.
- Thomas, W.P., & Collier, V.P. (2012). *Dual language education for a transformed world.* Albuquerque, NM: Fuente Press.

What do administrators need to know about bilingual and ESL programs?

There are two types of bilingual and ESL programs with the following goals:

- the acquisition of English via the use of sheltered practices (ESL)
- the acquisition of English using the student's native language as well as English (bilingual)

The goals of both programs include the academic success of students as measured through annual state assessments. ESL programs use English as the language of instruction, while bilingual programs use both English and the student's native language during instruction.

In Texas, there are two approved program models for ESL programming: ESL Pull-Out and ESL Content-Based. There are four approved bilingual program models: Transitional Bilingual Early Exit, Transitional Bilingual Late Exit, Dual Language One-Way, and Dual Language Two-Way.

A district must provide a bilingual program for ELLs when twenty or more ELLs in the same grade – district-wide – speak the same native language. The bilingual program is provided in the native language in pre-K through grade 5. Grade 6 is included when that grade is clustered with elementary grades.

For all other ELLs, the district is required to provide an ESL program. It is possible for a campus or a district to operate more than one bilingual/ESL program.

ESL Pull-out (PO)

- Can be delivered in a separate setting or within the general education setting.
- An ESL-certified teacher provides English language arts instruction.
- Exit typically occurs between two and five years after enrollment.
- In high school, ELLs receive sheltered instruction in all content areas.

ESL Content-Based (CB)

- Program services are provided in content area classrooms where English is developed through sheltered content area instruction.
- K-grade 8: Content area instruction is provided by ESL-certified teachers.
- In high school, ELLs receive sheltered instruction in all content areas.

Transition Bilingual Early Exit (EE)

- Instruction in literacy and academic content areas is provided in ELLs' first language.
- Development of oral and academic English is provided.
- Over time, ELLs transfer to all-English instruction.
- Exit typically occurs between two and five years after enrollment.

Transition Bilingual Late Exit (LE)

- Using both the ELL's first language and English, cognitively challenging academic work is provided.
- High levels of academic achievement and full proficiency in both languages are promoted.
- Over time, ELLs transfer to all-English instruction.
- Exit occurs no earlier than six and no later than seven years after enrollment.

Establishment of Programs

Dual Language Immersion One-Way (DL1W)

- A biliteracy model for ELLs integrates language learning with content instruction.
- Academic subjects are taught in both languages.
- Full bilingualism, biliteracy, and cross-cultural awareness are emphasized.
- Over time, ELLs transfer to all-English instruction.
- Exit occurs no earlier than six years and no later than seven years after enrollment.

Dual Language Immersion Two-Way (DL2W)

- A bilteracy model for ELLs and English dominant students integrates language learning with content instruction. Academic subjects are taught in both languages.
- Full bilingualism, biliteracy, and cross-cultural awareness are emphasized.
- Over time, ELLs transfer to all-English instruction.
- Exit occurs no earlier that six years and no later than seven years after enrollment.

How do administrators select an appropriate second language program model?

It is important for administrators to check with their school district leaders to envision the future of district bilingual/ESL program models. There may/may not be a local policy about programs offered on district campuses. If not, it is important to work with district personnel to identify program models to best serve district ELLs.

Knowing the history of bilingual/ESL programs in district and on campus provides administrators with an understanding of how current programming was developed. Gathering stakeholders, i.e., community members, parents, district/campus leaders, teachers, and even students together to discuss the history of the program and to envision future directions for bilingual/ESL programs supports and enhances the decision-making process.

When making a decision about which of the four program models to implement, it is important to keep in mind that community support for the program model is essential. Many times, superintendents/district leaders identify bilingualism in district mission statements as a goal for all students. As a result, program models are selected because the community expresses a desire to provide enrichment language programs.

Administrators must consider student language needs to ascertain the best ways to meet those needs. For example, it is necessary to:

- review teaching certifications, expertise, and experience of all teachers on campus.
- include a professional development plan focused on the program model selected
- consider resource allocations for program books and materials.

Program Models

Program models refer to specific frameworks for using the student's language (L1) and the target language (L2) while delivering standards-based instruction.

LEGAL LINEAGE

- TEC, Title 2, Subtitle F, Chapter 28, Subchapter A, Sec. 28.0051
- TEC, Title 2, Subtitle F, Chapter 29, Subchapter B, Sec. 29.055;
- TAC Title 19, Part II, Chapter 89, Subchapter BB, §89.1201 (d); §89.1210(b),(d),(e),(g)

JUST ENOUGH INFORMATION

★ Need to Know

- The specific program model used in the district (Bilingual: EE, LE, DL1W, DL2W; ESL: PO; CB)
- The rationale for the selection and/or continued use of the program

★ Need to Do

- Provide services as described in the law
- Meet cognitive, linguistic, and affective needs of ELLs
- Ensure that TEKS and ELPS are the foundations of instruction within the program model

QUESTIONS

1. What is the difference between an early-exit bilingual program model and a late exit program model?
2. Why might ELLs need an ESL class in addition to a language arts class for English language learners?
3. What is the difference between one-way and two-way dual language programs?
4. How do dual language program models differ from transitional bilingual program models?
5. What are the specific characteristics of a dual language approach?

FOR MORE INFORMATION (FMI)

- Bilingual/ESL Programs in Texas – TEA Texas English Language Learners Portal
- Ong. F. (Ed.). (2010). *Improving education for English learners: Research-based approaches* (pp. 251-321). Sacramento, CA: California Department of Education.
- Saunders, W., Goldenberg, C., & Marcelletti, D. (2013). English language development: Guidelines for instruction. *American Educator,* Summer 2013, 13-25.
- Thomas, W.P., & Collier, V.P. (2012). *Dual language education for a transformed world.* Albuquerque, NM: Fuente Press.

Program Models

What is the difference between an early exit bilingual program model and a late exit program model?

Early exit models are those in which ELLs receive bilingual instruction for 1-3 years. In this model, ELLs build initial literacy and basic academic content in their first language. During instruction, teachers use the English Language Proficiency Standards (ELPS) to develop English oral and academic language. Transition to instruction in English is accomplished rapidly, usually by the end of third grade.

Late exit models are those in which ELLs receive bilingual instruction for 1-5 years. ELLs build both literacy and academic skills through rigorous instruction in both their native language and English. Teachers use the ELPS to develop proficiency in listening, speaking, reading, and writing in English. Transition to all-English instruction is gradual and is usually accomplished by the end of the elementary grades.

Not every ELL begins school in Texas as a kindergarten student; some students arrive in later grades. To accommodate the needs of new arrivals, teachers need to differentiate instruction. As these students transfer to secondary schools, they may be in need of continuing program services. In that case, they will be served through either an ESL or bilingual program if the district has extended these programs beyond the required grades.

Why might ELLs need an ESL class in addition to a language arts class for English language learners?

When an ELL arrives in school with large gaps in schooling, a lack of literacy development in a native language, or little to no English language proficiency, the Language Proficiency Assessment Committee (LPAC) may determine that the student needs additional time with an ESL-certified teacher to address particular needs. ELLs, identified as non-English speaking or very limited English speaking, benefit from intensive, focused instruction in the foundations of the English language.

At the elementary level, where ELLs may be in a self-contained classroom, the ESL-certified teacher may be able to adequately differentiate individual needs with various grouping strategies. In departmentalized settings, it becomes more of a challenge to provide the initial language development support in content area classrooms. Some campuses may provide additional time for the student with an ESL-certified teacher or specialist to ensure that they acquire the English proficiency and vocabulary skills they need for grade level instruction.

ESL classes that are elective classes are commonplace in secondary settings in Texas. Sometimes districts/campuses create sections of reading improvement or writing classes composed entirely of ELLs. In these classes, ELLs have additional time provided for intensive instruction in the foundations of the English language.

Administrators often struggle with how to place the English language learner, i.e., a sheltered English language arts class, a separate class for English language development (ESL/ESOL), or some combination of the two. The best current research indicates that English language learners do benefit from instruction specifically designed for second-language learners focused on English language development (Saunders, Goldenberg, & Marcelletti, 2013). Therefore, in addition to sheltered instruction, some English language learners, especially those at early levels of proficiency, would perform better if they had ESL instruction in addition to enrollment in sheltered courses. Administrators should be aware that chapter 74.4 subsection b(4) states that, "ELLs in grade 3 or higher who are at the beginning or intermediate level of English language proficiency…require focused, targeted, and systematic second language acquisition instruction." This instruction must include a "foundation of English language vocabulary, grammar, syntax, and English mechanics necessary to support content-based instruction and accelerated learning of English." It is very difficult for teachers in heterogeneous sheltered classes to provide this kind of instruction for English language learners.

The primary goal of sheltered content instruction is not English language development. Instead, it is to make content comprehensible while students are developing English language proficiency. In an ESL class, the focus is on English language development in both social and academic language. Students in ESL classes may understand content, but may not have opportunities to receive instruction in English grammar.

What is the difference between one-way and two-way dual language programs?

One-way dual language programs are composed of students who speak one primary language, i.e. Spanish speakers.

Two-way dual language programs are comprised of students who speak at least two languages, i.e. Spanish speakers and English speakers.

How do dual language program models differ from transitional bilingual program models?

Dual language programs are models of bilingual education that strive to maintain the native language of the student who is acquiring a second language. The goals of dual language program models (one-way and two-way) are to develop full biliteracy and bilingualism while developing appreciation for both cultures.

The instructional goals of transitional bilingual education programs include the development of proficiency in English and academic success as measured by the annual state assessments and other evidence, such as teacher-subjective evaluations. Transitional bilingual programs (both early exit and late exit) do not include the goal of maintaining the native language of the student.

What are the specific characteristics of a dual language approach?

Dual language instruction is an effective method of language learning with instruction that promotes bilingualism and biliteracy in two languages, i.e., Spanish and English. Students receive instruction in both languages beginning with a kindergarten cohort through fifth grade. Some districts have chosen to extend dual language program models into middle and high school.

Program Goals

Program goals are specific student outcomes for mastery of academic content and language development.

LEGAL LINEAGE

- Elementary and Secondary Education Act of 1965, Title III, Part A, Sec. 3102; Subpart 1, Sec. 3115 (a)(1-4)
- TEC, Title 2, Subtitle F, Chapter 29, Subchapter B, Sec. 29.051
- TAC Title 19, Part II, Chapter 89, Subchapter BB, §89.1201 (b) (c) and §89.1210 (d)(1-4), (e)

JUST ENOUGH INFORMATION

★ Need to Know

- Local demographics
- Program outcomes
- The process of second language acquisition/English language development
- The benefits of bilingualism

★ Need to Do

- Ensure that program goals are reflected in district and campus mission statements
- Ensure that the ESL and bilingual program goals are included in the district/campus improvement plans

QUESTIONS

1. What are the goals of ESL programs?
2. What are the goals of bilingual programs?
3. How are the goals for dual language program models different from transitional bilingual program models?

FOR MORE INFORMATION (FMI)

- Alford, B., & Niño, M.C. (2011). *Leading academic achievement for English language learners.* Thousand Oaks, CA: Corwin.
- Escamilla, K., Butvilofsky, S., Hopewell, S., Sparrow, W., Ruiz-Figueroa, O., Soltero-González, L., & Hernández, J. M. P. A. (2013). *Literacy squared® phase II: Colorado case study technical report year three, 2011-2012.* University of Colorado, Boulder: BUENO Center for Multicultural Education.
- *Guiding Principles for Dual Language Education* – Center for Applied Linguistics website
- Hamayan, E., & Field, R. (2012). *English language learners at school: A guide for administrators.* Philadelphia, PA: Caslon Publishing.
- Secretaría de Educación Pública (SEP). (2008). *El enfoque intercultural en educación: Orientación para maestros de primaria.* Coordinación General de Educación Intercultural y Bilingüe. México, D.F.: Secretaría de Educación Pública.

What are the goals of ESL programs? [§89.1201 (c)]

- ELLs will become competent in listening, speaking, reading, and writing in English through the integrated use of second language methods.
- ELLs will be academically successful.
- ELLs will participate equitably in school.

What are the goals of bilingual programs? [§89.1201 (b)]

- ELLs will become competent in listening, speaking, reading, and writing in English through the development of literacy and academic skills in the primary language and English.
- ELLs will be academically successful.
- ELLs will participate equitably in school.

How are the goals for dual language program models different from transitional bilingual program models? [§89.1210 (d) (3-4)]

All four bilingual program models share the same program goals. However, dual language program models have these additional goals:

- Develop fluency and literacy in English and another language for all students, with special attention given to English language learners participating in the program.
- Integrate English speakers and English language learners for academic instruction, in accordance with the program design and model selected by the school district board of trustees. Whenever possible, 50% of students in a program should be dominant English speakers and 50% of students should be native speakers of another language at the beginning of the program.
- Promote bilingualism, biliteracy, cross-cultural awareness, and high academic achievement.

Program Monitoring and Evaluation

To ensure an effective and successful program, administrators should monitor and evaluate the implementation and the impact of program services.

LEGAL LINEAGE

- Elementary and Secondary Education Act of 1965, Title I, Part A , Sec. 1112 (g)(1-5)
- Elementary and Secondary Education Act of 1965, Title III, Part A , Subpart 1, Sec. 1116 (c)
- Elementary and Secondary Education Act of 1965, Title III, Part A , Subpart 2, Sec. 3121
- Elementary and Secondary Education Act of 1965, Title III, Part B, Subpart 5, Sec. 3253
- TEC, Title 2, Subtitle F, Chapter 7, Subchapter A, Sec. 7.028 (b)
- TEC, Title 2, Subtitle F, Chapter 29, Subchapter B, Sec. 29.062
- *TEC, Title 2, Subtitle F, Chapter 39, Subchapter B, Sec. 39.0545 (added by HB5)*
- TEC, Title 2, Subtitle F, Chapter 39, Subchapter E
- TAC Title 19, Part II, Chapter 89, Subchapter BB, §89.1265, §89.1267

JUST ENOUGH INFORMATION

★ Need to Know

- Which languages are used/should be used and to what extent within a given program model
- Essential components of bilingual/ESL instruction
- Longitudinal data of ELLs, i.e., academic performance and English language acquisition

★ Need to Do

- Monitor the implementation of instructional accommodations for English language learners
- Strategically disaggregate ELL data for various purposes
- Facilitate teacher awareness of the relationship between ELPS, PLDs, and TELPAS

QUESTIONS

1. How do administrators monitor ELL program implementation?
2. How do administrators evaluate ELL programs for effectiveness?
3. How do administrators monitor instructional and assessment accommodations for ELLs?
4. How do administrators monitor English language development and ensure that ELLs are making appropriate progress in English language acquisition?
5. How will the district meet the requirement to evaluate second language programs in House Bill 5 (HB5)?

FOR MORE INFORMATION (FMI)

- Division of Program Monitoring and Interventions – TEA webpage
- Educator Guide to TELPAS – TELPAS Resources webpage at TEA
- Integrated Intervention Guidance and Resources – TEA webpage
- HB5
- Performance-Based Monitoring – TEA webpage
- Performance-Based Monitoring Manual – Performance-Based Monitoring webpage at TEA

How do administrators monitor ELL program implementation?

It is important to observe classroom instruction on a regular basis to ensure that teachers are meeting the affective, linguistic, and cognitive needs of ELLs. In addition, it is important and beneficial to meet with teachers periodically to discuss the:

- classroom climate and learning environment.
- strengths and/or concerns about instruction.
- ways an administrator can be helpful to the teacher and to students.

Administrators should use the data collected during classroom observations to revise and update the campus/district improvement plans for next year. A sample chart can be found on page 268.

How do administrators evaluate ELL programs for effectiveness?

The board of trustees for each district/school is responsible for ensuring compliance with all state educational program requirements. If noncompliance is discovered within a program, the board must be informed, and they must discuss and act upon the issue/s [TEC Sec. 7.028 (b)].

The Texas Administrative Code, Chapter 89, §89.1265 describes annual evaluation activities for bilingual/ESL programs to meet this requirement. To begin, campus administrators must have student-level data for each ELL, i.e., the level of academic success and progress towards acquiring English language proficiency that determines exit levels from program services. Progress and program exit data must be described. Progress refers to the number of students who advance at least one level every year in the TELPAS composite rating; the progress data can be accessed from STAAR and TELPAS reports. The exit data can be accessed from the LPAC records and PEIMS reports.

In addition, administrators need to know the kinds of professional development district ELL teachers have received and the impact of that training. To describe the impact, administrators need to monitor instruction for ELLs consistently to ascertain that teachers are using appropriate sheltered instruction practices and that ELLs are speaking and writing in English class during instruction.

Finally, administrators need to document appropriate certification for all teachers of ELLs; teachers must be certified for their teaching assignment in the bilingual/ESL program/s.

In order to determine the effectiveness of the program models implemented on campus, administrators need to conduct an evaluation of the programs as described above. A determination of the effectiveness of each program can be made by analyzing the data described and by examining anecdotal evidence, such as surveys and feedback from stakeholders, i.e., teachers, students, and parents. These informal sources of information can also be very valuable when evaluating the success of programs in place on campus.

Program Monitoring and Evalution

How do administrators monitor instructional and assessment accommodations for ELLs?

Instructional and assessment accommodations for ELLs can be measured by supervising instruction and by participation in the LPAC meetings. Formal and informal classroom visits should focus on both instructional accommodations and assessment accommodations. In the simplest terms, upon entering an ELL classroom, students should be actively engaged in learning and interacting with their peers (both linguistic peers and native English speakers). Accommodations that are common to sheltered instruction practices should be observed. See sample walk-through forms on pages 269-272.

The LPAC determines what, if any, assessment accommodations are needed for the ELL to access the language of the STAAR and EOC tests. The LPAC Decision-Making materials on the TEA website identify acceptable accommodations for ELLs. In addition, ELLs are eligible for all general testing accommodations available to all students. For ELLs with a disability, Admission, Review, Dismissal (ARD) and the LPAC together determine what, if any, accommodations are appropriate – based upon the student's particular disability.

For classroom-based and benchmark assessments, ELLs should test with the accommodations they will be using during STAAR/EOC testing, if possible. Also, accommodations that are in addition to those for state assessments may be used if the teacher feels they will enable the student to fully demonstrate mastery of learning. Administrators should be aware of these accommodations to be sure that all ELLs are receiving the assessment accommodations they need.

How do administrators monitor English language development and ensure that ELLs are making appropriate progress in English language acquisition?

Monitoring English language development is similar in many ways to monitoring content area knowledge and skill development. Begin with an accurate assessment of the knowledge and skills of ELLs based upon the TELPAS rubrics or on the results of an Oral Language Proficiency Test (OLPT).

After establishing ELL proficiency levels, establish checkpoints throughout the year to re-assess students. These checkpoints show the levels of progress made in English language proficiency. In addition, teachers can monitor the levels of comprehension in both instruction and oral interaction of ELLs in social settings and cooperative groups. This data will inform the TELPAS rater when it comes time to assign a rating for Listening and Speaking.

Following each checkpoint, teachers can review the assessments to adjust instruction that provides language practice opportunities and comprehensible input appropriate to ELL proficiency levels. The instruction adjustments are reflected in lesson plans that include language practice opportunities. The language of the lesson plan includes stems aligned to proficiency levels and reading passages that help ELLs attain higher levels of proficiency. In addition, administrators must endeavor to ensure sufficient opportunities for free voluntary reading for ELLs, as they have demonstrated value in developing fluency.

How will the district meet the requirements to evaluate second language programs in House Bill 5 (HB5)?

With the final passage of HB5, Section 39.0545 is added to Chapter 39 of the Texas Education Code. This section requires the district to engage in:

- the evaluation of district and campus programs.
- compliance with statutory reporting and policy requirements.

Among other programs, second language programs are included in this new statute.

Using criteria developed by a local committee, each district will evaluate the performance and compliance for each program listed in the new statute, including second language programs. Before August 8th of each year, the district will report to the TEA a performance rating assigned using the locally developed criteria.

Ratings include:

- Exemplary
- Recognized
- Acceptable
- Unacceptable

When evaluating second language programs, district and campus administrators can examine the following performance and compliance indicators:

- Annual Measurable Achievement Objectives (AMAOs)
- Performance-Based Monitoring Analysis System (PBMAS)
- STAAR and TELPAS achievement data
- Compliance with program requirements under Chapter 89
- Teacher certification
- Required training (LPAC Framework, LPAC Decision-Making for State Assessments, TELPAS Rater Training)
- Implementation of ELPS
- Implementation of Sheltered Instruction
- Inclusion of ELLs in strategic and significant ways in Campus and District Improvement Plans
- Compliance with LPAC Framework

SYSTEMS & PROCESSES

Enrollment and Registration

Administrators should be aware of best practices related to the initial enrollment and registration systems and processes for English language learners.

LEGAL LINEAGE

- TEC, Title 2, Subtitle F, Chapter 29, Subchapter B, Sec. 29.056, Sec. 29.0561; Sec. 29.058
- TAC Title 19, Part II, Chapter 89, Subchapter BB, §89.1215; §89.1220 (g), (j); §89.1225 (f)

JUST ENOUGH INFORMATION

★ Need to Know

- Home Language Survey (HLS)
- Identification requirements for English language learners
- Timeline for completion of identification for English language learners

★ Need to Do

- Ensure that every student record has one HLS
- Ensure that tests for identification, placement, and exit are current (see *List of Approved Tests for Assessment of Limited English Proficient Students*) and sufficient in number to meet campus needs
- Ensure that required identification activities for the LPAC are concluded within the first 20 days of student enrollment
- Ensure that necessary staff are included in the enrollment process

QUESTIONS

1. What is the Home Language Survey (HLS), and how is it important to the initial identification of ELLs?
2. What school staff should be included in the enrollment/registration process for ELLs?
3. What should the enrollment/registration process look like for ELLs?
4. What options do administrators and school staff have when scheduling classes for ELLs?

FOR MORE INFORMATION (FMI)

- 2013 – 2014 *Student Attendance Accounting Handbook* (SAAH), Sec. 6.3, Sec. 6.11.1 – TEA webpage

What is the Home Language Survey (HLS), and how is it important to the initial identification of ELLs?

The Home Language Survey (HLS) is a document that every new student receives upon entering a school district. This document needs to be signed by the parent/guardian in grades K-8 or by the student in grades 9-12. The original copy of the survey must remain on file.

Districts must provide the HLS to the parent/guardian in their home language. This survey has two questions:

(1) What language is spoken in your home most of the time?

(2) What language does your child speak most of the time?

When the response to the survey is a language other than English, the student must be tested and the LPAC committee must:

- classify the student as ELL/non-ELL.
- place student in a bilingual, ESL, or general education program.

Which school staff should be included in the enrollment/registration process for ELLs?

Members of the school staff that may be involved in the enrollment and registration process include:

- Administrator
- Counselor
- Bilingual/ESL teacher
- Staff member who will conduct initial assessments for identification as ELL
- Nurse

What does the enrollment/registration process for ELLs look like?

Administrators are responsible for establishing policies and procedures for registration and enrollment on campuses. When enrolling ELLs, there are required activities that are part of the identification process outlined in TAC Chapter 89, §89.1215 and §89.1220.

It is important that the screening tests for identification be administered as quickly as possible to ensure proper scheduling of classes for the student pending the outcome of the initial LPAC meeting. Several staff members come in contact with students and their parents/guardians during these processes, and each campus should have staff members who can speak the language of the bilingual programs. To the greatest extent possible, all registration materials should be available in English and the language of the bilingual programs. If another language is used by the parents/guardians or student, all efforts should be made to attain an interpreter to assist them in the enrollment and registration process. This function is often filled by someone at the district office. Sometimes the parents/guardians will bring a friend to act as interpreter, and this is a welcome support.

If the parents/guardians indicate a language other than English on the HLS during the enrollment process, the person responsible for initiating the identification process should be notified. It may be that a staff member will cover a teacher's class so s/he can meet with the parents/guardians and student for a brief meeting. During this meeting, the teacher can answer any questions they might have about the enrollment process. They can also offer their contact information to parents/guardians to reassure support during the student's first few days of school.

The family may need assistance locating a clinic in order to secure the proper vaccinations and records to complete the enrollment process. A staff member who may fulfill this role in the initial enrollment process for ELLs is the school nurse. However, this function may be offered at an off-campus location.

What are the scheduling options for ELL classes?

Pending results of the initial LPAC meeting, students whose parents/guardians have indicated a language other than English on the HLS and who have scored Limited English Proficient on either the Oral Language Proficiency Test (OLPT) in grades pre-K through 12 or who have scored below the fortieth percentile on a state-approved standardized achievement test (grade 2 and above) may be placed in the appropriate bilingual or ESL classroom.

Apart from certification requirements, the counselor should work with the lead bilingual or ESL teacher to identify teachers who are effective with ELLs in order to make the best possible placement decisions for newly-enrolled ELLs. Whenever possible, avoid placing beginner and intermediate ELLs with teachers who are also responsible for significant numbers of students with disabilities. The needs of ELLs are quite distinct and should not be confused with the needs of students receiving special education services.

Equally important, is the review of any transcripts the student may have brought. In the absence of transcripts, an interview with the parents can offer information about any other services their child may have been receiving in a previous educational setting. If a student participated in advanced academics, it is important to schedule them accordingly.

In elementary schools providing bilingual programming, the student is placed with a bilingual-certified teacher for his/her grade level. Spanish is the language of most of the bilingual programs in Texas; however, there are districts providing bilingual programs in other languages. If an ELL does not speak the language of the bilingual program in the district, they will be served through an ESL program.

For students enrolling in a school that only provides ESL programming, the student is placed with an ESL-certified teacher. Depending on the program model (ESL, Pull-Out, or ESL Content-Based), other scheduling decisions are made. If the grade level provides departmentalized instruction, this will also impact scheduling decisions for an ELL.

In middle school settings, ELLs are placed with teachers according to the certification requirements of the program model in place. In an ESL Pull-Out model, the ELL must be placed with at least one ESL-certified teacher who will be responsible for providing language arts instruction using second language approaches. All other teachers will provide sheltered instruction support in classes with ELLs. In an ESL Content-Based model, all content area teachers must be ESL-certified. Other teachers of ELLs can use sheltered instruction approaches to support the ELLs in their classes.

In high school, ELLs may be served through a combination of supports identified by the LPAC as outlined in TAC Chapter 89, §89.1210. All teachers of ELLs at the high school level must provide sheltered instruction to ELLs.

At all secondary levels, additional class periods of ESL or English Language Development (commonly referred to as ELD) may be scheduled for ELLs at the Beginning or Intermediate levels of English language proficiency in order to accelerate their acquisition of the English language.

The state of Texas also recognizes some innovative courses for ELLs, and these can be found on the Innovative Courses webpage at TEA. These courses carry state credits. Local courses for local credit may also be developed to meet the specific needs of ELLs. In some cases, Newcomer Programs make extensive use of these courses when designing a schedule for recent immigrant arrivals.

Funding

There are both federal and state funding sources for the establishment and support of bilingual and ESL programs.

LEGAL LINEAGE

- Elementary and Secondary Education Act of 1965, Title III, Part A, Subpart 1, Sec. 3114, Sec. 3115 (b)(g)
- TEC, Title 2, Subtitle F, Chapter 28, Subchapter B, Sec. 28.0217
- TEC, Title 2, Subtitle F, Chapter 29, Subchapter B, Sec. 29.081(b)(2)
- TEC. Title 2, Subtitle F, Chapter 42, Subchapter A, Sec. 42.001-Sec. 42.003
- TEC, Title 2, Subtitle F, Chapter 42, Subchapter B, Sec. 42.152 (a-d), Sec. 42.153
- TAC Title 19, Part II, Chapter 89, Subchapter BB, §89.1245 (c)

JUST ENOUGH INFORMATION

★ Need to Know

- District personnel responsible for funding allocation related to English language learners
- The order in which funds are to be accessed
- Basic differences between *supplement* and *supplant*

★ Need to Do

- Document expenditures for each funding source
- Ensure that money spent has impact on the academic achievement and English language development of ELLs

QUESTIONS

1. Which students can generate Average Daily Attendance (ADA) for the bilingual/ESL allotment?
2. Which students cannot generate Average Daily Attendance (ADA) for the bilingual/ESL allotment?
3. Can teachers receive salary supplements to teach in a bilingual/ESL program?
4. Which funding sources provide professional development for teachers in bilingual, ESL, or sheltered instruction programs?
5. What funds support parental involvement?
6. What funds can be used for materials and resources for ELLs?
7. What are the rules regarding the use of Title III, Part A funds?

FOR MORE INFORMATION (FMI)

- 2013 – 2014 *Student Attendance Accounting Handbook* (SAAH) – Sec. 6.2, Sec. 6.2.1, Sec. 6.3
- TEA School Transportation Allotment Handbook – TEA website
- Title III, Part A – English Language Acquisition, Language Enhancement, and Academic Achievement Act – TEA webpage
- Title III Guidance Document – on TEA webpage listed above

Which students can generate an Average Daily Attendance (ADA) for the bilingual/ESL allotment?

English language learners participating in the bilingual or ESL programs and enrolled in grades pre-K and up can generate bilingual/ESL ADA allotment. The Parent Permission Code used to note this must be one that generates this specifically. The Parent Permission Codes that DO generate bilingual/ESL ADA include:

A	Parent/guardian has denied placement of a Limited English Proficiency (LEP) student in the required bilingual program, but has approved placement of a LEP student in an ESL program.
B	Parent/guardian has approved placement of a grade pre-K-8 LEP student in the required ESL program.
D	Parent/guardian has approved placement of a LEP student in the bilingual program.
E	Parent/guardian has approved placement of a LEP student in the bilingual program, but the district has or has requested an exception approved under 19 TAC §89.1207; parent has therefore approved placement of a LEP student in an ESL program.
F	Parent/guardian of a grade 9-12 LEP student has approved services in accordance with the LPAC plan. The LPAC plan may include English I for Speakers of Other Languages, English II for Speakers of Other Languages, and/or modified (sheltered) courses for LEP students. Modified (sheltered) courses for LEP students may be taught by non ESL-certified teachers who have received training in modified (sheltered) instruction, but English I for Speakers of Other Languages and English II for Speakers of Other Languages must be taught by ESL-certified teachers.
J	Parent/guardian has approved placement of a LEP student in the ESL program, but the program is an alternative language program approved by the Texas Education Agency [TAC 19.89.1207]. Districts that use Parent Permission Code J have or should have submitted a waiver to the TEA ESL program.

Which students cannot generate Average Daily Attendance (ADA) for the bilingual/ESL allotment?

ELLs whose parents/guardians have denied bilingual or ESL program services for their student cannot generate a bilingual/ESL allotment. In addition, non-ELLs whose parents request placement in a bilingual or ESL classroom cannot generate this allotment. Students below the age of three who are only served in a Preschool Program for Children with Disabilities (PPCD) program cannot generate this allotment. Finally, dominant-English speakers who are participating in a Dual Language Two-Way program model cannot generate this allotment.

Parent Permission Codes that DO NOT generate bilingual/ESL ADA include:

3	Parent/guardian has requested placement of a non-LEP student in the bilingual program
7	Parent/guardian did not respond
8	Parent/guardian was not contacted
C	Parent/guardian has denied placement of a LEP student in any Special Language Program

Funding

G Parent/guardian has approved the placement of a recently exited non-LEP student in a bilingual or English as a Second Language special language program.

H Parent/guardian has requested placement of a non-LEP student in the English as a Second Language program.

Can teachers receive salary supplements to teach in a bilingual/ESL program?

According to TEC Chapter 42, Sec. 42.153 and TAC Chapter 89, §89.1245 (c), teachers may receive salary supplements. Under §89.1245 (d), school districts may compensate teachers and aides assigned to the bilingual or ESL programs for participating in continuing education programs intended to increase their skills or that lead to bilingual or ESL certification.

Which funding sources provide professional development for teachers in bilingual, ESL, or sheltered instruction programs?

Any school under a bilingual exception or an ESL waiver approved by TEA is required to expend a minimum of 10% of the bilingual allotment to fund a training program to improve the skills of the certified teachers assigned to teach the program [TAC §89.1207 (a)(1)(D) and (b)(1)(E)].

The state of Texas may allocate funding for specific training, i.e. General Revenue Riders. The state may also allocate funds to the regional education service centers to provide professional development and technical assistance to district personnel.

At the local level, funding sources include:

- Local funds
- Title I, Part A
- Title I, Part C
- Title II, Part A
- Title III, Part A
- Foundation School Funding
- State Compensatory Education Funds
- State Bilingual/ESL Allotment

Which funds support parental involvement?

Title I funds can be used to support parental involvement activities on campus. Education Service Center, Region 16, along with the TEA, manages the Statewide Title I School Support/Parental Involvement Initiative.

House Bill 5, passed in 2013, includes a requirement stating that districts report annually on student and parental engagement. The TEA is developing some resources that will guide districts in meeting this new requirement.

To meet parental involvement goals, strategies, and activities identified in district and campus improvement plans, local and state funding sources may be used.

Which funds can be used for materials and resources for ELLs?

According to Chapter 89, Subchapter BB, §89.1210 (c)(f), state adopted materials for bilingual and ESL programs, as well as supplemental materials, will be used as curriculum tools. Each district is entitled to an annual Instructional Materials Allotment from the state for each biennium. PEIMS student enrollment data determines the amount of the allotment. This allotment can be used to purchase instructional materials adopted by the State Board of Education or the Commissioner of Education. In addition, the IMA can be used to purchase instructional materials not on the adopted lists as well as technology services and technological equipment.

As an administrator of bilingual/ESL programs, it is important to prioritize these purchases to meet the instructional needs of ELLs in a manner that is equitable and commensurate with their needs and with the level of materials currently available to teachers of ELLs.

What are the rules regarding the use of Title III, Part A funds?

All Title III funds are allocated at the district-level. District leaders decide how to apportion those funds, often in consultation with campus leadership teams.

There are some fundamental rules regarding the use of these federal funds that are helpful for campus administrators to know.

The TEA Title III, Part A web page posts a Title III, Part A Guidance document and Frequently Asked Questions document regarding the allowable use of Title III, Part A funds. Perhaps the most important concept to remember as an administrator is the "supplement, not supplant" rule. This means that funds from Title III, Part A cannot be used in place of local, state, or other federal funds. They cannot fund any program required by state law. These funds can only be used to supplement state-required programs and services. If a program, initiative, or service for ELLs is currently provided through another funding source, it cannot be funded through Title III, Part A funding. A good way to think about it is to ask the question, "But for these funds, would this (program, initiative, activity) be provided?" If the answer is "no," it might be allowable under Title III, Part A, subject to the allowable use of funds requirements. For more information about the specifics related to the required use of Title III, Part A funds and Allowable Use of Title III, Part A funds, see the Title III, Part A Policy Guidance document on the TEA webpage.

Language Proficiency Assessment Committee (LPAC)

The Language Proficiency Assessment Committee (LPAC) is a team of knowledgeable people who meet periodically about English language learners regarding: identification, program placement, instructional needs, assessment, and reclassification.

LEGAL LINEAGE

- Elementary and Secondary Education Act of 1965, Title I, Part A , Sec. 1112 (g)(1-5)
- TEC, Title 2, Subtitle F, Chapter 29, Subchapter B, Sec. 29.056, Sec. 29.063
- TAC Title 19, Part II, Chapter 89, Subchapter BB, §89.1220

JUST ENOUGH INFORMATION

★ Need to Know

- Required membership for the LPAC
- Required meetings for the LPAC
- Required documentation for the LPAC

★ Need to Do

- Build the LPAC
- Secure parent volunteers for the LPAC
- Document decisions for the LPAC
- Maintain documentation of training, confidentiality, and rosters for the LPAC

QUESTIONS

1. What is the Language Proficiency Assessment Committee (LPAC)?
2. What is the best way to ensure that the LPAC operates efficiently and with a high degree of quality?
3. How often should the LPAC meet?
4. Which kinds of documentation are required for the LPAC?
5. What documentation should be maintained in the ELL's record?
6. Which LPAC documentation should be maintained at the campus/district level?

FOR MORE INFORMATION (FMI)

- Language Proficiency Assessment Committee (LPAC) Assessment Resources – TEA webpage
- LPAC Decision-Making Resources – documents located on the TEA webpage listed above
- LPAC Framework – ESC 20 webpage

SYSTEMS & PROCESSES

What is the Language Proficiency Assessment Committee (LPAC)?

The Language Proficiency Assessment Committee (LPAC) is a required entity under state law (TEC Chapter 29, and TAC Chapter 89) and meets for specific purposes as outlined in the law.

There are two areas of Language Proficiency Assessment Committee (LPAC) activities for campus and district leaders to understand and to lead: the LPAC Framework and LPAC Decision-Making.

LPAC Framework

Activity	Statutory Reference	Leadership Implications
Establishment of the LPAC	• TAC §89.1220 (a) • TAC §89.1220 (a) • TAC §89.1220 (e) • TAC §89.1220 (f) • TAC §89.1220 (f)	• Ensure that the LPAC is established and operated by local board policy. • Ensure there are local board policy and procedures for selecting, appointing, and training of members of the LPAC. • Ensure there is an adequate number of LPACs to carry out responsibilities in a timely and effective manner. • Ensure that all members of the LPAC are trained by the school district and understand they are acting for the school district. • Ensure that confidentiality of discussions and actions related to individual students is observed.

Language Proficiency Assessment Committee (LPAC)

LPAC Framework		
Activity	**Statutory Reference**	**Leadership Implications**
Composition of the LPAC	• TEC Sec. 29.063 • TAC §89.1220 (b)(c)(d)	• A campus administrator is a required member of all LPACs, both bilingual and ESL. (Campus Principal or Assistant Principal must be coded as function 23 – as defined by the Financial Accountability System Resource Guide.) • In a bilingual LPAC, a professional transitional language educator must be included. The definition of this term is an ESL-certified teacher or a general education teacher, according to the TEA LPAC Framework Manual PPT on the LPAC Framework webpage housed at ESC, Region 20. • Ensure that the parent representative is not an employee of the district.
Duties of the LPAC	• TAC §89.1210 (a) • TAC §89.1220 (g)	• Ensure that the LPAC: properly identifies ELLs, designates ELL instructional plans and level of academic achievement, facilitates ELL participation in other state and federally funded special programs (when eligible), reclassifies ELLs as non-LEP in PEIMS, and releases them from program services in accordance with the exit criteria.
Monitored Students	• TEC Sec. 29.0561 • TAC §89.1220 (k)	• Ensure that monitoring of recently exited students is ongoing and that LPACs are meeting whenever a monitored student fails any subject in the foundation curriculum during any grading period.

LPAC Framework		
Activity	**Statutory Reference**	**Leadership Implications**
Maintenance of documentation in the student's permanent record	• TAC §89.1220 (l)	• Ensure that the LPAC folders are regularly audited to confirm proper documentation of the LPAC activities and student progress. • When asked, forward the LPAC information of transferring ELLs to receiving districts.
Testing and Classification of Students	• TAC§89.1225 (a-f) • TAC §89.1225 (g) • TAC §89.1225 (h-j) • TAC §89.1225 (k) • TAC §89.1225 (l)	• Ensure the correct tests are administered for identification of students as Limited English Proficient and that personnel giving the test are trained and are proficient in the language of the test. • Ensure the student is identified and enrolled in the appropriate program within 20 school days of initial enrollment in the district. • Ensure that the LPAC follows the procedures for exiting a student from the bilingual or second language program. • Ensure that the LPAC and ARD committees are working in conjunction on behalf of any student who is served by both bilingual or second language programs and special education. • Ensure the tests being used by the LPAC to identify, place, and exit students are on the *List of Approved Tests for Assessment of Limited English Proficient Students* published by the TEA each year.

Language Proficiency Assessment Committee (LPAC)

LPAC Framework		
Activity	**Statutory Reference**	**Leadership Implications**
Parental Authority and Responsibility	• TAC §89.1240 (a) • TAC §89.1240 (b) • TEC Sec. 29.056 (a) • TAC §89.1240 (b)	• Ensure that parents are notified of their child's classification as an ELL and provide them with all relevant program information. • Ensure that parents are notified of the student's reclassification to non-LEP and his/her exit from program services. • Ensure that documentation of parental approval for both program entry and program exit are maintained in the student's permanent record.

LPAC Decision-Making		
Activity	**Statutory Reference**	**Leadership Implications**
Schedule the LPAC meetings to determine appropriate assessments for ELLs.	• TAC §89.1220 (h) • TAC §101.1005 (a)	• Ensure that all members of the LPAC receive training in assessment decision-making using materials distributed by the TEA.
Determine whether STAAR Spanish is the appropriate assessment.	• TAC §101.1005 (b)	• Ensure that the LPAC is properly documenting all testing decisions.
Determine eligibility for participation in STAAR L testing.	• TAC §101.1005 (b)	• Ensure that the LPAC is properly documenting all testing decisions.
Determine eligibility for Special Provisions for English I and English II End of Course (EOC) tests.	• TAC §101.1005 (e)	• Ensure that the LPAC is properly documenting all testing decisions.

LPAC Decision-Making		
Activity	**Statutory Reference**	**Leadership Implications**
Determine eligibility for asylee or refugee provisions.	• TAC §101.1005 (c)(d) • TEC Sec. 39.027 (a-1)	• Ensure that the LPAC is properly documenting all testing decisions.
Document testing decisions for parental denials.	• TAC §101.1005 (f)	• Ensure that the LPAC understands the impact of the denial of required services on testing decisions for ELLs.
Work in conjunction with ARD to make testing decisions for ELLs served by special education.	• TAC §101.1005 (a) (e)	• Ensure that an LPAC member is part of the ARD committee meeting when making decisions about ELLs served by special education. • Support a flow of communication between the LPAC and the ARD committees.
Determine what testing accommodations (linguistic, general, disability-based) are available and appropriate for each ELL.	• TAC §101.1005 (a) (c)	• Ensure that LPAC members have been trained in LPAC Decision-Making using materials distributed by the TEA. • Ensure that all decisions regarding accommodations are properly documented.
Meet all requirements for TELPAS.	• TAC §101.1003 (a) • Federal requirement	• Ensure that all ELLs participate in TELPAS. • Ensure that the LPACs document all TELPAS decisions.
Work with ARD to determine what parts of the TELPAS and what accommodations are required for an ELL receiving special education services.	• TAC §101.1003 (b)(c)	• Ensure that all decisions are documented by the ARD and the LPAC committees.

Language Proficiency Assessment Committee (LPAC)

What is the best way to ensure that the LPAC operates efficiently and with a high degree of quality?

The beliefs that the LPAC meetings are about signatures and completion of forms are outdated. In the current climate of attention to student-level data and student-by-student monitoring of interventions and progress, administrators are responsible for ensuring that LPACs are deliberative bodies that act with high regard for each ELL they discuss.

There are some steps that administrators can take to ensure that LPACs are operating at a high degree of efficiency and effectiveness.

- Ensure there are enough LPACs to complete the work in a timely manner since some of the work done by LPACs must be completed within a specified time frame. For example, the process of identification, placement, and request for parental permission must be completed within the first twenty school days of enrollment. The decisions regarding annual state testing must be made prior to the opening of the testing window. End-of-year LPACs must be completed before the last day of the school year.
- Ensure that administrators and members of LPACs are trained and updated annually regarding the LPAC Framework.
- Ensure that administrators and members of the LPAC are trained annually on state-assessment decision-making.
- Model the level of discourse required to ensure that decisions are thoughtful, relevant to the individual student, and realistic at the LPAC meetings.
- Ensure there is adequate documentation of the LPAC discussion and the suggested TEA forms included in the student's record.

Administrators may serve a dual role in and Admission, Review, Dismissal (ARD) meeting. For example, they may serve as an administrator for both committees as well as serving as the LPAC representative to the ARD committee. If the administrator is also asked to serve as an interpreter in an ARD committee, it will be extremely difficult to adequately fulfill all roles. An administrator might also serve as administrator and interpreter in an LPAC meeting.

How often should the LPAC meet?

LPACs are required to meet:

- for initial identification and placement.
- for the purpose of decision making for annual state testing.
- at the end of the year to review student performance, progress, and placement for the next year.
- at the end of any grading period in which a student – in the two-year monitoring period – fails a class or course in a grading period.
- at any time deemed necessary to meet the needs of individual students.

Which kinds of documentation are required for the LPAC?

LPACs are required to document all actions taken with individual ELL students. The state has provided a set of Suggested Forms which can be accessed on the ESC, 20, LPAC Framework webpage (under L in the A-Z index, select LPAC Framework). In addition, the LPAC should include minutes of discussions and deliberations in each ELL's record. With the requirements to document all the LPAC decisions, it is often helpful if the administrator be a note-taker during the LPAC meetings. In this way, they can fulfill an important function in creating a record of the main point of discussion for each student.

Many of the forms used by LPACs require signatures of the LPAC members. In these cases, the signatures of all required members are necessary for proper documentation of the LPAC activity.

What documentation should be maintained in the ELL's record?

Documentation related to the initial LPAC meeting:

- Home Language Survey (original HLS only)
- Oral Language Proficiency Tests (English and Spanish, if district offers bilingual programs)
- Agency-Approved Norm-Referenced Achievement Tests
- LPAC Initial Placement/Recommendation
- Parent Notification of Placement
- Parent Permission for Placement (signature on letter)
- Parent Denial (if applicable)

Annual Documentation:

- Oral Language Proficiency Tests
- Agency Approved Norm-Reference Achievement Tests
- State Assessment Results
- TELPAS Results
- Letter to the Parents Regarding Student Achievement and Progress in Acquiring English
- Parental Notification of Exit
- Parental Permission for Exit (signature on letter)

Which LPAC documentation should be maintained on the campus/district level?

- Parent responses to the LPAC Parent Membership Request Letter
- LPAC Member Roster
- LPAC Confidentiality Statements
- Certificates of required trainings
- LPAC Meeting Rosters

Summer School

ELLs who are entering kindergarten or first grade are eligible to attend summer school as identified in the law.

LEGAL LINEAGE

- TEC, Title 2, Subtitle F, Chapter 29, Subchapter B, Sec, 29.060
- TAC Title 19, Part II, Chapter 89, Subchapter BB, §89.1250, §89.1265

JUST ENOUGH INFORMATION

★ Have to Know

- Who is eligible for summer school
- Time frame for a summer school program
- Process for enrollment
- Transportation requirements
- Funding sources

★ Need to Do

- Send survey letter
- Staff for number enrolled
- Report on student progress to parents
- Maintain records of eligibility, attendance, and progress

QUESTIONS

1. What do administrators need to know about ELLs and the summer school program?
2. What is the purpose of the required summer school program for ELLs?
3. Which students are eligible to attend the required summer school for ELLs?

FOR MORE INFORMATION (FMI)

- Colorín Colorado - website
- Intercultural Development Research Association (IDRA) - website
- *To the Administrator Addressed* (TAA) letters dated April 10, 2013 and April 19, 2013

What do administrators need to know about summer school programs for ELLs?

Under TEC Chapter 29, Sec. 29.060 and Sec. 29.053, school districts must provide a summer school program to eligible bilingual/ESL students entering grades K-1. The summer school program is not available for students with parental denials.

Each year, TEA posts a *To the Administrator Addressed* letter regarding the summer school program for ELLs. The letter informs districts that funding has been set aside to cover program expenses for eligible students. The letter also serves as a reminder to arrange for staffing, facilities, transportation (if provided by the district), calendars, and instruction.

The letter identifies the amount budgeted per group of 18 students, and the budget fund code is included. The district is required to submit cost data to the state, and accurate recordkeeping is essential. Data from the required ELL summer school program is part of Submission 4 for the 101 Student Demographic Record (aka "snapshot").

TAC Chapter 89, §89.1250 describes the summer school program requirements, data collection requirements, and reporting requirements.

As stated by law, the summer school program:

- is optional.
- is provided for a half-day (minimum 3 hours per day) for 8 weeks or a total of 120 hours.
- cannot count recess or meals as part of the required hours.
- is operated with an 18:1 student-teacher ratio.
- does not require transportation to be provided.

The school district:

- must report student progress to parents and teachers.
- may join other districts to provide the program.
- must not use this program as a substitute for other required programs.
- must use state and local funds and may use federal funds consistent with guidelines for the expenditure of those funds.
- must maintain records of eligibility, attendance, and student progress.

What is the purpose of the summer school program for ELLs?

The goals of the program are to:

- give students a head start on language development.
- provide students with necessary knowledge and skills for success in grades K-1.
- instruct students while meeting their affective, linguistic, and cognitive needs.

Summer School

Which students are eligible to attend the required summer school program for ELLs?

English language learners, eligible for admission into kindergarten and first grade at the beginning of the next school year, may attend the required summer school program. In addition, the parent/guardian must have approved placement of the student in the district bilingual or ESL program as a result of the LPAC determination of limited English proficiency. Limited English proficiency for students at this age is determined through the use of an Oral Language Proficiency Test (OLPT) from the *List of Approved Tests for Assessment of Limited English Proficient Students* published annually by TEA.

COMPLIANCE ★

Accommodations for ELLs

There are two main categories of accommodations for ELLs —those that pertain to instruction and those that pertain to assessment.

LEGAL LINEAGE

Instructional Accommodations:

- Elementary and Secondary Education Act of 1965, Title III, Part A, Sec. 3102; Subpart 1, Sec. 3111 (b)(2)
- TEC, Title 2, Subtitle F, Chapter 29, Subchapter B, Sec. 29.055
- TAC Title 19, Part II, Chapter 89, Subchapter BB, §89.1210 (a)

Assessment Accommodations:

- TEC. Title 2, Subtitle F, Chapter 29, Subchapter B, Sec. 29.063
- TEC, Title 2, Subtitle F, Chapter 39, Subchapter B, Sec. 39.023, Sec. 39.027
- TAC Title 19, Part II, Chapter 74, Subchapter A, §74.4 (b)(2)(3)(4)
- TAC Title 19, Part II, Chapter 89, Subchapter BB, §89.1220 (h)
- TAC Title 19, Part II, Chapter 101, Subchapter AA, §101.1005

JUST ENOUGH INFORMATION

★ Need to Know

- What accommodations are required and what accommodations are optional for ELLs
- How accommodations are determined for each ELL
- How accommodations are documented
- How accommodations are monitored

★ Need to Do

- Participate in the LPAC meetings where accommodations are discussed
- Ensure that instructional and assessment accommodations are identified for each ELL
- Ensure that accommodations for ELLs are documented and monitored

QUESTIONS

1. What are the differences between accommodations for instruction and accommodations for assessment?
2. In a bilingual district, what accommodations are provided for non-Spanish speaking students?
3. Who determines the accommodations provided to ELLs?

FOR MORE INFORMATION (FMI)

- Accommodation Resources - TEA webpage
- Language Proficiency Assessment Committee (LPAC) Assessment Resources - TEA webpage
- Seidlitz, J. (2008a). *Navigating the ELPS: Using the new standards to improve instruction for English learners.* San Clemente, CA: Canter Press.
- Seidlitz, J. (2010). *ELPS flip book: A user-friendly guide for academic language instruction.* San Clemente, CA: Canter Press.
- TEA/Project Share Courses: TELLIT Courses (Math, Science, Social Studies)
- Texas English Language Learners Portal – TEA sponsored website

Accommodations for ELLs

What are the differences between accommodations for instruction and accommodations for assessment?

ELLs require accommodations in materials, instruction, and pacing [TAC §89.1210 (a)]. In providing these accommodations, ELLs are afforded a full opportunity to meet the essential knowledge and skills for the grade or courses in which they are enrolled.

Since instruction must meet the cognitive, linguistic, and affective needs of ELLs, instructional accommodations may be aligned to each of these needs. The TEA TELLIT (Texas English Language Learner Instructional Tool) courses for math, social studies, and science (housed on Project Share) organize instructional accommodations similarly.

Instructional accommodations may also be aligned to ELL proficiency levels in English. The *Navigating the ELPS* series and *The ELPS Flip Book*, published by Seidlitz Education, provide instructional accommodations organized by levels of English language proficiency (Seidlitz, 2008a; Seidlitz, 2010).

For state assessments, TEA has identified the following accommodations: there are general accommodations available to all students; linguistic accommodations for certain qualifying ELLs; and accommodations for some eligible ELLs with disabilities who are served by Special Education. To learn more about these accommodations, visit the TEA webpage Accommodation Resources.

In a bilingual district, what kinds of accommodations are provided for non-Spanish speaking students?

Elementary schools in Texas with highly effective bilingual programs often face the challenge of meeting the needs of students who do not speak the language of the bilingual program. In addition to having highly skilled bilingual teachers to meet the needs of ELLs, at least one certified ESL teacher and a bilingual teacher (who supports the language of the non-Spanish speaking ELL) must be available at each grade level.

ESL teachers need to be trained in: Total Physical Response (TPR), Teaching Proficiency through Reading and Storytelling (TPRS) language experience approach, and other ESL methodologies appropriate for second language acquisition. In addition, these teachers must be familiar with state adopted resources for use in ELL instruction.

Depending upon the number of non-Spanish-speaking ELLs, many campuses are able to have one ESL teacher work with students at a variety of grade levels. The role of the ESL teacher in this context is not only to provide support for the students participating in heterogeneous, content area classes, but to teach English as a second language to the non-Spanish speaking students. Bilingual districts may choose to concentrate the ESL program at a select number of campuses if the numbers are small.

COMPLIANCE

Who determines the accommodations provided to ELLs?

Instructional accommodations for ELLs are most often determined by the classroom teacher. The LPAC may recommend certain accommodations based upon subjective teacher input from previous years' teachers. In addition, other specialists or administrators may require certain accommodations to be routinely provided; for example, the use of language objectives, sentence stems, and visuals may be the norms or expectations for all teachers, even though they are considered instructional accommodations for ELLs.

In the case of assessment accommodations, the LPAC is responsible—in consultation with the classroom teachers—to determine which, if any, of the approved assessment accommodations will be provided to an ELL during the state assessments. These decisions are documented and maintained in the student's record. Any accommodation that is provided in a state assessment must be routinely used and requested by the student throughout the year.

For ELLs served by Special Education, the LPAC and ARD committees work collaboratively to make these important decisions. The ARD may determine that an ELL served by Special Education requires a modified curriculum or modified assessments. Modifications are different from accommodations in that they alter the required curriculum or the assessment. Instruction and assessment may be conducted at a lower grade level and/or the learning expectations may differ from those for the grade level or course. In the case of modified assessments, TEA has determined that these are not considered general assessments

Beginning/Intermediate ELLs

ELLs at TELPAS Beginning or Intermediate levels of proficiency in English require additional instructional supports. These supports must be provided to ELLs in grade 3 or higher.

LEGAL LINEAGE

- Elementary and Secondary Education Act of 1965, Title III, Part A, Sec. 3102 (1); Subpart 1, Sec. 3111 (b)(2)(c)(ii)
- TAC Title 19, Part II, Chapter 74, Subchapter A, §74.4 (b)(4)

JUST ENOUGH INFORMATION

★ Need to Know

- Which ELLs on campus or in the district are at Beginning or Intermediate levels of English language proficiency
- What are appropriate supports for ELLs at Beginning and Intermediate levels of proficiency

★ Need to Do

- Ensure that teachers know which ELLs are at Beginning or Intermediate levels of English language proficiency
- Ensure that teachers are providing required additional instructional supports to ELLs at Beginning and Intermediate levels of proficiency
- Ensure that teachers have necessary resources to provide additional supports to ELLs at Beginning and Intermediate levels of proficiency

COMPLIANCE

QUESTIONS

1. What are the characteristics of ELLs at the Beginning and Intermediate levels of English proficiency?
2. What are the characteristics of instruction that is designed to meet the needs of ELLs at the Beginning and Intermediate levels of English language proficiency?
3. What do the words *focused, targeted,* and *systematic* mean in TAC Chapter 74, §74.4(b)(4)?

FOR MORE INFORMATION (FMI)

- *Double the Work: Adolescent Newcomers* - Center for Applied Linguistics (CAL) website
- Foundations of Intensive Language Acquisition and Support (FILAS) - Currently Approved Innovative Courses - TEA webpage
- Krashen, S. D. (1985). *The input hypothesis: Issues and implications* (Vol. 1, p. 985). London: Longman.
- National Clearinghouse for English Language Acquisition – website
- *Newcomers Module* – TEA online course on Project Share from A&M Corpus Christi
- Seidlitz, J., & Perryman, B. (2011). *Seven steps to a language-rich interactive classroom.* San Clemente, CA: Canter Press.
- *TEA Best Practices Clearinghouse Newsletter (*BPC News), Jan. 2011, Volume 2, Issue 1
- TPRS Publishing - website A&M Corpus Christi

Beginning/Intermediate ELLs

What are the characteristics of ELLs at the Beginning and Intermediate levels of English proficiency?

The listening, speaking, reading, and writing skills for students at the Beginning and Intermediate levels of language proficiency are described in the TELPAS Proficiency Level Descriptors (PLDs). The following chart summarizes these skills in a general way; however, these summaries are not appropriate to use in formal TELPAS rating activities.

SUMMARIES OF ELPS: Proficiency Level Descriptors

Level	Listening (d1: k-12) *The student comprehends...*	Speaking (d2: k-12) *The student speaks...*	Reading (d4: 2-12) *The student reads...*	Writing (d6: 2-12) *The student writes...*
Beginning (A)	1A(i) few **simple conversations** with linguistic support 1A(ii) **modified conversation** 1A(iii) few words, **does not seek clarification,** watches others for cues	2A(i) using **single words and short phrases** with practiced material; tends to give up on attempts 2A(ii) using **limited bank of key vocabulary** 2A(iii) with **recently practiced familiar material** 2A(iv) with frequent **errors** that hinder communication 2A(v) with **pronunciation that inhibits communication**	4A(i) little except recently practiced terms, **environmental print,** high frequency words, **concrete words represented by pictures** 4A(ii) **slowly, word by word** 4A(iii) with very limited sense of English structure 4A(iv) with comprehension of **practiced, familiar text** 4A(v) with need for **visuals and prior knowledge** 4A(vi) modified and **adapted text**	6A(i) with **little ability to use English** 64A(ii) **without focus** and coherence, conventions, organization, voice 6A(iii) labels, lists, and copies of printed text and **high-frequency words/ phrases**, short and simple, practiced sentences primarily in **present tense with frequent errors** that hinder or prevent understanding
Intermediate (B)	1B(i) unfamiliar language with **linguistic supports** and adaptations 1B(ii) unmodified conversation with **key words** and phrases 1B(iii) with **requests for clarification** by asking speaker to repeat, slow down, or rephrase speech	2B(i) **with simple messages** and hesitation to think about meaning 2B(ii) using **basic vocabulary** 2B(iii) with **simple sentence structures** and present tense 2B(iv) with **errors** that inhibit unfamiliar communication 2B(v) with **pronunciation generally understood** by those familiar with English language learners	4B(i) **wider range of topics,** and everyday academic language 4B(ii) **slowly** and **rereads** 4B(iii) basic language structures 4B(iv) simple sentences **with visual cues, pre-taught vocabulary,** and **interaction** 4B(v) **grade-level texts** with difficulty 4B(vi) at high level with **linguistic accommodation**	6B(i) with **limited ability to use English** in content area writing 6B(ii) best on **topics that are highly familiar** with simple English 6B(iii) with **simple oral tone in messages**, high-frequency vocabulary, loosely connected text, repetition of ideas, **mostly in the present tense**, undetailed descriptions, and **frequent errors**

Level	Listening (d1: k-12) *The student comprehends...*	Speaking (d2: k-12) *The student speaks...*	Reading (d4: 2-12) *The student reads...*	Writing (d6: 2-12) *The student writes...*
Advanced (C)	1C(i) with some processing time, **visuals, verbal cues, and gestures; unfamiliar conversations** 1C(ii) most unmodified interaction 1C(iii) with occasional **requests** for the speaker to slow down, repeat, rephrase, and **clarify meaning**	2C(i) in conversations with some **pauses to restate, repeat, and clarify** 2C(ii) using **content-based and abstract terms** on familiar topics 2C(iii) with **past, present, and future** 2C(iv) using **complex sentences** and grammar with some errors 2C(v) with **pronunciation usually understood** by most	4C(i) abstract, grade appropriate text 4C(ii) **longer phrases and familiar sentences** appropriately 4C(iii) while developing the ability to construct meaning from text 4C(iv) at **high comprehension** level with **linguistic support** for unfamiliar topics and to clarify meaning	6C(i) grade appropriate **ideas with second language support** 6C(ii) with extra need for second language **support when topics are technical and abstract** 6C(iii) with a grasp of basic English usage and some understanding of complex usage with **emerging grade appropriate vocabulary** and a more academic tone
Advanced High (D)	1D(i) longer **discussions on unfamiliar topics** 1D(ii) spoken information nearly **comparable to native speaker** 1D(iii) with few requests for speaker to slow down, repeat, or rephrase	2D(i)in **extended discussions** with few pauses 2D(ii) using **abstract content-based vocabulary** except low frequency terms; using idioms 2D(iii) with grammar **nearly comparable to native speaker** 2D(iv) with **few errors** blocking communication 2D(v) **occasional mispronunciation**	4D(i) **nearly comparable to native speakers** 4D(ii) **grade appropriate familiar text** appropriately 4D(iii) while constructing meaning at near native ability level 4D(iv) with high level comprehension with **minimal linguistic support**	6D(i) grade appropriate **content area ideas with little need for** linguistic **support** 6D(ii) develop and demonstrate **grade appropriate** writing 6D (iii) nearly **comparable to native speakers** with clarity and precision, with **occasional difficulties,** and with naturalness of language.

These summaries are not appropriate to use in formally identifying student proficiency levels for TELPAS. TELPAS assessment and training materials are provided by the Texas Education Agency Student Assessment Division.

Beginning/Intermediate ELLs

Often, ELLs at the Beginning or Intermediate levels of English language proficiency are new to schooling in the US, and these designations do little to indicate the educational levels in their native language. In addition, they do not provide information about the academic achievement of these students. With an understanding of student academic/educational background, administrators can make good decisions in term of placement for cognitive, linguistic, and affective supports.

Note: Beginners and Intermediates may also be classified as immigrants, refugee/asylee students, or US born. Therefore, the rapid acquisition of English sufficient to function in general education classrooms is an immediate goal.

What are the characteristics of instruction designed to meet the needs of ELLs at the Beginning and Intermediate levels of English language proficiency?

Linguistic accommodations for students at the Beginning and Intermediate levels of English language proficiency focus on ensuring that students receive adequate comprehensible input. At the Beginning level, teachers allow a "silent period" to let students become accustomed to the sounds and patterns of English even though the need for silence opposes the demands placed on teachers to accelerate the acquisition of English language proficiency for Beginning ELLs (Krashen, 1985).

TAC Chapter 74, §74.4(b)(4) requires that Beginning and Intermediate level students receive intensive, ongoing English language development that is focused, targeted, and systematic. Some students may require support to develop foundational literacy in English and can include such skills as: the alphabetic principle, phonology (sounds of English), directionality of print, translating sounds into writing, and basic sight vocabulary. Many of these skills may not be available in a general educational setting and may require intensive support by an ESL-certified teacher or specialist. This can often be accomplished in the context of an ESL classroom.

The following chart notes the kind of accommodations that are appropriate for students at the Beginning and Intermediate levels. In addition, Advanced and Advanced High levels are shown.*

**Guidelines at specific proficiency levels may be beneficial for students at all levels of proficiency depending on the context of instructional delivery, materials, and students' background knowledge.*

LINGUISTIC ACCOMMODATIONS for each Proficiency Level

Sequence of Language Development	Communicating and Scaffolding Instruction			
	Listening *Teachers...*	Speaking *Teachers...*	Reading *Teachers...*	Writing *Teachers...*
Beginning Students (A)	• Allow use of same language peer and **native language support** • Expect student to struggle to understand simple conversations • Use **gestures and movement** and other linguistic support to communicate language and expectations	• Provide short **sentence stems** and single words for practice before conversations • **Allow some nonparticipation** in simple conversations • Provide **word bank** of key vocabulary • Model **pronunciation of social and academic language**	• Organize reading in **chunks** • Practice **high frequency, concrete terms** • Use **visual and linguistic supports** • Explain classroom **environmental print** • Use adapted text	• Allow **drawing and use of native language** to express concepts • Allow student to use high frequency recently memorized, and **short, simple sentences** • Provide **short, simple sentence stems** with present tense and high frequency vocabulary
Intermediate (B)	• Provide **visuals, slower speech, verbal cues, and simplified language** • **Preteach vocabulary** before discussions and lectures • **Teach phrases** for student to request speakers repeat, slow down, or rephrase speech	• Allow extra **processing time** • Provide **sentence stems** with simple sentence structures and tenses • Model and provide practice in **pronunciation of academic terms**	• Allow wide range of reading • Allow grade-level comprehension and **analysis of tasks** including **drawing** and use of **native language** and peer collaboration • Provide high level of **visual and linguistic supports** with adapted text and **pretaught vocabulary**	• Allow **drawing and use of native language** to express academic concepts • Allow writing on **familiar, concrete topics** • **Avoid assessment of language errors** in content area writing • Provide simple **sentence stems and scaffolded writing assignments**
Advanced (C)	• Allow some **processing time, visuals, verbal cues, and gestures** for unfamiliar conversations • Provide opportunities for student to **request clarification,** repetition, and rephrasing	• **Allow extra time** after pauses • Provide **sentence stems** with past, present, future, and **complex grammar,** and vocabulary with **content-based and abstract terms**	• Allow abstract grade-level reading comprehension and analysis with **peer support** • Provide **visual and linguistic supports** including **adapted text** for unfamiliar topics	• Provide **grade-level appropriate writing tasks** • Allow abstract and technical writing with linguistic support including teacher **modeling and student interaction** • Provide complex **sentence stems** for **scaffolded writing assignments**
Advanced High (D)	• Allow some **extra time** when academic material is complex and unfamiliar • Provide **visuals, verbal cues, and gestures** when material is complex and unfamiliar	• Provide opportunities for extended **discussions** • Provide **sentence stems with** past, present, future, and **complex grammar** and vocabulary with **content-based and abstract terms**	• Allow abstract grade-level reading • Provide minimal **visual and linguistic supports** • Allow grade level comprehension and **analysis tasks** with **peer collaboration**	• Provide complex **grade-level appropriate writing tasks** • Allow abstract and technical writing with **minimal linguistic support** • Use **genre analysis** to identify and use features of advanced English writing

Beginning/Intermediate ELLs

These accommodations may be provided in the context of an ESL classroom or through some other intervention mechanism using ESL specialists. When they are not, content area teachers in general education classes can use sheltered instruction approaches to support ELLs at all levels of English language proficiency, including Beginners and Intermediates. (See Sheltered Instruction on page 84.)

What do the words *focused, targeted,* and *systematic* mean in TAC Chapter 74, §74.4(b)(4)?

The words *focused, targeted,* and *systematic* identify the kind of instruction for students at the Beginning and Intermediate levels of English language proficiency, at third grade or higher. Focused, targeted, and systematic English language instruction is not equivalent to linguistic accommodations in a general education setting. Instead, this language refers to the accelerated English language instruction specially designed for students at the Beginning and Intermediate levels. More information is provided in the chart on the next page.

COMPLIANCE

UNDERSTANDING THE ELPS FRAMEWORK
Foundations of Second Language Acquisition Instruction for Beginning and Intermediate ELLs Grades 3-12

Second language acquisition instruction must be:	What is it?	What are some examples?
Focused	**Concentrated effort centered on student acquisition** of vocabulary, grammar, syntax, and English mechanics necessary to support content-based instruction and accelerated learning of English.	• Explicit instruction in English vocabulary and language structures • Lesson plans include cross curricular student expectations from the ELPS • Use of sentence structures of increasing complexity in vocabulary, grammar, and syntax
Targeted	**Specific goals and objectives** align with vocabulary, grammar, syntax and English mechanics necessary to support content-based instruction and accelerated learning of English.	• Content objectives for ELLs align with the TEKS • Language objectives for ELLs align with ELPS and language skills necessary for TEKS • Formal and informal assessments align with content and language assessments
Systematic	**Well organized structure** in place to ensure students acquire vocabulary, grammar, syntax, and English mechanics necessary to support content-based instruction and accelerated learning of English.	• ELPS integrated into district curriculum frameworks • **Comprehensive plan for students in grades 3-12 at Beginning or Intermediate** level for integrating language and content instruction • Comprehensive plan for assessing the implementation of focused, targeted instruction for beginning and intermediate students in grades 3-12 • Periodic review of progress of ELLs through formal and informal assessment

COMPLIANCE

Community Engagement/ Parental Involvement

Community engagement refers to the collaboration between administrators, teachers, and families/caregivers for the growth and development of all students and the success of the program.

LEGAL LINEAGE

- Elementary and Secondary Education Act of 1965, Title III, Part A, Sec. 3102 (6)
- Elementary and Secondary Education Act of 1965, Title III, Part A, Subpart 1, Sec. 3116 (b)(4)
- TEC, Title 2, Subtitle F, Chapter 11, Subchapter F, Sec. 11.253 (d)(9)
- TEC, Title 2, Subtitle F, Chapter 29, Subchapter B, Sec. 29.056 (a)
- *TEC, Title 2, Subtitle F, Chapter 39, Subchapter B, Sec. 39.0545 (added by HB5)*
- TAC Title 19, Part II, Chapter 89, Subchapter BB,§ 89.1240
- TEC Chapter 29, Subchapter B, 29.056 (a)

JUST ENOUGH INFORMATION

★ Need to Know

- Community history
- Community demographics
- Ways to communicate with community
- Benefits of bilingual/ESL programs

★ Need to Do

- Act as an advocate for ELLs and district programs
- Provide information about ELLs and existing program to stakeholders
- Gather information through surveys, questions, and interviews
- Make the school/district a culturally responsive, welcoming environment

QUESTIONS

1. How do administrators promote parental involvement of ELLs?
2. How can administrators recruit students into the dual language program?
3. How can administrators create community support for the second language programs on campus?
4. How will the district meet the requirement to evaluate parent/student engagement as required in HB5?

FOR MORE INFORMATION (FMI)

- Cultural Orientation Resource Center (website sponsored by CAL)
- HB5
- Parent Involvement Conference - ESC, Region 16
- Parent Involvement Modules - ESC, Region 20

How do administrators promote parental involvement of ELLs?

It is important for administrators to create a welcoming climate for parents because their participation in campus activities is not only vitally important, it is valuable. Many steps can be taken to ensure a close partnership between parents and schools. Parents can get involved in:

- a parent resource center directed by a staff person/parent who can act as parent liaison.
- decision-making processes related to bilingual/ESL programs on campus. This helps establish a sense of ownership that usually leads to increased participation. For example, if a campus accepts Title I funds, parents of ELLs must be included in decision-making meetings about the services to be provided. Administrators can ensure that these opportunities are offered at different times during the day to help accommodate the schedules of working parents.
- school functions, such as Meet the Teacher, Open House, report card night, PTA, Donuts for Dad, and any academic event that brings parents and teachers together.

To increase parental participation, administrators need to communicate effectively with parents. Be sure to:

- communicate with parents in their native language.
- send all campus communications in English and the native language of the students. In this manner, value is given to the home language.
- make phone calls to student homes with an interpreter available.
- consider using the marquee as a means of connecting with parents. List the daily message and/or event in English on one side and the native language of the parents on the other side.
- include contact information for parents who need assistance with reading the district website.
- provide interpreters for all campus events so that parents can receive assistance in translating. This sets a positive tone for parents of ELLs.
- offer parent liaisons who know and can explain the bilingual/ESL models to parents.
- distribute regular newsletters to parents to inform them of school events and functions.
- appropriately assign bilingual-certified teachers and document their proficiency in the languages of instruction.

Community Engagement/Parental Involvement

How can administrators recruit students into the dual language program?

Students can enter the dual language program by:

- hosting information sessions at the campus and in the community. These information sessions must be held in the native language of the parents and in English.
- inviting teachers, current students, and parents to dual language program information sessions to provide first-hand information about the effectiveness of the program.

It is interesting to note that the "consumer" on the elementary level is the parent – making the decision for the student. When the program extends to secondary settings, the student becomes the "consumer" in that they make course selection/elective decisions which may drive their placement in academics or cohorts of learners. It is strongly advisable for the district/campus to build a sufficient number of dual language cohorts/classrooms in order to ensure adequate numbers of students in the upper grades.

How can administrators create community support for the second language programs on campus?

One of the best ways to create community respect for second language programs is to act as an advocate for the program, both on campus and in the community.

To advocate for ELLs, administrators can:

- visit bilingual and ESL classrooms frequently.
- interact with ELLs and their parents on campus and in the community. Consider regular meetings with parents at a location off-campus.
- provide resource and funding allocations to support and enhance the bilingual/ESL programs.
- inform the Board of Trustees and the community of the positive impact and student/teacher achievements of the district's second language programs.
- put the needs of ELLs first in decisions that regard the academic needs and goals of the bilingual/ESL programs on campus.
- ensure that the campus improvement plan includes specific goals, strategies, and activities that support the goals of the bilingual/ESL programs.

Administrators should have a clear understanding of the goals, instructional strategies, and outcomes of the bilingual/ESL programs on campus. With such information administrators can articulate the rigor and relevance of the second language program on campus. In addition, it is important to be familiar with student performance data to help confirm the effectiveness of the second language program.

How will the district meet the requirements to evaluate parent/student engagement as required in HB5?

Section 39.0545 is added to Chapter 39 of the Texas Education Code with the final passage of HB5. This section requires the district to engage in:

- the evaluation of district and campus programs.
- compliance with statutory reporting and policy requirements.

Among other programs, community/parental involvement programs are included in this new statute. When evaluating community/parental involvement, the district should address:

- opportunities for parents to assist students in preparing for state assessments.
- tutoring programs designed to support students taking assessments.
- opportunities for students to participate in community service projects.

Using criteria developed by a local committee, districts will evaluate the performance and compliance for each program listed in the new statute, including community/parental involvement. Before August 8th of each year, the district will report a performance rating to the TEA using the locally developed criteria.

Ratings include:

- Exemplary
- Recognized
- Acceptable
- Unacceptable

Campus and district administrators should include community/parental involvement criteria, a combination of ELL parents and any community-based organizations that support the ELL programs in district or on campus.

COMPLIANCE

Facilities for ELLs

Bilingual and ESL programs must be located in facilities in compliance with state law.

LEGAL LINEAGE

- TEC, Title 2, Subtitle F, Chapter 29, Subchapter B, Sec. 29.057
- TAC Title 19, Part II, Chapter 89, Subchapter BB, §89.1235

JUST ENOUGH INFORMATION

★ Need to Know

- The rules regarding facilities that house bilingual and ESL programs
- The demographics for the ELL population

★ Need to Do

- Ensure that all eligible ELLs are receiving program services in appropriate settings
- Ensure that the campus enrollment of ELLs does not exceed limits

QUESTIONS

1. Are there any housing restrictions for ELL programs?
2. What do administrators need to know about facilities and classes for ELLs?
3. What requirements apply to providing facilities for ELLs assigned to newcomer programs?
4. What requirements apply to the enrollment of non-ELLs in bilingual program classes?

FOR MORE INFORMATION (FMI)

- Local district boundaries and campus attendance zones
- Local policy
- Local transportation guidelines
- TEA School Transportation Allotment Handbook – on TEA website

Are there any housing restrictions for ELL programs?

Per TEC Chapter 29, Sec. 29.057, bilingual and ESL programs must be located in regular public schools in the district and may not be operated in separate facilities in the community. TAC Chapter 89, §89.1235 provides additional explanation of this requirement. It is permissible to concentrate the bilingual or ESL programs at a limited number of campuses within the district. However, the enrollment of ELLs at these campuses may not exceed 60% of the total campus enrollment.

What do administrators need to know about facilities and classes for ELLs?

ELLs are to be placed in classes with other students of the same/approximate age and level of educational attainment. Instruction for ELLs must be appropriate for their level of attainment [TEC Sec. 29.057] and commensurate with their levels of English language proficiency [TAC§ 89.1210 (b)(e)].

What requirements apply to providing facilities for ELLs assigned to newcomer programs?

ELLs assigned to Newcomer Programs or centers away from their home campus must not spend more than two years after initial enrollment at the separate facility. Some newcomer programs or centers are located in district-managed buildings, which may or may not be operated as a district campus.

What requirements apply to the enrollment of non-ELLs in bilingual program classes?

Students who are not ELLs may participate in bilingual program classes with the approval of the school district and the student's parents. The number of non-ELLs may not exceed 40% of the total enrollment of students enrolled in the program [TEC Sec. 29.058 and TAC §89.1233].

In a dual-language two-way program model, the mix of the class is ideally 50% dominant English speakers and 50% native speakers of the other language [TAC §89.1210 (3)(B)].

Once an ELL has met exit criteria, he/she may continue receiving program services and participate in the program with school district and parental approval, however, the district will no longer receive the bilingual allotment for that student. Districts that continue bilingual programs, especially those with dual language program models, may elect to continue those programs for ELLs who are reclassified as non-ELL because they have met the exit criteria.

Required Training and Professional Development

Teachers of ELLs require specialized training to enable them to effectively implement the required curriculum and applicable standards in bilingual/ESL programs as well as in general education classrooms.

LEGAL LINEAGE

- Elementary and Secondary Education Act of 1965, Title III, Part A, Sec. 3102 (8); Subpart 1, Sec. 3115 (c)(2)
- Elementary and Secondary Education Act of 1965, Title III, Part B, Subpart 3, Sec. 3231
- TEC, Title 2, Subtitle F, Chapter 11, Subchapter F, Sec. 11.251 (d), Sec. 11.252 (a)(3)(F)
- TEC, Title 2, Subtitle F, Chapter 29, Subchapter B, Sec. 29.061 (a)(b)
- TAC Title 19, Part II, Chapter 74, Subchapter A, §Chapter 74.4 (a)(b)
- TAC Title 19, Part II, Chapter 89, Subchapter BB, §89.1210, §89.1220 (a)(g), §89.1245 (f)(g), §89.165 (b)(d)

JUST ENOUGH INFORMATION

★ Need to Know

- What training LPAC members need
- What training TELPAS raters need
- What training teachers of ELLs need
- When required trainings occur
- Professional development options for teachers of ELLs

★ Need to Do

- Ensure that LPAC members are trained in their roles and responsibilities
- Ensure that TELPAS raters receive required training
- Ensure that teachers receive required training in sheltered instruction
- Ensure that teachers receive training in implementing the ELPS in instruction and planning

COMPLIANCE

QUESTIONS

1. What kind of training is required for Language Proficiency Assessment Committee (LPAC) members?
2. What kind of training is required for Texas English Language Proficiency Assessment System (TELPAS) raters?
3. What are some examples of appropriate professional development for bilingual, ESL, and sheltered teachers?
4. What kind of training do teachers need in order to implement the English Language Proficiency Standards (ELPS) in instruction?
5. What kind of training do teachers need for sheltered instruction?

FOR MORE INFORMATION (FMI)

- BUENO Center – Colorado
- Center for Applied Linguistics (CAL) – website
- Educator Certification – TEA webpage
- ELPS Instructional Alignment Guide Training – ESC, Region 20
- Escamilla, K., Hopewell, S., Butvilofsky, S., Sparrow, W., Soltero-González, L., Ruiz-Figueroa, O., Escamilla, M. (2013). *Biliteracy from the start; Literacy Squared© in action.* Philadelphia, PA: Caslon Publishing.
- Gómez, R. (2006). Promising practices: Dual language enrichment for ELL students K-12. *TABE Journal*, 9(1), 46-63.
- Guided Language Acquisition and Development (GLAD) - Project GLAD website
- *Implementing the ELPS, A+ Rise Online Tutorial,* and *Accelerating Language Acquisition for Secondary English Language Learners* online courses – TEA sponsored Project Share website
- Intercultural Development Research Association (IDRA) – website
- *Keystone* curriculum materials – Pearson Education
- Lara, M. (2011). *Siete pasos para crear un aula interactiva y rica en lenguaje: Estrategias para un aprendizaje significativo en aulas bilingües.* San Clemente, CA: Canter Press.
- Linguistic Instructional Alignment Guide (LIAG) – ESC, Region 20
- LPAC Framework Training Materials – ESC, Region 20 webpage
- Quality Teaching for English Language Learners (QTEL) – WestEd website
- *Reach, Edge,* and *National Geographic ELPS (NGELPS)* curriculum materials – National Geographic/Hampton Brown
- Regional Education Service Centers (ESCs)
- Seidlitz, J. (2010). *ELPS flip book: A user-friendly guide for academic language instruction.* San Clemente, CA: Canter Press.
- Seidlitz, J. (2008a). *Navigating the ELPS: Using the new standards to improve instruction for English learners.* San Clemente, CA: Canter Press.
- Seidlitz, J. (2008b). *Sheltered instruction plus: A comprehensive plan for successfully teaching English language learners.* San Clemente, CA: Canter Press.
- *Sheltered Instruction Observation Protocol* (SIOP) – CAL website
- State Board for Educator Certification (SBEC) – TEA webpage
- *Student Attendance Accounting Handbook*, Section 6.10
- TELLIT for Instructional Leaders – on TEA sponsored Project Share website
- TELPAS Resources – TEA webpage
- Texas English Language Learners Portal – TEA sponsored website
- Texas English Language Learners Portal (TEA sponsored website) – Professional Development and Additional Resources section

Required Training and Professional Development

What kind of training is required for LPAC members?

Chapter 89 (§89.1220) requires that LPAC members receive training in their duties and responsibilities. There are two annual trainings that all LPAC members receive in order to meet the statutory requirement. They are: LPAC Framework (training and annual update) and LPAC Decision-Making for State Assessments. Both trainings provide current information related to all aspects of bilingual and ESL programs and any assessments pertaining to ELLs. ESC, Region 20 is responsible for maintaining training resources on the ESC, 20 website (look under "L" on the A-Z index, and click on LPAC Framework). In addition to the training materials, there are valuable resources for parents and translations of LPAC materials and resources for training purposes.

Before the state assessment windows open each year, LPACs are required to receive training on the decision-making process with regard to ELL participation and accommodations for assessments. The training is provided by the Student Assessment Division of TEA - ELL Assessments. The materials and resources for this training are located on the TEA webpage, Language Proficiency Assessment Committee (LPAC) Assessment Resources.

What kind of training is required for TELPAS raters?

Teachers selected as ELL TELPAS raters and staff members selected to ensure Data Verification or Supplementary Support Providers (SSP) for raters must receive training in order to do their work. Some training is provided through Pearson Texas Training Center, while other training is available on the TEA webpage, TELPAS Resources.

What are some examples of appropriate professional development programs for bilingual, ESL, and sheltered instruction teachers?

To begin, visit the TEA website – Texas English Language Learners Portal – to see a section devoted to professional development resources provided by TEA or recommended by the state as effective for ELL teachers. Courses available in TEA's Project Share include TELLIT courses, Implementing the ELPS, A+ Rise Online Tutorial, and Accelerating Language Acquisition for Secondary English Language Learners Online Course.

Next, there are a variety of resources and staff development opportunities that districts can use for teachers who work with ELLs. The first resource is the local regional education service center (ESC). ESCs often offer specific workshops on various approaches to sheltered instruction, bilingual education, and strategies for bilingual/ESL teachers. Other resources for ELL teachers are with local universities and university professors who provide consulting and training for districts.

In addition to regional service centers and universities, textbook publishers are often great resources for staff development of bilingual and ESL teachers. For example:

- National Geographic/Hampton Brown provides training for teachers who have adopted the *Reach* textbook at the elementary level and the *Edge* textbook at the high school level. They also provide training for their National Geographic ELPS (NGELPS) program.
- Pearson Education provides staff development on the *Keystone* ESL textbook series.
- Information about state adopted textbooks can be found on the TEA webpage, Instructional Materials and Educational Technology.
- The Center for Applied Linguistics (CAL) provides some training and many resources for bilingual and ESL teachers. CAL also provides training on two-way immersion bilingual program models.
- Some districts in Texas have used the services of the Bueno Center in Colorado for training with emergent bilinguals.
- Many districts throughout Texas have used the services of the Intercultural Development Research Association (IDRA) – based in San Antonio – to support their bilingual teachers.
- Other districts have received support based on specific methodologies being used within their bilingual or dual language program model – for example: *Literacy Squared®* (Escamilla, et al., 2013), the *Dual Language Enrichment* Model (Gomez, 2006), and the *Siete Pasos* delivery model (Lara, 2011). In addition, Seidlitz Education offers many resources and training opportunities for ELL teachers. Information about these professional development options and teacher/administrator resources are available on the Seidlitz Education website.

Required Training and Professional Development

What kind of training do teachers need in order to implement the ELPS in instruction?

According to TAC Chapter 89, the *Student Attendance Accounting Handbook,* and TAC Chapter 74, §74.4, all content area teachers must integrate the ELPS into lesson planning and delivery. To do this, teachers must receive adequate training, and many resources offer this training. TEA provides courses for math, science, and social studies teachers –available on Project Share, at no cost. The courses, identified as TELLIT, are organized to address the cognitive, linguistic, and affective learning environments referred to in TAC Chapter 89, §89.1210.

Campus administrators are responsible for monitoring the implementation of linguistically accommodating instruction aligned to the ELPS. A TELLIT course on Project Share for instructional leaders (Professional Service Provider Course for Campus/District Leaders) includes a useful walk-through tool for effective monitoring of ELL instruction. In addition, an overview of the content area TELLIT courses for teachers is included.

Other courses available in Project Share include *Implementing the ELPS, A+ Rise Online Tutorial,* and *Accelerating Language Acquisition for Secondary English Language Learners* online courses.

ESC, Region 20 also provides TEA-sponsored *ELPS Instructional Alignment Guide Training* on the *Linguistic Instructional Alignment Guide.*

In addition, Seidlitz Education provides *Navigating the ELPS* (Seidlitz, 2008a) and *The ELPS Flip Book* (Seidlitz, 2010) workshops for English Language Arts/Reading, Science, Math, and Social Studies teachers. The charts found on pages 268-274 provide support for administrators who are responsible for ensuring that the ELPS are being properly implemented in classrooms with ELLs (Seidlitz, 2008b).

What kind of training do teachers need for sheltered instruction?

According to the *Student Attendance Accounting Handbook*, published annually by TEA, all teachers of ELLs must receive training in sheltered instruction. There are a variety of opportunities for teachers in Texas to receive training for sheltered instruction, as well as training in the sheltered instruction model their district has in effect.

Districts within Texas use a variety of sheltered instruction models on their campuses.

- The TEA provides courses designed to equip teachers with sheltered instruction approaches that are research-based. Through a set of courses in Project Share, teachers can meet the state requirement for sheltered instruction training. Although not required, these courses have no cost, do not remove the teacher from instructional time with students, and are self-paced.
- Many districts use the research-based Sheltered Instruction Observation Protocol (SIOP) model of sheltered instruction developed in 1999 at the Center for Applied Linguistics (CAL). Materials and resources continue to be developed and expanded. SIOP training and resources are available from CAL and from Pearson Education.
- Many Texas districts have used the Sheltered Instruction Plus Model developed by John Seidlitz (2008b). Key elements of this model were researched in 2010 through the University of Arizona (ITELL/Institute for Teachers of English Language Learners). Training on the model is available from Seidlitz Education and from MELCAST educational consulting.
- Other professional development options for sheltered instruction include GLAD (Guided Language Acquisition and Development), provided by Project GLAD, and QTEL (Quality Teaching for English Language Learners) available from WestEd.

Staffing and Certification

Staffing a bilingual or ESL program involves assigning properly certified personnel to teach in classes that are providing program services as well as in general education classrooms where ELLs are present. Staffing also involves ensuring that all ELLs with parent denials are receiving instruction that is designed to address their linguistic needs and to ensure their progress in acquiring English language proficiency.

LEGAL LINEAGE

Staffing

- Title III, Part A, Sec. 31111 (b)(2)(A)
- TEC, Title 2, Subtitle F, Chapter 29, Subchapter B, Sec. 29.054, Sec. 29.055(a), Sec. 29.057(b)(c), Sec. 29.061
- TAC Title 19, Part II, Chapter 89, Subchapter BB, § 89.1201(a), §89.1207, §89.1245

Required Certification

- TEC Chapter 29, Subchapter B, Sec. 29.061 (a)(c)
- Title 19, Part VII of TAC
- TAC Chapter 89, Subchapter BB, §89.1201(3), §89.1207(a)(b), §89.1245
- *Student Attendance Accounting Handbook,* Sec. 6.4, 6.10
- State Board for Educator Certification (SBEC)

JUST ENOUGH INFORMATION

★ Need to Know

- Certification requirements for the program models on campus or in the district
- Exceptions and Waivers process
- Roles and responsibilities of teachers and staff with regard to providing services to ELLs

★ Need to Do

- Ensure that there are sufficient numbers of teachers assigned to bilingual/ESL programs
- Ensure that teachers of ELLs are properly certified
- Ensure that all staff understand their role in supporting the bilingual/ESL programs and ELLs

QUESTIONS

1. What do administrators need to know about certification for teachers of ELLs?
2. What actions do administrators take if teachers of ELLs are not properly certified for the program model(s) on campus?
3. What is the role of the ESL teacher?
4. What is the role of the bilingual director?
5. What are the roles of instructional specialists, e.g., coaches, interventionists, facilitators?
6. What should administrators consider when hiring teachers for bilingual and ESL programs?
7. What should administrators consider when hiring teachers for dual language program models?
8. How do administrators assign educational assistants/paraprofessionals to bilingual/ESL classrooms?

FOR MORE INFORMATION (FMI)

- Educator Certification – TEA webpage
- Exceptions and Waivers Training Webinar – on Texas English Language Learners Portal, TEA sponsored website
- State Board for Educator Certification-Administrative Rules – TEA webpage
- State Board for Educator Certification (SBEC) – TEA webpage
- *Student Attendance Accounting Handbook* (SAAH), Sec. 6.4, 6.10
- *To the Administrator Addressed* (Sept. 11, 2013) – TEA webpage

Staffing and Certification

What do administrators need to know about certification for teachers of ELLs?

Teachers assigned to a bilingual classroom must be bilingual-certified. This means that they are trained in second language acquisition strategies and have demonstrated oral and written proficiency in the native language of the students in their classrooms. This requirement applies to all teachers of core content-area instruction regardless of program model. For example, if a teacher is assigned to a dual language two-way program model, and is assigned the responsibility of instruction of a core content area in English, that teacher must be bilingual-certified as well as being certified for the teaching assignment. In bilingual and dual language program models, teachers responsible for the ESL portion of the instructional day (where the ELPS are implemented), must be bilingual-certified. Recent state guidance states that all content area teachers of ELLs in bilingual programs (including both dual language program models) must be bilingual-certified [TEC Sec. 29.061 and TAC §89.1245].

Teachers assigned to the ESL program must have an ESL certificate. This means that they are trained in second language acquisition strategies, but they are not required to be proficient in the native language of the students they serve. Teachers in ESL Content-Based programs pre-K–8 who teach core content (English/reading, math, science, social studies) classes must be ESL-certified. In ESL Pull-Out programs, at least one teacher of the ELLs in the program must be ESL-certified, and that teacher is responsible for meeting the linguistic needs of the students [TEC Sec. 29.061 and TAC §89.1245]. Most often, that teacher is the reading, English language arts, or ESL class teacher.

High school requirements are different for ESL services. As stated in TAC Chapter 89, §89.1210(e), *"the English as a second language program shall be consistent with graduation requirements under Chapter 74 of this title. The language proficiency assessment committee may recommend appropriate services that may include content courses provided through sheltered instructional approaches by trained teachers, enrollment in English as a second language courses, additional state elective English courses, and special assistance provided through locally determined programs."* Because of the different requirements for the high school program for ELLs, the requirement for certification is replaced by the requirement that all ELLs receive sheltered instruction in all content areas [TAC §89.1210 (g)(1)(2)]. The *Student Attendance Accounting Handbook,* Section 6.10 states that all teachers of ELLs must receive sheltered instruction training. So, it is possible that an ELL at the high school level would not receive instruction from an ESL-certified teacher. An exception to this is in the case of ESOL I or ESOL II, the two state-approved courses that may replace English I or English II for ELLs at the Beginning or Intermediate levels of English language proficiency. Teachers of ESOL I and II must be dually certified in English and in English as a Second Language (ESL).

All general education teachers who teach ELLs must have sheltered instruction training (*Student Attendance Accounting Handbook,* Sec. 6.10) and must incorporate the ELPS into their planning and instruction [TAC §74.4].

What actions do administrators take if teachers of ELLs are not properly certified in the district program model/s on campus?

To be in compliance, administrators need to direct teachers to certification resources provided by the school district, the local Educational Service Center (ESC), and area universities. In addition, administrators need to file an exception (bilingual programs) or a waiver (ESL programs) with TEA each year until teacher certification requirements are in compliance. The ESC can assist with filing. A description of the Exceptions and Waivers process and responsibilities of the district can be found in Chapter 89, §89.1207. In addition, the TEA provides resource guides for filing exceptions and waivers at the TEA-sponsored Texas English Language Learners Portal website.

What is the role of the ESL teacher?

The role of the ESL teacher is to provide support to ELLs as they are acquiring English. The ESL teacher is trained to use a variety of second language acquisition strategies to support student learning. The ESL teacher has the responsibility of building knowledge of English for all ELLs. In addition, the ESL teacher, along with all other teachers of ELLs, is responsible for ensuring that the students make at least one level of progress each year until they meet exit criteria (from Beginning, to Intermediate, to Advanced, to Advanced High).

Depending on teaching assignments, an ESL-certified teacher may:

- provide all content area instruction in a self-contained setting.
- provide instruction in the content area in a departmentalized setting.
- offer elective classes for ELLs.
- support ELLs in general education classes in an inclusionary way.
- serve as a resource for general education teachers.
- serve as a campus or district specialist and assist in program implementation.

What is the role of the bilingual director?

The bilingual/ESL director at the district level is responsible for the implementation, maintenance, and evaluation of all bilingual/ESL programs offered in the district. The director may:

- work with specialists who provide support to individual campuses.
- have content expertise and valuable knowledge of program goals across the district.
- visit individual campuses to talk with administrators and staff about program implementation, assessment, evaluation, etc.
- coordinate staff in order to assist administrators with professional development.
- be responsible for completing all state documentation requirement forms.
- complete applications and reports for federal funds allocated to bilingual programs.
- develop and circulate district bilingual/ESL program guidelines.
- oversee the LPAC operations to ensure they are compliant with Chapter 89.
- ensure that testing materials from the *List of Approved Tests for Assessment of Limited English Proficient Students* are available to districts.

Staffing and Certification

- coordinate purchases of state-approved texts and materials for second language programs.
- manage district and campus testing coordinators regarding ELLs taking state assessments (STAAR, TELPAS).
- be the representative of bilingual programs for the Board of Trustees.
- present the required annual report of bilingual programs and their performance to the Board of Trustees.
- oversee the required summer school programs for ELLs entering kindergarten and first grade.

What is the role of instructional specialists, e.g., coaches, interventionists, facilitators?

ELL coaches are specialists at the campus or district level that provide support to teachers of ELLs assisting with lesson planning, instructional delivery, and student assessment. These specialists do not just work in bilingual or ESL classrooms. They are often effective in supporting general education teachers who teach ELLs. They are often asked to provide local professional development or training. They might model successful instructional strategies for the teachers they support.

What should administrators consider when hiring teachers for bilingual and ESL programs?

When hiring bilingual teachers, administrators should interview teachers who have:

- bilingual certification.
- experience teaching the bilingual education program model used on campus.
- training in a variety of second language instructional strategies.
- a desire to embrace their role as advocate for the bilingual program and for the goals of students in those programs.

It is wise to consider the needs of students when recruiting teachers from other countries and when recruiting teachers, in general, who have had experience with students similar to the population of students on campus.

When hiring ESL teachers, seek teachers who are:

- properly certified.
- understand second language acquisition.
- have experience in providing ESL program services to ELLs.

These teachers should embrace the cultural differences in students and their families. They should be clear advocates for the ESL program, both on campus and in the community.

When hiring general education teachers, it is helpful to determine if they have ESL certification. These teachers can support ELLs in general education classes. Some districts have local policy that requires all teacher applicants to have ESL certification– or that they will attain that certification within a specified timeframe when hired.

What should administrators consider when hiring teachers for dual language program models?

Dual language programs require teachers to deliver high quality lessons in both English and Spanish. Therefore, when hiring teachers for those programs, it is important to have a protocol in place to measure their ability to read and write in both languages to a high degree of mastery. In addition, they need to be well versed in second language acquisition methodologies and have working knowledge of research-based instructional practices that best meet the needs of ELLs (English Language Learners) and SLLs (Spanish Language Learners).

In meeting the goals of dual language program models, teachers must encourage and develop students' appreciation for other cultures. A candidate for employment as a dual language teacher should have knowledge not just of the two languages taught in the program, but also possess a strong understanding (if not personal experience) with the cultures represented by the students enrolled.

Teachers in dual language classrooms are charged with the ongoing literacy development in both languages for their students. In contrast to transitional bilingual programs (in Texas early exit and late exit), literacy development in the home language continues throughout the students' participation in the program. The goal is full biliteracy and full bilingualism. Teachers who wish to teach in a dual language setting must be comfortable in meeting these program model goals.

How do administrators assign educational assistants/paraprofessionals to bilingual/ESL classrooms?

Administrators can assign educational assistants to classrooms based on the learning and linguistic needs of students in specific grade levels and classrooms. Of particular concern are the areas that need the most support, i.e., the early grades (K-1) for literacy development or content support in the testing grades (3-5). In secondary settings, paraprofessionals can provide significant support to students and teachers. For example, they may float from class to class to provide native language support and small group or individual interventions. They may also proctor testing with linguistic supports – in and out of class.

CURRICULUM & INSTRUCTION

Required Curriculum and Best Practices

All English language learners are instructed in accordance with state adopted standards for knowledge and skills (TEKS) and English language development (ELPS).

LEGAL LINEAGE

- Elementary and Secondary Education Act of 1965, Title III, Part A, Sec. 3102; Subpart 1, Sec. 3115 (c)(1), (d)(1-8)(e)
- TEC, Title 2, Subtitle F, Chapter 4, Sec. 4.002,
- TEC, Title 2, Subtitle F, Chapter 7., Subchapter D, Sec. 7.102 (c)(4)
- TEC, Title 2, Subtitle F, Chapter 28, Subchapter A, Sec. 28.002, Sec. 28.005, Sec. 28.0051,
- TEC, Title 2, Subtitle F, Chapter 39, Subchapter B, Sec. 39.021
- TAC Title 19, Part II, Chapter 74, Subchapter A
- TAC Title 19, Part II, Chapter 74, §74.4 (c)
- TAC Title 19, Part II, Chapter 89, Subchapter BB, §89.1210 (a)(c)(f)
- TAC Title 19, Part II, Chapters 110-115, 118, 126-128, 130*

* Reference only – text not supplied in this resource

JUST ENOUGH INFORMATION

★ Need to Know

- Which standards apply to English language learners
- Relationship between TEKS and STAAR
- Relationship between ELPS and TELPAS

★ Need to Do

- Ensure teachers understand relationship between TEKS/STAAR-EOC and TEKS
- Ensure teachers understand relationship between ELPS/TELPAS
- Ensure teachers are implementing both TEKS and ELPS for ELLs

QUESTIONS

1. What are the Texas state standards that describe what students should know and do?
2. How do the Texas Essential Knowledge and Skills (TEKS) apply to ELLs?
3. What are the state standards for English language development?
4. Which teachers are responsible for implementing the English Language Proficiency Standards (ELPS)?
5. How do administrators ensure that teachers are implementing both TEKS and ELPS in planning and instruction?
6. Which instructional resources support ELLs?
7. Where can administrators find appropriate resources for ELLs (in English and other languages)?
8. How do administrators ensure free voluntary reading for ELLs in their home language?

FOR MORE INFORMATION (FMI)

- 2013 – 2014 *Student Attendance Accounting Handbook* (SAAH), Sec. 6.10 – TEA Webpage
- ELPS Academy Linguistic Instructional Alignment Guide (LIAG) – available on ESC, Region 20 website
- Krashen, S. D. (2011). *Free voluntary reading.* Santa Barbara, CA: Libraries Unlimited, ABC-CLIO, LLC.
- Seidlitz, J. (2008a). *Navigating the ELPS: Using the new standards to improve instruction for English learners.* San Clemente: CA. Canter Press.
- Texas Essential Knowledge and Skills – TEA webpage

Required Curriculum & Best Practices

What are the Texas state standards that describe what students should know and do?

In Texas, the Texas Essential Knowledge and Skills (TEKS) are the set of standards for all grade levels and courses. These standards are published in the Texas Administrative Code (TAC), Title 19, Part II, Chapters 110-188, 126-128, and 130.

In addition, specific standards and guidelines for students are set in the English Language Proficiency Standards (ELPS), College and Career Readiness Standards (CCRS), and Pre-kindergarten Guidelines.

The TEKS are available in Spanish (for grades K-6) on the Texas Essential Knowledge and Skills webpage of the Curriculum Division at TEA.

How do the Texas Essential Knowledge and Skills (TEKS) apply to ELLs?

ELLs are required to demonstrate mastery of the TEKS annually, just as their native English-speaking peers do. Teachers are required to provide linguistically accommodated instruction to ELLs using sheltered instruction practices to ensure mastery of the grade level or course TEKS. If an ELL has a gap in prior schooling or lacks background knowledge for the TEKS, supplemental content instruction or accelerated English language instruction is provided.

What are the Texas state standards for English language development?

In Texas, the English Language Proficiency Standards (ELPS) outline which skills ELLs must master in listening, speaking, reading, writing, and learning strategies. The extent to which an ELL masters the listening, speaking, reading, and writing ELPS is measured through the annual, summative assessment of English language proficiency – TELPAS (Texas English Language Proficiency Assessment System).

Which teachers are responsible for implementing the English Language Proficiency Standards (ELPS)?

TAC Chapter 74, §74.4(a)(b) states that states that the ELPS are part of the required curriculum and apply to grades K-12 in all subjects in the required curriculum. Instruction in the foundation and enrichment curriculum must be linguistically accommodated for ELLs commensurate with their levels of English language proficiency.

Per the *Student Attendance Accounting Handbook*, Sec. 6.10, teachers of ELLs are required to receive sheltered instruction training which prepares them to linguistically accommodate planning and instruction for ELLs.

How do administrators ensure that teachers are implementing both TEKS and ELPS in planning and instruction?

There is no specific method required for implementing the TEKS and ELPS, therefore many districts in Texas monitor implementation in a variety of ways.

- Administrators can include language and

content objectives in lesson plans that are aligned to the TEKS and the ELPS.

- Administrators can require teachers to complete linguistic accommodation charts based on ELL proficiency levels.
- Administrators can integrate evidence of TEKS/ELPS implementation into walk-throughs, observation documents, and other teacher feedback opportunities such as:
  - posted content and language objectives.
  - observable opportunities for reading, writing, listening, and speaking for ELLs.
  - use of linguistic accommodations appropriate to students' proficiency levels. (See chart on page 51.)

Which instructional resources support ELLs?

Apart from adopted texts and related supplemental materials, teachers of ELLs can access various materials to enhance instruction. Administrators can confirm the campus budget allocates funds for this purpose. Some of these materials might be maintained in the classrooms while others may be housed in the school library or literacy center. Examples of these resources include:

- Adapted level texts
- Native language materials
- Library resources
- Classroom resources
- Online resources ELLs can access from home

Where can administrators find appropriate resources for ELLs (in English and other languages)?

Administrators can connect teachers to resources in English as well as other languages through:

- Local libraries
- Publishing companies that specialize in materials for ELLs
- Campus and community liaisons
- Local institutions, i.e. Catholic Charities, Mexican Consulate

How do administrators ensure access to free voluntary reading for ELLs in their home language?

ELLs benefit from access to materials in their home language that are suitable for independent reading, i.e., high interest level, low vocabulary level. During Silent Sustained Reading (SSR) or other free reading opportunities, ELLs should have the option to select a book in their home language, if they prefer. Stephen Krashen's, *Free Voluntary Reading* (2011) reviews current research and findings regarding the value of free voluntary reading.

In order to encourage free voluntary reading in classrooms, teachers should:

- maintain a large, classroom library with a variety of reading levels and topics.
- include books with a high interest level, but low vocabulary level.
- create student interest surveys for information about student preferences; there are a number of surveys shared by teachers on the Internet.
- schedule trips to the library.
- read aloud to students.

English Language Proficiency Standards (ELPS)/ Proficiency Level Descriptors (PLDs)

The English Language Proficiency Standards (ELPS) are cross-curricular student expectations for English language development. The Proficiency Level Descriptors (PLDs) identify characteristics of the four levels of English language proficiency (Beginning, Intermediate, Advanced, Advanced High). Teachers use the ELPS to plan instruction that addresses the proficiency levels of each ELL and ensures their continued progress in English language acquisition.

LEGAL LINEAGE

- Elementary and Secondary Education Act of 1965, Title III, Part A, Subpart 1, Sec. 3111 (b)(2), Subpart 2, Sec. 3111 (b)(2), Sec. 3111 (2)(C)(iii)
- TAC Title 19, Part II, ,Chapter 74, Subchapter A, §74.4 (c)(d)

JUST ENOUGH INFORMATION

★ Need to Know

- Administrators' responsibilities with regard to the ELPS
- What the cross-curricular student expectations look like
- The characteristics of the four proficiency levels
- How teachers use the PLDs in planning and implementing instruction

★ Need to Do

- Ensure that teachers and leaders are trained in the ELPS
- Monitor teachers' integration of the ELPS into planning and instruction
- Monitor teachers' alignment of the PLDs in instruction

QUESTIONS

1. How does a campus/district develop appropriate curriculum for ELLs?
2. What are content and language objectives, and why are they required in many districts?
3. What are the English Language Proficiency Standards (ELPS)?
4. What are an administrator's responsibilities for implementing instruction using the ELPS?
5. What are the Proficiency Level Descriptors (PLDs)?
6. How do the ELPS and the PLDs work together?
7. How do administrators ensure teachers use the ELPS and PLDs to linguistically accommodate instruction for ELLs?

FOR MORE INFORMATION (FMI)

- Introductory Training on the PLDs (grades K-1 or grades 2-12) – TELPAS Resources webpage at TEA
- Linguistic Instructional Alignment Guide (LIAG) ELPS Academy training webinar – ESC, Region 20 ELPS webpage
- Making the ELPS-TELPAS Connection - Grades K-12 Overview –TELPAS Resources webpage at TEA
- Seidlitz, J. (2008a). *Navigating the ELPS: Using the new standards to improve instruction for English learners.* San Clemente, CA: Canter Press.
- Seidlitz, J. (2010). *ELPS flip book: A user-friendly guide for academic language instruction.* San Clemente, CA: Canter Press.
- TEA/Project Share Courses: *TELLIT Courses (Math, Science, Social Studies, ELA coming soon), ELPS Academy, Implementing the ELPS in ELAR, Implementing the ELPS in Math, Implementing the ELPS in Science, Implementing the ELPS in Social Studies, Accelerating Language Acquisition for Secondary English Language Learners, A+Rise Online Tutorial*
- Texas English Language Learners Portal – TEA sponsored website

English Language Proficiency Standards (ELPS)/ Proficiency Level Descriptors (PLDs)

How does a campus/district develop appropriate curriculum for ELLs?

As with other special populations, ELLs receive instruction that reflects the Texas Essential Knowledge and Skills (TEKS) for their grade level or course. In addition to the TEKS, curriculum and planning for instruction of ELLs must incorporate the English Language Proficiency Standards (ELPS). When working with the ELPS, teachers need to know:

- cross-curricular student expectations in the ELPS.
- appropriate linguistic accommodations that are aligned to the proficiency levels of each ELL.

The cross-curricular student expectations can be found in TAC Chapter 74, §74.4 (c). These include specific language skills that content area teachers must integrate into every subject of the required curriculum. These skills include: learning strategies, listening, speaking, reading, and writing. The most common integration methods in Texas involve language objectives in lessons. First, teachers identify a content objective that aligns with the TEKS, and with a clear content objective, teachers write a language objective that aligns with the ELPS. Sample language objective stems can be found on page 273. Many teachers throughout Texas find these language objective stems helpful.

Linguistic accommodations are specific adjustments made during instruction to meet the needs of ELLs. Some accommodations focus on ways to make content more comprehensible for ELLs. Other accommodations address ways to facilitate English language development for ELLs. The chart found on page 51 identifies specific accommodations matching each proficiency level. The chart on page 274 arranges the information into three-columns. Either chart would assist teachers in organizing accommodations when planning instruction.

It is important to remember that integrating the cross-curricular student expectations into every required course is not optional within the state of Texas. In addition to being mandated by the state, research demonstrates the advantages of focusing on English language development and providing linguistic accommodations for ELLs.

To facilitate this process, it is imperative that teachers have adequate time to integrate ELPS aligned language objectives and to plan specific ways to linguistically accommodate curriculum.

What are content and language objectives, and why are they required in many districts?

To ensure that ELLs are successful at understanding content, it is important for teachers to have clear objectives aligned to the TEKS. These objectives are referred to in sheltered classes as content objectives. To ensure that ELLs advance in language proficiency, specific language goals are also set by the teacher in every lesson. These language goals align with the ELPS, and they are called language objectives. Most models of sheltered instruction in Texas, i.e., SIOP, Sheltered Plus, GLAD, and QTEL, use language objectives as a way of integrating the ELPS and ensuring that sheltered instruction teachers focus on developing language within the context of math, science, social studies, and language arts classes.

What are the English Language Proficiency Standards (ELPS)?

The ELPS are English Language Proficiency Standards, adopted by the State of Texas in December 2007 [TAC §74.4]. The ELPS meet the requirements of Title III, Part A with regard to instruction and assessment of English language development for ELLs.

They are divided into four different subsections described below.

Subsection a: INTRODUCTION

This subsection indicates that:

- The ELPS are part of the required curriculum.
- ELLs need social and academic language proficiency to be successful.
- Instruction must integrate social and academic English.
- ELLs must read, write, listen, and speak with increased complexity.
- Student expectations of ELPS apply to K-12 students.
- Level descriptors are not grade-specific and serve as a road map.

Subsection b: DISTRICT RESPONSIBILITIES

This subsection indicates that districts must:

- Identify students' proficiency levels.
- Provide linguistically accommodated content instruction.
- Provide linguistically accommodated content-based language instruction.
- Provide focused, targeted, and systematic language instruction for beginning and intermediate ELLs (grade 3 or higher).

Subsection c:
CROSS-CURRICULAR STUDENT EXPECTATIONS

This subsection contains student expectations for:

- Learning Strategies
- Listening
- Speaking
- Reading
- Writing

(See Section II for the full text of the statute)

Subsection d:
PROFICIENCY LEVEL DESCRIPTORS (PLDs)

This subsection contains the levels of proficiency and their descriptors by language domain aligned to the Texas English Language Proficiency Assessment System (TELPAS):

- Beginning
- Intermediate
- Advanced
- Advanced High

(See Section II for the full text of the statute)

English Language Proficiency Standards (ELPS)/ Proficiency Level Descriptors (PLDs)

The ELPS replaced the ESL TEKS and are required to be implemented within each subject of the required curriculum. The most common way districts integrate the ELPS is by using language objectives aligned with the cross curricular student expectations outlined in Subsection c, and linguistic accommodations aligned with the proficiency level descriptors outlined in Subsection d. See the following page for more information.

What are an administrator's responsibilities for implementing instruction using the ELPS?

According to TAC Chapter 74, §74.4, school districts in Texas are required to implement the ELPS as "an integral part of each subject in the required curriculum." It is important to note that they are not to be implemented gradually, subject by subject. Just as with the TEKS, school districts must implement the ELPS in each subject in which ELLs are taught.

While administrators must ensure that teachers implement the standards, the exact method of implementation can vary from district to district. Best practices for implementing language standards suggests that teachers write language objectives aligned to the ELPS for each ELL lesson. In addition, teachers of ELLs need to provide appropriate linguistic accommodations to students based upon their TELPAS proficiency levels. Administrators must ensure that teachers know the proficiency levels of their ELLs and that lesson plans include appropriate accommodations aligned to proficiency levels of ELLs.

What are the Proficiency Level Descriptors (PLDs)?

The Proficiency Level Descriptors (PLDs) are part of the TELPAS assessment of ELLs conducted each year within the state of Texas. Teachers use the PLDs to identify critical attributes of English language proficiency in the four domains– listening, speaking, reading, and writing. Students are rated annually in all four domains. For each domain, the ELL's level of English language proficiency is identified as either Beginner, Intermediate, Advanced, or Advanced High. A chart summarizing the proficiency level descriptors can be found on pages 48-49.

How do the ELPS and the PLDs work together?

TEA has produced a PowerPoint titled *Making the ELPS-TELPAS Connection – Grades K-12 Overview.* This presentation, along with the *Introductory Training on the PLDs* (grades K-1 or grades 2-12), is an excellent resource for teachers who are unfamiliar with the ELPS and the PLDs. The presentations assist teachers in providing the required standards (ELPS) and monitoring progress in English language acquisition (required for all TELPAS raters).

The presentations are located on the TELPAS Resources web page at TEA.

How do administrators ensure that teachers use the ELPS and PLDs to linguistically accommodate instruction for ELLs?

Linguistic accommodations are specific adjustments made to the curriculum in order to meet the needs of ELLs. Linguistic accommodations need to be aligned to students' specific language proficiency levels as determined by the TELPAS. In order to do this, teachers must be aware of student proficiency levels, and they must understand the accommodations appropriate to each proficiency level. For students – not yet assessed using the TELPAS – teachers can use the initial oral language proficiency test and classroom observations to identify a student's level of language development. The TELPAS proficiency level descriptors are recommended to facilitate this process. It is important for teachers to understand that they are responsible for helping students show progress of at least one level of language proficiency every year.

The purpose of providing linguistically accommodated curriculum is twofold. First, teachers provide linguistic accommodations to help students understand the subject matter of the required curriculum; second, teachers help students progress one level of language proficiency on the TELPAS every year. Perhaps one of the best ways administrators can help teachers linguistically accommodate curriculum is to be a part of the process of disaggregating TELPAS data with their teachers. While disaggregating the data, they can fully articulate the expectation that students will progress one level of language proficiency every year.

The following actions outline a process for ensuring that linguistic accommodations are being provided to ELLs:

1. Teachers of ELLs receive training on TELPAS proficiency level descriptors.
2. Teachers of ELLs received training on linguistic accommodations appropriate to each level of language proficiency.
3. Leaders assist teachers of ELLs disaggregate the TELPAS data.
4. Teachers of ELLs identify their students' levels of language proficiency and specific accommodations appropriate for that level of language development.
5. Teachers of ELLs integrate linguistic accommodations in their lesson plans and instructional delivery.
6. Leaders monitor and provide feedback to teachers of ELLs on the implementation of appropriate linguistic accommodations.

Sheltered Instruction

Sheltered instruction is an approach for ELLs that emphasizes the importance of making content comprehensible as students develop academic language.

LEGAL LINEAGE

- Elementary and Secondary Education Act of 1965, Title III, Part A, Sec. 3102 (4)(9)
- TAC Title 19, Part II, Chapter 74, Subchapter A, §74.4 (B)
- TAC Title 19, Part II, Chapter 89, Subchapter BB, §89.1210 (c)(2)(3), (e), (f)(2)(3)

JUST ENOUGH INFORMATION

★ Need to Know

- Characteristics of effective sheltered instruction
- Ways to support ELLs in developing academic language
- Who is required to provide sheltered instruction

★ Need to Do

- Identify specific approach to sheltered instruction in place on the campus or in the district
- Ensure that all teachers of ELLs receive ongoing training in implementing sheltered instruction
- Monitor sheltered instruction practices through walk-throughs and other sources of data

QUESTIONS

1. What is sheltered instruction?
2. What is comprehensible input?
3. Who is required to provide sheltered instruction?
4. In what settings does sheltered instruction occur?
5. Why do teachers need to focus on social language (Basic Interpersonal Communication Skills – BICS) and academic language (Cognitive Academic Language Proficiency – CALP) with their ELLs?
6. What does high-quality sheltered instruction look like?
7. Who needs to receive sheltered instruction training?
8. Should ELLs in math, science, and social studies – at the middle school and high school levels – be clustered for instruction?

FOR MORE INFORMATION (FMI)

- Castillo, M. (2012). *Guiding educators to praxis: Moving teachers beyond theory to practice.* (ProQuest, LLC., Ed . D. Dissertation). Arizona State University.
- CREATE (Center for Research on the Educational Achievement and Teaching of English Language Learners) - website
- Cummins, J. (1991). Interdependence of first-and second-language proficiency in bilingual children. Language processing in bilingual children, 70-89.
- Goldenberg, C., & Coleman, R. (2010). *Promoting academic achievement among English learners: A guide to the research.* Thousand Oaks, CA: Corwin.
- IDRA (Intercultural Development Research Association)
- Krashen, S. D., & Terrell, T. D. (1983). *The natural approach: Language acquisition in the classroom.* San Francisco: CA. The Alemany Press.
- Project GLAD (Guided Language Acquisition Design) - United States Department of Education, OBEMLA, Project of Academic Excellence, and California Department of Education Exemplary Program
- QTEL (Quality Teaching of English Learners) – WestEd website
- Regional Education Service Centers
- Seidlitz, J. (2008b). *Sheltered instruction plus: A comprehensive plan for successfully teaching English language learners.* San Clemente, CA: Canter Press.
- Seidlitz, J., & Castillo, M. (2011). *Language & Literacy for ELLs: Creating Systematic Change for Academic Achievement.* San Clemente, CA: Canter Press.
- Seidlitz, J., & Perryman, B. (2011). *Seven steps to a language-rich, interactive classroom.* San Clemente, CA: Canter Press.
- Short, D., & Echevarria, J. (1999). *The Sheltered Instruction Observation Protocol: A tool for teacher-researcher collaboration and professional development.* UC Berkeley: Center for Research on Education, Diversity and Excellence.
- SIOP (Sheltered Instruction Observation Protocol) – Center for Applied Linguistics, Pearson Education
- *Student Attendance Accounting Handbook* (SAAH), Sec. 6.10 – on TEA website
- TEA/Project Share Courses: TELLIT Courses, ELPS Academy, Accelerating Language Acquisition for Secondary English Language Learners, A+Rise Online Tutorial
- Walqui, A., & Van Lier, L. (2010). *Scaffolding the academic success of adolescent English language learners.* San Francisco, CA: WestEd.
- Wright, W. (2010). *Foundations for teaching English language learners: Research, theory, policy, and practice.* Philadelphia, PA: Caslon Publishing.

Sheltered Instruction

What is sheltered instruction?

The term sheltered instruction was first used in 1983 to describe an approach to instruction of English language learners. (Krashen & Terrell, 1983). By definition, it means that ELLs receive comprehensible input about content area subject matter while developing English language proficiency. According to Wright (2010), in order to ensure that ELLs participate fully and achieve academically, teachers in sheltered instruction classes teach content-area language at grade level.

There are several popular models of sheltered instruction. The most commonly used in Texas are:

Sheltered Instruction Observation Protocol (SIOP): The SIOP Model was initially developed by Deborah Short and Jana Echevarria in 1999 in order to measure the quality of instructional delivery of sheltered practices in elementary and secondary classrooms. It consists of eight components and thirty features, each measured on a scale ranging from Not Evident (0) to Highly Evident (4) for each feature. For more information on the SIOP model, visit the SIOP Institute on the Internet.

Sheltered Instruction Plus, A Guide for Texas Teachers of ELLs: This model was developed by John Seidlitz to help Texas teachers integrate the ELPS into their approach to sheltered instruction. This research-based approach is organized according to the *Seven Steps to a Language-Rich Interactive Classroom* and the use of targeted linguistic accommodations aligned with TELPAS proficiency level descriptors. Many districts in Texas have shown gains after implementing this approach with ELLs (Seidlitz & Perryman, 2011).

For more information on research related to *Sheltered Instruction Plus, A Guide for Texas Teachers of ELLs* (2008b) and specific districts that have used this approach, visit the Seidlitz Education website on the Internet.

Quality Teachers for English Learners (QTEL): This approach was developed by WestEd under the direction of Aida Walqui as a pragmatic methodology grounded in socio-cultural theory. Teachers implementing this approach use the resource titled *Scaffolding the Academic Success of Adolescent English Language Learners* by Aida Walqui and Leo van Lier. Teachers in Austin ISD were involved in some of the research related to the QTEL approach.

Six principles guide QTEL's work with and on behalf of teachers and students:

- Sustain Academic Rigor
- Hold High Expectations
- Infuse Metaprocesses in the Educational research related to QTEL
- Engage in Quality Teacher and Student Interactions
- Sustain a Language Focus
- Develop a Quality Curriculum

For more information on the QTEL approach, visit the WestEd website on the Internet.

Guided Language Acquisition Design (Project GLAD): This approach to ELL instruction was developed and field-tested in the Fountain Valley School District in California. The model involves explicitly teaching ELL educators with research-based approaches, followed by observations of the model with students. The model has been popular with some districts in Texas, particularly at the elementary level.

For more information related to Project GLAD, visit the Project GLAD website on the Internet.

What is comprehensible input?

Comprehensible input happens whenever a second language learner understands English. It is important to realize that without comprehensible input, there is no language development. Hearing English does not automatically create English language development. To develop a second language, the words heard or read must be made comprehensible in some manner to a second language learner. For beginning and intermediate ELLs, this requires teachers to use effective techniques for providing comprehensible input such as:

- Visuals
- Total Physical Response (TPR)
- Gestures
- Speech appropriate for proficiency levels
- Opportunities for clarification with teacher or peer
- Use of native language resources/peers to build background about topic

The most important factor in providing comprehensible input is a clear intention by the teacher to communicate and ensure understanding by the second language learner. With these language comprehension goals in mind, teachers will use appropriate visuals, gestures, and speech in the classroom to focus on communication and understanding.

Sheltered Instruction

Who is required to provide sheltered instruction?

According to the *Student Attendance Accounting Handbook*, Sec. 6.10, all teachers of ELLs are required to receive sheltered instruction training in order to linguistically accommodate instruction and provide comprehensible input for ELLs in class.

Since the goal of sheltered instruction is to provide comprehensible input and develop academic language, content area teachers bear a special responsibility to provide quality sheltered instruction to ELLs.

In what settings does sheltered instruction occur?

A sheltered approach is required in Texas schools when ELLs receive instruction in general education content area classes or when they are taught content in a bilingual or ESL classroom conducted in English. According toTAC Chapter 89, §89.1210, the "English language learner receives sheltered instruction in all content areas" in ESL pull-out or content-based programs.

This requirement is also stated in the *Student Attendance Accounting Handbook*, Sec. 6.10.

Why do teachers need to focus on social language (Basic Interpersonal Communication Skills – BICS) and academic language (Cognitive Academic Language Proficiency – CALP) with their ELLs?

Both social and academic language are significant for ELLs. Jim Cummins (1981) coined the term BICS (Basic Interpersonal Communication Skills) to refer to social language and CALP (Cognitive Academic Language Proficiency) to refer to academic language.

Social language is the language of everyday interaction. It is often informal, incorporates many idioms, and occurs during everyday interactions – outside of academic and formal contexts.

Academic language is the type of language usually found in academic contexts. It includes the kind of language found in academic text, such as in academic articles and textbooks, as well as the kind of language heard in academic lectures and conversations.

Social language can usually be acquired within one or two years, but growth in conversational language continues over many years –as ELLs become more proficient in a second language. Academic language takes from 7 to 9 years to fully develop.

It is important for teachers to realize that both academic and social language are necessary for ELLs in classroom contexts. In order to develop social language, ELLs need opportunities to interact and receive comprehensible input. This interaction needs to take place not only in ESL classes but also in content area and elective classes.

Also, teachers should be aware that ELLs need explicit vocabulary instruction in core content vocabulary. Methods for direct vocabulary instruction will vary across content areas, but all teachers of ELLs must emphasize content area vocabulary development for ELLs to be successful. In addition, ESL teachers and language arts teachers can greatly enhance vocabulary acquisition for ELLs by providing free voluntary reading opportunities so that students can read engaging, culturally-relevant texts.

What does high-quality sheltered instruction look like?

Although there are a variety of models of sheltered instruction, some essential practices are common to every model. Saunders, Goldenberg, and Marcelletti (2013) offer a basic list of instructional strategies that facilitate the learning of grade-level academic content in content-based sheltered classes. They include:

- building on student experiences and familiar content
- providing students with necessary background knowledge
- using graphic organizers
- making instruction and learning tasks extremely clear
- using pictures, demonstrations, and real-life objects
- providing hands-on, interactive learning activities
- providing redundant information using gestures and visual cues
- giving additional practice and time for discussion of key concepts
- designating language and content objectives for each lesson
- using sentence frames and models to help students talk about academic content
- providing instruction differentiated by students' English language proficiency

Sheltered Instruction

Who needs to receive sheltered instruction training?

Because all ELLs must receive sheltered instruction in their content area classes, all secondary teachers who instruct ELLs in any courses that form part of the required curriculum must receive some sheltered training. It is also recommended that those instructional assistants and other support staff who directly instruct ELLs receive some training on sheltered approaches.

At the elementary level, teachers also benefit from using sheltered approaches to deliver content area instruction in English. Such approaches use research-based methods to effectively make content comprehensible and to help the ELLs develop academic language.

Regardless of which model of sheltered instruction is selected, a one-day staff development event on sheltered instruction is not sufficient to make a difference in the achievement of ELLs. In many cases, districts may be in compliance with regard to teacher training, but still may not provide appropriate instruction and linguistic accommodations for ELLs. The problem with such "paper compliance" is that it fails to result in gains for ELLs and does not narrow the achievement gap, since the training is not reflected in daily instructional delivery.

A US Department of Education study, conducted through the University of Arizona, examined the integration of theory and practice in implementing a sheltered approach. ELLs made significant gains because their teachers received extended support and implemented the *Seven Steps to a Language-Rich Interactive Classroom* model used by many districts in Texas (Seidlitz & Perryman, 2011). Over a period of eighteen months, educators were given knowledge about ELLs, opportunities to practice what they were learning in and out of training sessions, and on-going collaboration and support as they worked with their students (Castillo, 2012). Survey data and interviews revealed that the sustained ongoing support was essential to the success of ELLs.

Should ELLs taking science, math, and social studies – at the middle and high school levels – be clustered for instruction?

There is no research that offers a definite answer to the question of clustering ELLs. The choices are to place students with teachers who have received intensive training on sheltered approaches or to train all content-area teachers on sheltered instruction. Often, districts with larger numbers of ELLs will avoid clustering whereas smaller districts are more likely to cluster students. To make good decisions about clustering ELLs, several issues need to be remembered. They are:

- The choice to cluster students should be made in the context of a well-defined plan that maximizes opportunities for language development for ELLs.
- If students are not clustered, all content area teachers must be trained to provide high quality sheltered instruction to meet the needs of these ELL students.
- Decisions should be focused on the needs of the ELL students, rather than on the needs of the teachers/system.
- Not all ELLs have the same needs. Campuses may want to cluster beginning/intermediate or SIFE (Students with Interrupted Formal Education) students with a specific group of teachers trained to work with them.
- Campus administrators should ensure that any decision regarding clustering allows each ELL to reach their full potential.

ELLs Served by Other Programs

ELLs may require support from more than one program in order to succeed academically and socially in school. This section describes other programs which may serve ELLs, in addition to bilingual or ESL programs.

LEGAL LINEAGE

- All programs – TAC Title 19, Part II, Chapter 89, Subchapter BB, §89.1220 (g)(4)
- Dyslexia – TEC, Title 2, Subtitle F, Chapter 38, Sec. 38.003; TAC Title 19, Part II, Chapter 74, §74.28*
- Gifted and Talented – TEC, Title 2, Subtitle F, Chapter 29, Subchapter D, Sec. 29.121- Sec. 29.123 and Chapter 42, Sec. 42.156*
- Response to Intervention (RtI) – Individuals with Disabilities Act (IDEA), Elementary and Secondary Education Act of 1965, Title I, Part A, and Response to Intervention Coordinating Council (state level)*
- Special Education – TEC, Title 2, Subtitle F, Chapter 29, Subchapter A; TAC Title 19, Part II, Chapter 89, Subchapter BB,§ 89.1220 (G)(4) and §89.1225 (k); TAC Title 19, Part II, Chapter 101, Subchapter AA, §101.1003*
- Preschool and PPCD - TEC, Title 2, Subtitle F, Chapter 29, Subchapter B, Sec. 29.060; Subchapter E, Kindergarten and Pre-kindergarten Programs

* Reference only – text not supplied in this resource

JUST ENOUGH INFORMATION

★ Need to Know

- Program participation data for ELLs
- Teachers in other programs that are coordinating services with bilingual/ ESL programs
- How to coordinate the delivery of program services for ELLs served by other programs

★ Need to Do

- Ensure that ELLs are afforded the same opportunity to receive services from other programs for which they are eligible
- Ensure that teachers and staff in other programs are aware of the needs of ELLs
- Ensure that teachers and staff in other programs— providing services to ELLs— are properly trained to support ELLs
- Ensure that a member of the LPAC is present at all ARD meetings that concern ELLs as well as 504 meetings, RtI team meetings, or other group meetings where ELLs are discussed individually

QUESTIONS

1. If ELLs participate in other programs, which ones would require coordination between the LPAC and the program?
2. How are ELLs identified for participation in Gifted and Talented programs?
3. How do administrators ensure that ELLs have equitable access to advanced academics?
4. How do the LPAC and ARD committees work together?
5. What documentation provides evidence of participation and monitoring of ELLs in other programs?
6. Should ELLs participate in RtI? If so, what would be the best way to provide those services?
7. How can teachers provide culturally-responsive instruction and interventions for ELLs who struggle behaviorally and academically?
8. Are students who receive services from the district prior to pre-kindergarten – for example, Preschool Program for Children with Disabilities (PPCD) – eligible for identification as ELLs? Can they receive bilingual/ESL program services? If not, how are their second language needs met prior to pre-kindergarten?

FOR MORE INFORMATION (FMI)

- 2013-2014 *List of Approved Tests for Assessment of Limited English Proficient Students* – TEA Bilingual Education web page
- Information on State Assessments for English Language Learners – TEA web page
- LPAC Framework Additional Resources – ESC, Region 20
- The National Center for Culturally Responsive Educational Systems - website
- *To the Administrator Addressed* (Sept. 19, 2013) – TEA webpage
- *Writing Preparation for Educators of ESL/ELL Students* – College Board website

Dyslexia

- Dyslexia Handbook and Dyslexia Informational PowerPoint – TEA Dyslexia Requirements for Educator Preparation Programs web page
- Regional and state assistance to districts, parents, and other entities in the area of dyslexia – ESC, Region 10

Gifted and Talented

- Equity in Gifted/Talented (G/T) Education – web page sponsored by TEA
- The Texas State Plan for the Education of Gifted/Talented Students and Gifted/Talented Frequently Asked Questions – TEA Gifted/Talented Education in Texas web page

Preschool and PPCD

- Services for Texas Students with Disabilities, Ages 3-5 – TEA webpage
- Texas Project First – TEA sponsored bilingual website
- Texas Pre-kindergarten Guidelines – TEA webpage

Response to Intervention (RtI)

- Gay, G. (2002). Preparing for culturally responsive teaching. *Journal of Teacher Education,* 53(2), 106-116.
- Response to Intervention Guidance Document and Question and Answer (Q&A) Document – TEA Curriculum Programs – Response to Intervention web page
- Seidlitz, J., & Jones C. (2011). *RtI for ELLs: Considerations for success with diverse learners* (2nd Ed.). San Clemente, CA: Canter Press.

Special Education

- Assessment for Special Populations Unit, Student Assessment Division, TEA
- Guidance Related to ARD Committee and LPAC Collaboration – TEA Accommodation Resources web page
- LPAC Framework – ESC, Region 20 webpage
- Process for Exiting LEP Students Receiving Special Education Services from Bilingual/ESL Programs – TEA Bilingual Education web page
- STAAR and TELPAS Accommodations – TEA Accommodation Resources web page

ELLs Served by Other Programs

If ELLs participate in other programs, which ones would require coordination between the LPAC and the program?

The following programs require coordination between the LPAC and the program:

- Special Education
- Response to Intervention
- Gifted/Talented
- Dyslexia
- 504
- Early Childhood/PPCD
- Advanced Academics

The degree of coordination between the LPAC and these programs – on behalf of ELLs – is determined by individual ELL needs and the academic/linguistic/social characteristics of each student.

In addition, the LPAC is expected to meet as needed to ensure the ELL has access to programs for which they might become eligible. Students can be dual-classified (for example ELL/SPED) based on their eligibility for participation. All decisions are made on an individual basis and are based upon personal academic needs and goals of ELLs.

How are ELLs identified for participation in Gifted and Talented (G/T) programs?

It is likely that the district has adopted local policy to determine participation in G/T programming. However, if ELLs are underrepresented in the program, it is helpful to share the screening tests approved for use in identifying ELLs for G/T services included in the *List of Approved Tests for Assessment of Limited English Proficient Students* published annually by the TEA.

If the G/T program pulls students from general education classrooms for additional services, then the same programming should be made available for ELLs in order for them to be offered equitable services.

How do administrators ensure that ELLs have equitable access to advanced academics?

One of the principle tenets of bilingual/ESL programs is that ELLs are entitled to equitable access to the same programs and extra-curricular activities as their native-English speaking peers. It can be challenging for teachers to understand this principle as it pertains to access and participation in advanced academics by ELLs.

If, on the other hand, a campus/district has a policy to identify eligibility for enrollment in advanced coursework, it is vital that ELLs have an equitable opportunity to meet the requirements. It is important to know the academic achievement levels and educational background for ELLs as their class schedules are built.

It is imperative that teachers of pre-AP, AP, IB, and other advanced courses be trained in sheltered instruction practices that support ELLs who qualify for participation in those classes. If a campus/district has an open enrollment policy for advanced coursework, ELLs cannot be prevented from participation simply because of linguistic differences. If the ELL is capable of mastering the content, the teacher is responsible for linguistically accommodating the ELL, i.e., the teacher must support ELL understanding in the language of instruction.

The College Board has developed training for teachers who are working with ELLs to prepare them for SAT testing. The training is titled, *Writing Preparation for Educators of ESL/ELL Students.* The workshop is intended to assist teachers prepare recently exited students for the writing section of the SAT.

How do the LPAC and ARD committees work together?

It is up to the LPAC and the ARD, working in conjunction, to determine the best placement and the best services to meet the needs of each ELL serviced by special education. The LPAC may determine that the student's second language needs can be best met in the IEP and not in the second language program. This determination is based upon the unique characteristics of student needs. Both English-dominant students and ELLs should be treated the same when it comes to program access. It would be advisable for the district to have developed policy regarding this situation.

Placement decisions for students with special needs in dual language classrooms are made by the Admission, Review, and Dismissal (ARD) committee and the Language Proficiency Assessment Committee (LPAC). These groups must review student objectives and performance data in order to make an informed placement decision.

The TEA webpage – Guidance Relating to ARD Committee and LPAC Collaboration – addresses topics such as: an overview of the collaborative process, student confidentiality, state resources, and technical assistance/ training contact information.

What documentation provides evidence of participation and monitoring of ELLs in other programs?

Participation in other programs is noted with PEIMS codes. Texas is transitioning all Local Education Agencies (LEAs) to the new Texas Student Data System (TSDS) from 2013 – 2017. In the interim, districts are using a variety of databases to identify student participation in special programs. A *To the Administrator Addressed* letter was posted on September 19, 2013 to explain the transition and implementation plan for the TSDS. This letter also includes a link to find out in which stage an LEA is located.

In addition, the LPAC is required to document discussions and decisions ensuring that ELLs have access to programs and services for which they are eligible. LPACs coordinate with other programs when determining student class schedules, teachers, and appropriate supports and accommodations for ELLs.

In determining bilingual/ESL program entry, annual state testing, and exit decisions, LPACs consult with other programs as needed to ensure good decision-making for ELLs. These contacts are to be documented in the LPAC minutes.

All documentation is to be maintained in the ELL's record folder on campus.

ELLs Served by Other Programs

Should ELLs participate in RtI? If so, what would be the best way to provide those supports?

Response to Intervention (RtI) is a process for ensuring high quality instruction for all struggling learners. RtI can be used to help educators determine if the ELL's academic or behavioral problems stem from an issue with acquisition of the English language or a true academic disability. Struggling students can be identified early and tiered interventions can be provided in the classroom or in small groups. RtI should not be implemented as a pathway to special education, but as a vital tool in the documentation that informs the decision-making process.

When considering the process of RtI with ELLs, the student's cultural background, as well as language proficiency in both the native language and English, should be considered. Research-based interventions which focus on the ELL's specific academic or behavioral needs should be implemented. One culturally and linguistically congruent approach to providing classroom-based intervention (Tier I) is the sheltered instruction approach.

In those cases where progress does not occur in spite of well-documented and well-delivered, differentiated and scaffolded classroom instruction, the teacher identifies the nature of the problem and implements interventions to address the student's academic and linguistic needs. The teacher may consult with fellow teachers or campus/district interventionists to develop an appropriate set of interventions to implement and monitor. Academic and behavioral interventions for ELLs must support the two goals of sheltered instruction; to enable the student to make sense of instruction of academic content, and to develop academic language through targeted instruction in the foundations of English language. One resource to access is *RtI for ELLs: Considerations for Success with Diverse Learners* (Seidlitz, J., & Jones, C., 2008b)

How can teachers provide culturally-responsive instruction and interventions for ELLs who struggle behaviorally and academically?

According to Gay (2002), "culturally responsive teaching means using the cultural characteristics, experiences, and perspectives of ethnically diverse students as conduits for teaching them more effectively." Culturally responsive teachers are:

- socio-culturally aware.
- positive towards students from diverse cultures.
- committed to more equitable schooling for culturally diverse students.
- capable of providing instructional supports in a challenging educational context.
- interested in learning about their culturally diverse students.
- committed to creating an inclusive, welcoming learning environment for all students.

If administrators find little or no evidence of culturally-responsive instruction among teachers, targeted professional development can ensure integration of these techniques.

It is important for administrators to review the RtI process on campus to determine the types of interventions teachers use with

ELLs. Some ELLs may be acting out behaviorally due to a lack of culturally responsive teaching. If they do not feel valued, welcomed, and significant, they might understandably act out. If teachers are trained in culturally responsive educational approaches, some ELLs might correct their inappropriate behavior.

For ELLs with purely academic problems, the RtI process might best be delivered in the student's native language (depending on their level of English language proficiency). This would be in keeping with a culturally responsive approach to RtI.

To learn more about culturally responsive teaching, visit The National Center for Culturally Responsive Educational Systems website on the Internet.

Are students who receive services from the district prior to pre-kindergarten – for example, Preschool Program for Children with Disabilities (PPCD) – eligible for identification as ELLs?

Can they receive bilingual/ESL program services?

If not, how are their second language needs met prior to pre-kindergarten?

According to the *Student Attendance Accounting Handbook*, section 6.2, students under the age of three and served only though Preschool Program for Children with Disabilities (PPCD) cannot generate average daily attendance for bilingual/ESL. Chapter 89 states that bilingual/ESL programs are only available in grades pre-K and up. Some districts offer pre-K classes for three-year-olds. If a child is enrolled in pre-K (not PPCD), he/she may be identified and served through the local bilingual/ESL program. The child must be coded in PEIMS as enrolled in pre-K.

Some districts split the day for these students, serving them for half of a day in PPCD or some other local program and half a day in pre-K. If the student is coded in PEIMS as enrolled in pre-K, the student may be identified using the LPAC process described in Chapter 89. The bilingual or ESL program services will be provided in the pre-K setting. During the other part of the day, the ARD, or local policy, will determine what, if any, second language support is to be provided in that setting.

Students who are served only through PPCD or a local program other than pre-K, can receive second language support through those programs. They cannot generate bilingual/ESL allotment for program participation and cannot be identified as an ELL. If a district secures a Home Language Survey, which indicates a language other than English upon initial participation in PPCD or another local program based on the campus, that HLS can be retained and then used to initiate the identification process once the student enrolls in pre-K and is coded in PEIMS for enrollment.

ELLs with Unique Characteristics

ELLs with unique characteristics include students who are: newcomers, migrant ELLs, students with interrupted formal education (SIFE), as well as students identified as long-term ELLs (receiving services for more than five years).

LEGAL LINEAGE

- Elementary and Secondary Education Act of 1965, Title I, Part C, Sec. 1301; Sec. 1304; Sec. 1308; Sec. 1309
- TEC, Title 2, Subtitle F, Chapter 39, Subchapter B, Sec. 39.027 (a)
- TAC Title 19, Part II, Chapter 74.4, §74.4 (b)(4)
- TAC Title 19, Part II, Chapter 89, Subchapter BB, §89.1210 (b)(e)(f) and §89.1220 (g)(3)(4)
- TAC Title 19, Part II, Chapter 101, Subchapter AA, §101.1005 (h) and §101.1007

JUST ENOUGH INFORMATION

★ Need to Know

- Definition for newcomers, migrant ELLs, students with interrupted formal education (SIFE), and long-term ELLs
- Requirement for serving these students
- Other staff responsible for these students
- 2013-2014 data collection requirements for certain populations of ELLs

★ Need to Do

- Ensure that all teachers know which ELLs have unique characteristics
- Ensure that all requirements for serving these students are met
- Monitor teachers to ensure best practices are in use

QUESTIONS

1. Which ELLs are considered newcomers?
2. How do administrators and teachers meet the needs of ELLs who are newcomers at the secondary level?
3. Which ELLs are considered long-term ELLs, and how can administrators and teachers meet their needs?
4. What are the characteristics of asylee/refugees, students with interrupted formal education (SIFE), and migrant ELLs?
5. How do administrators ensure that the needs of asylee/refugees, students with interrupted formal education (SIFE), and migrant ELLs are met?

FOR MORE INFORMATION (FMI)

- 2013-2014 District and Campus Coordinators Manual (DCMM) – on TEA website
- 2013-2014 Fall ELL Assessments Update – TEA PPT presentation
- Assessments for Special Populations Unit, Student Assessment Division – TEA webpage
- Center on Instruction - website
- Cultural Orientation Resource Center - website sponsored by Center for Applied Linguistics (CAL)
- *Double the Work: Adolescent Newcomers* - Center for Applied Linguistics (CAL) website
- ELL Solutions Forum, Best Practices Clearinghouse - TEA webpage
- Goldenberg, C., & Coleman, R. (2010). *Promoting academic achievement among English learners: A guide to the research.* Thousand Oaks, CA: Corwin.
- Identification and Recruitment of Migrant Students (ID&R) *Letter to the Administrator Addressed* (Aug. 2006) – TEA webpage
- K-12 Databases - TEA Long Range Plan for Technology webpage
- Krashen, S. D. (1985). *The input hypothesis: Issues and implications* (Vol. 1, p. 985). London: Longman.
- Krashen, S. D. (2011). *Free voluntary reading.* Santa Barbara, CA: Libraries Unlimited, ABC-CLIO, LLC.
- LPAC Framework Additional Resources – ESC, Region 20 LPAC Framework webpage
- Obamehenti, F., & Seidlitz, J. (2013). *Texas student refugee framework: A collaborative approach.* San Clemente, CA: Seidlitz Education.
- Refugee Intake Assessment (in document listed above)
- Saunders, W., Goldenberg, C. & Marcelletti, D. (2013). English language development: Guidelines for instruction. *American Educator,* Summer 2013.
- Seidlitz, J., & Kenfield, K. (2011). *38 great academic language builders.* San Clemente, CA: Canter Press.
- Seidlitz, J., & Perryman, B. (2011). *Seven Steps to a language-rich interactive classroom.* San Clemente, CA: Canter Press.
- Title I, Part C - Texas Migrant Education Program – TEA web page
- USDE Office of Migrant Education webpage
- *Welcome to the United States: A Guidebook for Refugees* – CAL website
- *Welcome to the United States: Orientation Video* – CAL website

ELLs with Unique Characteristics

Which ELLs are considered newcomers?

In general, ELLs are considered newcomers if they are in their first three years of enrollment in US schools and their levels of English language proficiency are at the Beginner or Intermediate level.

In Texas, the English Language Proficiency Standards (ELPS) identify the newcomer population as students (grade 3 or higher) in need of "focused, targeted, and systematic language acquisition instruction to provide them with the foundation of English language vocabulary, grammar, syntax, and English mechanics necessary to support content-based instruction and accelerated learning of English" [TAC §74.4 (b)(4)].

ELLs who are newcomers may be served in a variety of instructional settings designed to meet their needs. A district may establish a newcomer center as described in Chapter 89, §89.1235 to house recent immigrant ELLs for up to two years after initial enrollment. The district may also concentrate bilingual/ESL programs at a limited number of schools within a district, provided the enrollment of ELLs in those campuses does not exceed 60% of the total enrollment at the facility.

If newcomers are integrated into regular campus settings, their needs are still a priority, and administrators must ensure provisions for the required language acquisition services. ELLs who are newcomers are often scheduled into one or two classes per day of intensive language acquisition and acceleration taught by ESL-certified teachers. In addition, their participation in general education content area courses is also heavily supported by both general education teachers and ESL specialists or other support staff. An administrator's responsibility is to monitor placement and support within these special settings.

The LPAC is also involved in determining the daily schedule of each ELL to ensure that their linguistic needs are met. Since administrators are required members of each LPAC meeting, they can help identify special supports for ELLs who are newcomers.

How do administrators and teachers meet the needs of ELLs who are newcomers at the secondary level?

Students who arrive at a secondary campus with a Beginning or Intermediate level of English language proficiency pose certain challenges for district administrators. First, there is great diversity in this population of ELLs who are newcomers. For example, some newcomers may:

- have grade level experience.
- have completed course work above grade level.
- be functioning below grade level or have very little school experience.
- speak a European language and are able to decode the English alphabet.
- not be familiar with the English alphabet and have greater levels of linguistic and cultural differences from their English-speaking peers.

The needs of ELLs who are newcomers can be addressed in a variety of ways. The first is to establish a newcomer center and classes just for ELLs.

Newcomer centers host beginners and sometimes intermediates at the secondary level. Here, newcomers spend the majority of the day in homogeneous groups to focus on English language development. Large districts often establish the center on one campus with newcomers traveling to the center from district schools. At the newcomer center:

- Homogeneous groups focus on a high degree of comprehensible input in math, science, and social studies.
- ESL classes focus on the needs of secondary beginners to facilitate rapid acquisition of social and academic English – necessary to function in a general education environment.

When districts are unable to establish newcomer centers, they organize homogeneously grouped, content area ESL classes that incorporate sheltered instruction. These classes use:

- state adopted textbooks.
- adapted materials.
- strategies such as Total Physical Response (TPR), Teaching Proficiency through Reading and Storytelling (TPRS), or the language experience approach.
- high levels of comprehensible input to facilitate rapid English language acquisition.

Sheltered instruction, by itself, may not be sufficient for many ELL newcomers. Chapter 74, §74.4 (b)(4) of the Texas Administrative Code (TAC) mandates that ELLs at the Beginning or Intermediate levels of English language proficiency receive focused, systematic language development that includes English language vocabulary, grammar, syntax, and mechanics to support content-based instruction and accelerated English acquisition. Like math, science, and social studies, ELA is a content area where great emphasis is placed upon students to read large amounts of text, and they do so in a heterogeneous language arts classroom with ELLs who are newcomers and native speakers. Therefore, it becomes challenging to provide the required focused language development.

ELLs with Unique Characteristics

Which ELLs are considered long-term ELLs, and how can administrators and teachers meet their needs?

Long-term ELLs are those who have attended school in the US for six or more years yet are still classified as ELLs. Many districts struggle to meet the needs of these students. Characteristically, they are often fluent in conversational English, yet cannot be reclassified because they are unable to perform at expected levels on the STAAR and TELPAS. Many long-term ELLs have gaps in comprehension and lack of communication skills in academic English.

To meet the needs of long-term ELLs, administrators at both the campus and district levels must identify the students as a group needing additional support. Teachers and administrators should know these students by name and know the data related to their academic performance. It becomes a priority to implement strategies that will result in the student advancing in their levels of English language proficiency. Campuses can take specific actions to help long-term ELLs, such as:

1. Establish relationships with positive academic role models. Long-term ELLs may lack a history of academic success and sometimes do not have positive relationships with peers/adults with a history of academic success. Inviting guest speakers from the same cultural and language background of the students and establishing partnerships with university and community organizations can help long-term ELLs identify the value of learning to read and communicate in academic English.
2. Increase the use of academic text in content area classes. Many academic terms and phrases simply do not occur during conversations. To improve comprehension of academic English, ELLs must have a wide variety of opportunities to encounter academic language. Goldenberg & Coleman's research (2010) shows that increased amounts of student reading – either individually or in small groups – in science, math, language arts, social studies, and other electives provides opportunities for ELLs to be exposed to academic terms/phrases that help them communicate effectively using that language.
3. Increase academic conversations in content area classes. Structured student-to-student conversations within content area classes provides long-term ELLs with a variety of benefits. They can: clarify academic concepts, hear new terms used in a variety of contexts, and practice new terminology.
4. Practice robust English language development through English language arts or ESL. Recent ELL research by Saunders, Goldenberg, and Marcelletti shows that advanced levels of proficiency indicate a need for specific instruction in English grammar, syntax, and word usage. In addition, direct instruction on advanced English vocabulary, form and function of language used in academic contexts, and approaches to reading and writing in specific genres is beneficial. ESL and ELAR teachers can use the state adopted textbooks and other commercially available resources to design instruction focused on academic language development for ELLs.

Instructional materials designed for general population students may not be best for ELLs.

5. Allow free voluntary reading. Research supports the value of free voluntary reading. Campuses have implemented a variety of SSR (sustained silent reading) programs to provide opportunities to develop independent reading habits for students. Krashen's research indicates that these strategies elevate language acquisition skills for long-term ELLs. (Krashen, 2011)
6. Include ELLs in Response to Intervention (RtI) initiatives on campus. RtI is a system of tiered interventions that addresses students struggling either academically or behaviorally. Teams of teachers, often by grade level, discuss students whose performance on universal screening tests indicates a potential academic problem or whose behavior indicates a need for additional support. Students are placed into tiered support interventions and are closely monitored to ensure that they close the gap in their performance or behavior, as needed.

Long-term ELLs may have missed important concept development or content knowledge in their early years in school due to limited English proficiency. As older students, their English language proficiency is at a level where they can participate meaningfully in RtI interventions appropriate to their needs. Their lack of academic success is likely due to this gap in concept development or content knowledge, rather than linguistic difficulties.

What are the characteristics of asylee/refugees, students with interrupted formal education (SIFE), and migrant ELLs?

An increasing challenge for districts involves meeting the needs of ELLs who:

- have interrupted schooling in their country of origin.
- have not been in US schools long enough to perform on grade level.

These are known as students with interrupted formal education (SIFE). Not all refugee students would be identified as SIFE and some SIFE students would not meet the criteria established by the US Department of State.

Some characteristics common to SIFE students include ELLs:

- with little or no formal education.
- whose education has been interrupted by war, migration, cultural/political/economic upheaval.
- who perform several years below their grade level in terms of academic knowledge and skills.
- who have low literacy levels in their native language.

ELLs with Unique Characteristics

These students need to rapidly and simultaneously learn English, acquire academic language, and learn grade level content.

Some ELLs qualify for services through Title I, Part C Federal Migrant Education programs. The TEA webpage for Title 1, Part C – Migrant Education Programs provides guidance and regulation related to these services. In Texas, the process for identification and recruitment of migrant children is generally handled at the district level in accordance with procedures provided by the Identification and Recruitment (ID&R) *Letter to the Administrator Addressed* from the TEA.

How do administrators ensure that the needs of asylee/refugees, students with interrupted formal education (SIFE), and migrant ELLs are met?

Many districts face the challenge of meeting the needs of ELLs who have not attended school in their country of origin or have not been in US schools long enough to perform on grade level. These students are referred to, in research literature, as students with interrupted formal education (SIFE).

It is important to note that not all refugee students would be identified as SIFE, and some students would not meet the criteria established by the US Department of State to be identified as refugee or asylee.

There are many things districts can do to help meet the needs of these students. First of all, it is important to know the knowledge and skills of the arriving students and to identify deficits that may not be revealed through the OLPT or the TELPAS assessment. For example, the Refugee Intake Assessment in the *Texas Student Refugee Framework: A Collaborative Approach* (Obamehenti & Seidlitz, 2013) addresses a broad range of student academic background knowledge. Although designed specifically for refugees, this tool can be useful with other populations of students who miss significant amounts of schooling for various reasons.

Once student needs have been assessed, specific goals for SIFE students should be established based on the results of the assessments and available resources. Students who have not attended school for some time may require targeted effort to help them acculturate to US schools.

Many districts in Texas have formed partnerships with cultural community organizations, religious organizations, and university student groups that are familiar with the culture and language of the student. These groups can be an invaluable resource in providing translation and explanations of campus culture, acting as role models, and communicating with parents.

Other resources for supporting SIFE students are located on the Center for Applied Linguistics (CAL) website. They include:

- *Welcome to the United States: A Guidebook for Refugees*
- *Welcome to the United States: Orientation Video*
- *Cultural Orientation Resource Center* (website sponsored by CAL)

These sources offer help to schools working with refugee populations – many identified as SIFE. In addition, to better understand the student, it is helpful to speak with family members and individuals who know the student's background and experiences.

ASSESSMENT

State of Texas Assessment of Academic Readiness (STAAR) / End-Of-Course (EOC) Testing

State of Texas Assessments of Academic Readiness (STAAR®) tests are the annual, summative assessments of student mastery of the Texas Essential Knowledge and Skills (TEKS). Current STAAR and End-of-Course (EOC) testing includes assessments in reading and math (grades 3-8), writing (grades 4 & 7), science (grade 5), social studies (grade 8), and EOCs in English I and II, Algebra I, Biology, and US History.

LEGAL LINEAGE

- Elementary and Secondary Education Act of 1965, Title I, Part A , Sec. 1111 (b)(1)
- Elementary and Secondary Education Act of 1965, Title III, Part A, Subpart 2, Sec. 3122 (a) (1)
- TEC, Title 2, Subtitle F, Chapter 39, Subchapter B, Sec. 39.022; Sec. 39.023 (l)(m); Sec. 39.027 (a)(2)
- TEC, Title 2, Subtitle F, Chapter 39, Subchapter C, Sec. 39.052; Sec. 39.053
- TAC Title 19, Part II, Chapter 89, §89.1220 (h)
- TAC Title 19, Part II, Chapter 101, Subchapter AA, §101.1005; §101.1007

JUST ENOUGH INFORMATION

★ Need to Know

- Student-level STAAR/EOC performance data as well as subgroup data (LEP)
- Decision-making process for LPACs
- STAAR/EOC Accommodations for ELLs
- Which STAAR/EOC tests determine whether an ELL is eligible for exit from program services
- Availability of STAAR L student tutorials and practice sets
- Special English I EOC Provisions
- Criteria for selecting STAAR Spanish
- Math TEKS adopted in 2012 will be addressed in 2014 STAAR testing, grades 3-8

★ Need to Do

- Ensure that all teachers know the data related to ELL achievement on STAAR/EOC
- Ensure LPAC Decision-Making training occurs before STAAR/EOC testing begins
- Ensure that all decisions regarding participation and accommodations are documented in the ELLs record

ASSESSMENT

QUESTIONS

1. Which ELLs participate in STAAR/EOC testing?
2. What are the rules regarding state testing participation for ELLs who have parent denials?
3. How do teachers help prepare ELLs for STAAR/EOC testing?
4. How can administrators ensure that good decision-making occurs for ELLs in STAAR/EOC testing regarding participation and provision of accommodations?
5. How does the LPAC determine which students will take STAAR L?
6. How does the LPAC determine the test language for ELLs in grades 3-5?
7. Are STAAR Spanish tests translations of STAAR tests in English?
8. How are STAAR Spanish and regular STAAR tests aligned?
9. Which linguistic accommodations are allowed for ELLs on STAAR/EOC tests?
10. What is the exemption for refugees and asylees?
11. How do administrators work with district and campus testing coordinators to ensure that STAAR/EOC testing is successful for ELLs?
12. What changes are occurring in STAAR/EOC testing as a result of House Bill 5?
13. What are the English I Special Provisions?
14. Which ELLs have to meet Student Success Initiatives (SSI) requirements?

FOR MORE INFORMATION (FMI)

- 2013-2014 Fall ELL Assessment Update – TEA PPT presentation
- 2014 Accommodations for Students with Disabilities taking STAAR, STAAR Spanish, STAAR L, STAAR Modified, and TELPAS – TEA webpage
- Accommodation Resources – TEA webpage
- HB5
- Information on State Assessments for English Language Learners – TEA webpage
- Language Proficiency Assessment Committee (LPAC) Assessment Resources – TEA webpage
- Online student tutorials for STAAR L – coming Spring 2014 – TEA website
- STAAR Resources - TEA webpage

State of Texas Assessment of Academic Readiness (STAAR) / End-Of-Course (EOC) Testing

Which ELLs participate in STAAR/EOC testing?

According to the TEA Student Assessment Division, all ELLs in grades 3-8 participate in the STAAR general assessment if they are not taking STAAR L, STAAR Spanish (available in grades 3-5 only), STAAR Modified, or STAAR Alternate. LPACs must make state assessment decisions based on individual student needs and must also document test participation decisions.

In grades 9-11, eligible students take the STAAR End of Course (STAAR/EOC) assessments, including ELLs who do not meet the criteria for Eligibility for STAAR English I Assessment Special Provisions as described on the LPAC form of the same name.

What are the rules regarding state testing participation for ELLs who have parent denials?

According to the TEA, ELLs with parent denials are required to take the STAAR or EOC assessments just as any student participating in a general education program would.

For parent denials there is /are no:

- testing in Spanish.
- linguistic accommodations.
- English I EOC Special Provisions.
- unschooled asylee/refugee provisions.

How do teachers prepare ELLs for STAAR/EOC testing?

The STAAR assessment requires the knowledge of academic language and higher-order thinking processes. To prepare ELL students for testing, administrators must expect teachers to:

- incorporate sheltered instruction to facilitate grade-level knowledge and skills (TEKS).
- incorporate English language development instruction which includes:
  - vocabulary
  - syntax
  - morphology
  - functions
  - conventions
- emphasize academic and conversational language when planning and delivering instruction, paying close attention to language standards (ELPS) and proficiency levels.
- incorporate reading and writing in daily instruction.
- incorporate meaning and communication to support language instruction.
- incorporate questioning techniques carefully at various levels of cognition.
- reinforce connections between content areas.
- address readiness content and skills.
- address supporting content and skills.

Online student tutorials have been developed and will be released in spring of 2014 for ELLs taking a STAAR L test. The tutorials help students become familiar with the TestNav interface and with accessing allowable accommodations as needed. Since test directions assume students are familiar with the interface and accommodations, there are no instructions on using the interface or accessing the linguistic accommodations during the actual test. Teachers need to ensure that ELLs go through the tutorials and address any issues prior to the testing session.

How can administrators ensure that good decision-making occurs for ELLs in STAAR/ EOC testing regarding participation and provision of accommodations?

STAAR L (grades 3-8 and end-of-course, EOC, mathematics, science, and social studies assessments), STAAR Modified, and STAAR Alternate are all tests designed to meet the linguistic or cognitive needs of certain students. All students enrolled on the date of an assessment are expected to participate in state testing. Students who need linguistically accommodated or modified forms of the tests are also expected to participate. Careful deliberation must occur at LPAC meetings for these assessments, on a student-by-student basis.

There are two categories of accommodations: instructional and assessment. When students receive accommodations routinely during instructional time, they may be eligible to receive those accommodations during testing (review testing manual for allowable accommodations).

In addition to assessment accommodations for students with disabilities and linguistic accommodations for testing, all students are eligible for general testing accommodations. All accommodations are posted to the 2014 Accommodations for Students with Disabilities taking STAAR, STAAR Spanish, STAAR L, STAAR Modified, and TELPAS webpage at TEA. These accommodations must be documented in the LPAC, 504, and/or ARD minutes when applicable.

How does the LPAC determine which students will take STAAR L?

The STAAR L assessment is a linguistically accommodated test for mathematics, science, and social studies. It is administered through an online interface which provides certain linguistic accommodations for eligible ELLs. The following students are eligible to take this test:

- students for whom the Spanish form of the test is not the most appropriate (grades 3-5)
- students who have not attained the rating of Advanced High on TELPAS reading
- students who have been in US schools for 3 years or less and started school in grade 1 (This also applies for qualifying unschooled asylee or refugee students.)

ELLs with parent denials are not permitted to take the STAAR L form of the assessments.

Accommodations built into the online STAAR L test include:

- clarification in English at word or phrase level for predetermined words/phrases. Clarification may involve simplified language, illustrations, or diagrams
- words read aloud at the word-by-word level

In 2013, roughly 35,000 ELLs took STAAR L tests.

State of Texas Assessment of Academic Readiness (STAAR) / End-Of-Course (EOC) Testing

How does the LPAC determine the test language for ELLs in grades 3-5?

Students placed in a bilingual program or in a dual language program model make academic progress and acquire English at varying levels. The LPAC determines the language of testing based upon student progress in English or Spanish. They also consider the language of instruction for each subject tested. If a student is a recent immigrant participating in an ESL program, the LPAC may determine that the best decision is to have a student take STAAR in Spanish, especially if they have been schooled in their own country.

STAAR Spanish is available for students in grades 3-5 for the following tests:

- Grades 3-5 Reading and Math
- Grade 4 Writing
- Grade 5 Science

Non-ELLs — for whom Spanish is the most appropriate measure of content mastery in the above listed tests — may take the Spanish STAAR. Often these students are participating in a Dual Language Two-Way program model. The LPAC will document this decision, even though the student is not an ELL. The LPAC will not meet or discuss non-ELLs at any other point, and the student is never coded as ELL in PEIMS. Non-ELLs are not tested annually through TELPAS and do not have to meet any criteria (identification or exit) as do ELLs.

Are STAAR Spanish tests merely translations of STAAR tests in English?

The STAAR Spanish Reading and Writing assessments are trans-adaptations of the STAAR assessment in English. That is, the items are developed taking into account cultural and linguistic differences. In Mathematics and Science, some items may be translated while others may be trans-adapted into Spanish. Whenever possible, the same items are used for both tests. When an item cannot be translated and remain linguistically and culturally appropriate, a trans-adapted item of the same complexity and grade-level expectation is developed. Bilingual educators review selected items each year.

How are STAAR Spanish and regular STAAR tests aligned?

The STAAR Spanish assessments follow the same guidelines for test development and test blueprints as the STAAR general assessments. They elicit the same cognitive complexity, and they expect similar student performance. STAAR Spanish is considered a general assessment; it is not considered a modified or off-level test.

Which linguistic accommodations are allowed for ELLs on STAAR/EOC tests?

ELLs taking STAAR Spanish tests are not eligible for any linguistic accommodations. The test is written in their native language, and consequently, the student's accessibility to the test language is not compromised.

However, there are linguistic accommodations for the STAAR, STAAR L, and STAAR Modified. They are:

Linguistic Accommodations for STAAR (English form only):	**Math, Science, Social Studies:** • Bilingual dictionary • Extra time (same day) **Reading, Writing:** • Grades 3-5 – Dictionaries of various types • Extra time (same day) • Clarification in English of word meanings in writing prompts (Writing only) **English I/II:** • Extra time (same day) • Clarification of words in short-answer reading questions and writing prompts *Note - Grades 6 and above: English, ESL/simplified English, and bilingual dictionary access is provided to all students and is not considered a linguistic accommodation.*
Linguistic Accommodations for STAAR L: *(STAAR L tests are only available in Math, Science, and Social Studies. There are no STAAR L Reading, Writing, or English tests.)*	**Math, Science, Social Studies:** • Bilingual dictionary • Extra time (same day) • Clarification in English of word meanings (provided in online interface) • Reading aloud of text (provided in online interface) *Note: If an ELL does not routinely need and use clarification in English and reading aloud of text, they should take STAAR, not STAAR L.*
Linguistic Accommodations for STAAR Modified: *(Eligibility for STAAR M testing is determined by the ARD; determination of linguistic accommodations is determined by the LPAC)*	**Math, Science, Social Studies:** • Bilingual dictionary • Extra time (same day) • Clarification in English of word meaning • Reading aloud of text • Oral translation **Reading, Writing:** • Dictionaries of various types • Extra time (same day) • Reading aloud of eligible text • Clarification in English of word meaning • Oral translation **English I, English II:** • Extra time (same day) • Reading aloud of eligible text • Clarification in English of word meaning • Oral translation

Note: *The Linguistic Accommodations for ELLs Participating in the STAAR Program document can be found on the TEA webpage, 2014 Accommodations for Students with Disabilities taking STAAR, STAAR Spanish, STAAR L, STAAR Modified, and TELPAS. On that same webpage, there is information that LPACs use when working with ARD committees to determine which assessment accommodations are appropriate for ELLs with disabilities.*

State of Texas Assessment of Academic Readiness (STAAR) / End-Of-Course (EOC) Testing

For more information about specific criteria and allowable use of bilingual dictionaries, English/ESL dictionaries, non-English monolingual dictionaries, and picture dictionaries, see the TEA LPAC Resources webpage. In addition, the STAAR Decision-Making Guide for LPACs and Linguistic Accommodations for ELLs Participating in the STAAR Program documents are very helpful.

What is the exemption for refugees and asylees?

Qualifying asylees and refugees in grades 3-8 may be eligible for a one-time exemption from testing during their first year in US schools. The LPAC makes the determination regarding this exemption, and the committee is responsible for documenting the exemption in the LPAC Decision-Making record for the student.

How do administrators work with district and campus testing coordinators to ensure that STAAR/EOC testing is successful for ELLs?

In August of 2013, TEA posted released STAAR tests on their website. In addition, Grade 4 Writing Scoring Guides can be accessed on the Student Assessment webpage. These resources can assist teachers in preparing students for the STAAR assessments.

In early 2014, STAAR L practice sets will be available online. Each set consists of about 25 items. Like TELPAS, these sets are intended to familiarize ELLs with the online interface. The sets can also serve as an indicator to teachers regarding student readiness for STAAR testing.

LPACs are responsible for making assessment decisions to meet the needs of ELLs. According to TEA, the campus LPAC coordinator must communicate with the campus/district testing coordinator(s) to make sure that appropriate accommodations are in place on the day of the test. A good flow of information between the testing coordinators and campus administrators ensures that testing arrangements, i.e., room and coverage assignments, are appropriate. Since test "Say" directions for test administrators may be translated upon student request, it is essential for the test administrator assigned to a particular testing room to be able to provide this support for students.

District and campus testing coordinators are responsible for ordering test forms and documents. For this, they need timely and correct information regarding test participation and demographic data/accommodations reporting.

ASSESSMENT

What changes are occurring in STAAR testing for ELLs as a result of House Bill 5?

Beginning 2014, English I and English II EOCs Reading and Writing tests will be administered as a single assessment given in one day. Students will receive a single score for both tests.

Districts may not administer more than two benchmark assessments for any grade/course STAAR assessment.

The Special Provisions for English I EOC will no longer extend to English II as this is now the test used to meet the graduation requirement for ELLs. ELLs will have to take and pass the English II assessment (without provisions) to graduate.

The requirements for days of attendance counting as a full year of enrollment have changed. The new ruling states that a student's full attendance year will count after being enrolled for 60 consecutive school days. This law will be in effect beginning in the 2013-2014 school year and is not retroactive.

What are the English I Special Provisions?

Under TAC Chapter 101, §101.1007, the LPAC determines if an ELL meets the criteria for English I Special Provisions and documents the decision on an approved LPAC meeting form. This is not an exemption to testing for students enrolled in the course.

In the recent past, these provisions also applied to certain ELLs in English II or ESOL II. However, with the passage of HB5, the number of exams required for graduation has decreased significantly. There will be no English III EOC. Therefore, since the EOC for English II will be the top level exam in the English content area, no special provisions will be allowed on the test.

ELLs who meet the criteria for STAAR English I Assessment Special Provision will not be required to:

- use the assessment score for graduation purposes.
- retake the assessment each time it is administered if the student passes the course but does not meet the passing standard on the test.

All these apply to ELLs enrolled in courses entitled English I or English for Speakers of Other Languages I (ESOL) who have:

- 3 years or less in US schools (five or less for unschooled asylees or refugees).
- not reached Advanced High level on TELPAS Reading.

ELLs with parental denials are not eligible for these provisions.

Which ELLs have to meet the Student Success Initiative (SSI) requirements?

Beginning with Spring 2014 STAAR testing, ELLs in grades 5 and 8 who take STAAR L tests in math will be held to the same SSI requirements for BOTH reading and math, including retesting, as students who take the general STAAR assessments. There is no STAAR L assessment for reading.

Texas English Language Proficiency Assessment System (TELPAS)

The Texas English Language Proficiency Assessment System is the state-developed annual, summative assessment that measures the Levels of English language proficiency of ELLs in four areas: listening, speaking, reading, and writing.

LEGAL LINEAGE

- Elementary and Secondary Education Act of 1965, Title I, Part A, Sec. 1111 (b) (2)(B); Sec. 1111(b)(6)(7)
- Elementary and Secondary Education Act of 1965, Title III, Part A, Subpart 2, Sec. 3111 (2)(C)(iii); Sec. 3121 (d); Sec. 3122
- TEC, Title 2, Subtitle F, Chapter 39, Subchapter B, Sec. 39.027 (e)
- TAC Title 19, Part II, Chapter 74, Subchapter A, §74.4
- TAC Title 19, Part II, §89.1225 (h)
- TAC Title 19, Part II, Chapter 101, Subchapter AA, §101.1003

JUST ENOUGH INFORMATION

★ Need to Know

- Each ELL (including parent denials) is assessed and rated annually in TELPAS
- TELPAS raters must be a teacher of record for the ELL
- TELPAS raters must be trained and calibrated in the system
- TELPAS rating activities occur within a specified window of time
- Release of TELPAS forms for all grade bands available in 2014
- Availability of TELPAS and student tutorials and practice sets
- Two different TELPAS Administration Manuals

★ Need to Do

- Identify a TELPAS rater for each ELL
- Ensure that raters are trained
- Maintain documentation of rater training and successful calibration
- Ensure that rating activities are completed within the specified window

QUESTIONS

1. What is the purpose of the Texas English Language Proficiency Assessment System (TELPAS)?
2. What does TELPAS measure?
3. What are the TELPAS dates to remember for 2014?
4. How do administrators work with district/campus testing coordinators to ensure that TELPAS online reading testing is successful?
5. How do administrators ensure that good decision-making is occurring regarding the participation of ELLs in TELPAS testing?
6. How can administrators support TELPAS raters?
7. How do administrators help teachers prepare ELLs for TELPAS?
8. What is the role of TELPAS in state and federal accountability and monitoring/intervention systems?
9. What role does TELPAS play in the Annual Measurable Achievement Objectives (AMAOs)?
10. How should TELPAS data be used by teachers and administrators to address the needs of ELLs?
11. How does TELPAS data impact instruction?
12. What data collection will be required for Spring 2014 through TELPAS?

FOR MORE INFORMATION (FMI)

- 2013-2014 Fall ELL Assessment Update – TEA PPT presentation
- Accommodation Resources - TEA webpage
- Assessments for Special Populations Unit, Student Assessment Division – TEA webpage
- District and Campus Testing Coordinator Manual – TEA webpage
- Educator Guide to TELPAS – TELPAS Resources webpage at TEA
- TELPAS Resources - TEA webpage
- Texas Training Center – Pearson Education website

Texas English Language Proficiency Assessment System (TELPAS)

What is the purpose of the Texas English Language Proficiency Assessment System (TELPAS)?

The Texas English Language Proficiency Assessment System (TELPAS) was created to meet the federal requirement that all states develop an annual measure of English language proficiency tied to a set of state-adopted standards. TELPAS assesses the progress ELLs make in acquiring social and academic English language proficiency.

TELPAS assesses the ELPS in the same way that STAAR assesses the TEKS. The ELPS were approved in 2007-2008 by the State Board of Education. They are standards that support ELLs in acquiring sufficient English language proficiency to master the TEKS for their subject, course, or grade level.

What does TELPAS measure?

In order to fulfill federal requirements, the Texas English Language Proficiency Assessment System (TELPAS) measures levels of English language proficiency in four domains: listening, speaking, reading, and writing in alignment with the English Language Proficiency Standards (ELPS).

Reading in grades 2-12 is assessed with an online multiple choice test. A holistic rating process is used to assess listening, speaking, and writing in grades 2-12 and reading in grades K-1.

The levels of proficiency are identified as Beginning, Intermediate, Advanced, and Advanced High. ELLs receive separate ratings in all four domains and a composite rating for all. Currently, the reading rating comprises 75% of the composite score, writing 15%, listening 5%, and speaking 5%.

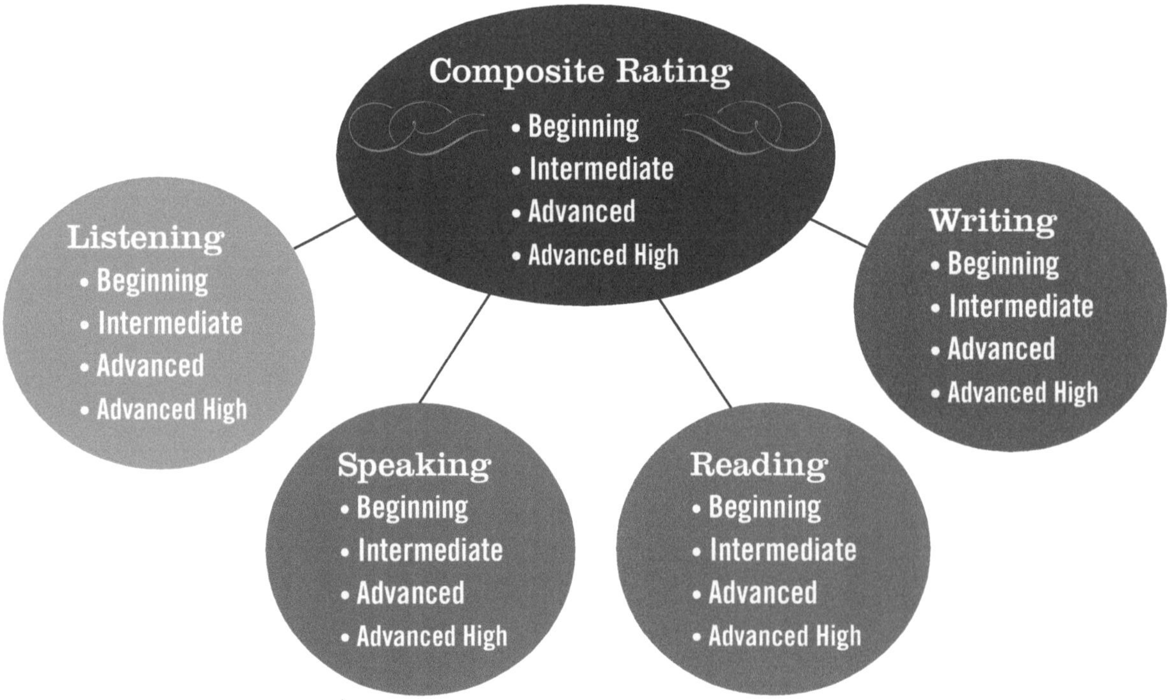

What are the TELPAS dates to remember for 2014?

The TELPAS assessment window for 2014 is March 17-April 9. The window for Data Verification is April 10-11.

The following dates are set for 2014:

- End date for District Campus Coordinator Training – January 24
- Online courses for TELPAS raters begins – Jan 27
- End date for Campus Coordinator Training – Feb 7
- Calibration window opens for raters – Feb 17
- End date for TELPAS rater training on administration procedures – Feb 17
- Earliest date to collect writing samples for writing collections – Feb 17
- Assessment window for TELPAS – March 17-April 9

How do administrators work with district and campus testing coordinators to ensure the success of the TELPAS Online Reading Test?

The training for district and campus testing coordinators is delivered at Education Service Centers (ESCs), and it identifies all of the technical and procedural guidelines for TELPAS testing. District or campus instructional technology staff may have a role in preparing the interface, online access for students, and/or loading of student rating data into the system.

Prior to the assessment window, a system for communication and responsibility must be developed at the district and campus level. During administration of the TELPAS Reading online test, all staff responsible in any way for the success of the system must be present and available. Those systems can include: broadband access and sufficiency, hardware configurations, space allocations, and scheduling alterations.

How do administrators work with district/campus testing coordinators to ensure that TELPAS online reading testing is successful?

All ELLs enrolled in K-12 and classified in PEIMS as LEP (Limited English Proficient), including parent denials, are required to participate in TELPAS. Both the LPAC (Language Proficiency Assessment Committee) and ARD (Admission, Review, and Dismissal) are required to work together to make decisions for students in special education, who on rare occasions may not participate in one or more domains – based solely on their disability.

Administrators are required to be present at all LPAC meetings for several reasons.

- Their input at state assessment decision-making meetings is critical in determining test locations and conditions for students.
- They must allocate sufficient support personnel to provide coverage for teachers who are with their ELLs during the online reading test.
- They can ensure that decisions are made on a student-by-student basis and are supported by teachers and staff.

Texas English Language Proficiency Assessment System (TELPAS)

How can administrators support TELPAS raters?

There are several things that can be done by campus/district level administrators to support TELPAS raters:

- Ensure that teachers focus on using the TELPAS Proficiency Level Descriptors (PLDs) for daily lesson delivery, paying close attention to key features to maximize student learning. This facilitates the use of rubrics during the TELPAS ratings in the spring.
- Remind teachers to pay close attention to opportunities for listening, speaking, reading, and writing on a daily basis during both formal and informal academic tasks.
- Inform teachers of face-to-face or online training opportunities.
- In addition to initial qualification requirements, make sure that TELPAS raters recalibrate their rater abilities yearly as required by the Texas Education Agency.

How do administrators help teachers prepare ELLs for TELPAS?

ELL students taking the TELPAS need opportunities to practice listening, speaking, reading, and writing on a regular basis, and they need to understand the essential parts of the online TELPAS Reading. Direct teachers, who are preparing students for online testing, to the TEA website. There, they will find online tutorials and practice items. Additionally, on the TELPAS Resources webpage, two PowerPoint presentations are available to assist teachers. They are:

- Making the ELPS-TELPAS Connection: K-12 Overview.
- Introductory Training on the PLDs (modules available for grades K-1 and 2-12).

In addition, the Educator Guide to TELPAS published by TEA is available on the website. It provides an extensive overview of the system and how the ELPS works with the TEKS to support second language learners. The TELPAS Administrators' Manual provides detailed information as well.

What is the role of TELPAS in state and federal accountability and monitoring/intervention systems?

Under the Elementary and Secondary Education Act (ESEA), reauthorized under No Child Left Behind Act of 2001 (NCLB), all districts that accept Title III, Part A funds for ELLs are accountable for ELL progress in acquiring English and for meeting the state achievement standards for their grade. TELPAS results data is used to measure these benchmarks.

In August 2013, TELPAS standards were reviewed and adjusted for reading tests in grades 2-12. Cut scores were adjusted for each proficiency level of each grade cluster test, and the new standards will be implemented in Spring 2014.

At TEA, the division of Program Monitoring and Interventions (PMI) is responsible for:

- state and federal accountability monitoring and interventions.
- monitoring and interventions for four program areas, including bilingual/ESL programs.
- data validation monitoring.

Using Performance-Based Monitoring (PBM) strategies to assign stages of intervention to districts, the PMI oversees district implementation of required integrated or single-program intervention activities. Annually, the Performance-Based Monitoring Analysis System (PBMAS) publishes a PBMAS Manual that explains the indicators used in the PBM process and the required intervention activities for each stage.

In 2013, there is a change to the bilingual/ESL indicators on Indicator 9 – TELPAS Reading Beginning Proficiency Level Rate. Indicator 9 measures the percentage of ELLs (tested over two years) who performed at the Beginning proficiency level on the TELPAS reading assessment in the current year. This indicator has moved from Report Only to an indicator with performance level assignments.

What role does TELPAS play in the Annual Measurable Achievement Objectives (AMAOs)?

The AMAOs use TELPAS data and state test achievement data of district ELLs to determine if the district met AMAO standards. The AMAOs measure ELLs through three lenses:

AMAO 1 – Progress: measures the progress ELLs are making in English language proficiency.

AMAO 2 – Attainment: measures the number of ELLs who attain English language proficiency.

AMAO 3 – ELL Accountability (System Safeguards): Due to the recent conditional approval from the USDE regarding the replacement of LEP AYP with system safeguards for ELL accountability, the third AMAO (AMAO 3) will now read ELL Accountability (System Safeguards). This AMAO measures how many of a district's ELLs meet the performance and participation targets for reading/ELA and math set by the state in student academic achievement standards.

How should TELPAS data be used by teachers and administrators to address the needs of ELLs?

Since TELPAS results are a direct reflection of instruction using the ELPS, teachers and administrators can use TELPAS data to evaluate the effectiveness of ELL instruction. Teachers and administrators need to know what trends are developing at the classroom, campus, and district levels with regard to ELL progress in acquiring English language.

Knowing which students have stalled in their progress through the four levels of proficiency is useful information. These students may require additional supports or interventions to continue making progress. Knowing if a particular domain (listening, speaking, reading, or writing) is lagging behind the others informs instructional decisions.

According to the Educator Guide to TELPAS (p.9), TELPAS data is used to:

- help parents monitor the progress their children make in learning English.
- inform instructional planning and program exit decisions for individual students.
- report performance to local school boards, school professionals, and the community.
- evaluate programs, resources, and staffing patterns.
- evaluate districts and campuses in a variety of state and federal accountability measures.

Texas English Language Proficiency Assessment System (TELPAS)

The LPAC uses TELPAS results and the ELPS/PLDs to monitor and maximize ELL acquisition of English language proficiency. At LPAC meetings, previous TELPAS data and current teacher input should:

- determine the rate of progress in acquiring English.
- review/adjust linguistic accommodations routinely used during instruction.
- determine the need for additional interventions/supports/RtI.
- determine the need for linguistic accommodations for state assessments.

Linguistic accommodations provided during instruction accelerate the rate at which ELLs acquire and master English. The more students understand instruction and master the English language, the less they need accommodations.

Any allowable accommodation, provided upon student request during state testing, should be routinely offered for classroom and local assessments as well. ELLs need to be familiar with the allowable testing accommodations and know how to request/use them during testing.

ELLs with disabilities may be able to use some accommodations from the Accommodations Triangle posted on the 2014 Accommodations for Students with Disabilities taking STAAR, STAAR Spanish, STAAR L, STAAR Modified, and TELPAS TEA webpage. TELPAS does not allow for any linguistic accommodations since the test is intended to measure the true level of English language proficiency of ELLs.

How does TELPAS data impact instruction?

Best practices suggest that instruction is more successful when it is data-driven. Therefore, student performance on TELPAS can be used to tailor lessons that better meet the specific needs of ELLs. When teachers know the language proficiency levels of their ELLs, they will be more intentional in selecting linguistic accommodations. Their decisions will help ELLs move to higher levels of English proficiency and accelerate student acquisition of social/academic English.

There are released TELPAS tests which can be used by classroom teachers to benchmark ELL growth in English. Information from these assessments can help teachers address specific areas during instruction and classroom activities.

What data collection will be required for Spring 2014 through TELPAS?

In 2014, data will be collected in two categories:

- unschooled asylees/refugees
- students with Interrupted Formal Education (SIFE)

This data will identify student needs and the numbers of students in each data reporting category.

ACCOUNTABILITY

Federal Accountability

Federal accountability for ELLs has been affected by the recent provisional approval of an Adequate Yearly Progress (AYP) waiver for Texas by the US Department of Education. LEP AYP will be replaced by ELL Accountability (System Safeguards). Performance-Based Monitoring and Program Monitoring and Interventions are two state systems for reporting and monitoring federal title programs related to ELLS.

LEGAL LINEAGE

- No Child Left Behind Act of 2001 (expiring without reauthorization in 2014-text not included in this resource)
- Elementary and Secondary Education Act of 1965, Title I, Part A, Sec. 1111 (b)(2)
- Elementary and Secondary Education Act of 1965, Title III, Part A, Subpart 2, Sec. 3116 (6)(d)(2-4), Sec. 3121 (d), Sec. 3122 (3) (b)
- TAC Title 19, Part II, Chapter 97, Subchapter AA, §97.1004, §97.1005

JUST ENOUGH INFORMATION

★ Need to Know

- New - Texas ELL Progress Measure
- Current status of federal accountability requirements as they are shared by TEA
- Local results for PBMAS
- The Division of Program Monitoring and Interventions at TEA is responsible for several activities related to Performance-Based Monitoring of federal and state accountability
- What the Annual Measurable Achievement Objectives (AMAOs) are, and what role they play in federal accountability for schools receiving Title III funds

★ Need to Do

- Become familiar with the Texas ELL Progress Measure
- Ensure that all stakeholders are aware of the progress ELLs are making in acquiring English, achieving required scores on STAAR and EOC exams, and exiting from the program
- Ensure that all required interventions are provided to ELLs as a result of federal indicators (AMAOs, staging through PBMAS)

ACCOUNTABILITY

QUESTIONS

1. What do administrators need to know about the current federal accountability system?
2. What do administrators need to know about the Annual Measurable Achievement Objectives (AMAOs)?
3. What were the main features of the previous federal accountability system in Texas?
4. What roles do the Division of Program Monitoring and Interventions, Performance-Based Monitoring, and the Performance-Based Monitoring Analysis System play in determining interventions based upon federal accountability for ELLs?
5. How administrators keep current about decisions regarding interventions required by the federal accountability system?
6. How does membership in a Title III, Part A, Shared Services Arrangement (SSA) affect accountability?
7. How will the new ELL Progress Measure result in individual ELL Progress Measure Plans?

FOR MORE INFORMATION (FMI)

- Annual Measurable Achievement Outcomes (AMAOs) Guidance Document – TEA webpage
- Division of Program Monitoring and Interventions – TEA webpage
- ELL Progress Measure document under What's New in Student Assessment section of the Student Assessment - TEA webpage
- *Letter to the Administrator Addressed* (TAA)– Nov. 1, 2013
- PBMAS Manuals – TEA webpage
- Performance-Based Monitoring - TEA webpage
- Regional Education Service Centers, including Shared Services Agreements (SSAs)
- TEA listservs that address Federal Accountability:
  - Bilingual/ESL Education
  - Grants Administration and Federal Program Compliance
  - No Child Left Behind
  - Performance Based Monitoring and Interventions
  - SBEC Rules
  - Student Assessment
  - To the Administrator Addressed (TAA)
- TETNs that address Federal Accountability for ELLs
- Title III, Part A – English Language Acquisition, Language Enhancement, and Academic Achievement Act – TEA webpage
- Title III Guidance Document – on TEA webpage listed above

Federal Accountability

What do administrators need to know about the current federal accountability system?

As the No Child Left Behind Act of 2001 approached the 2014 mandatory achievement standards of 100% success for all students in state achievement tests, Texas applied for waivers for certain accountability requirements. While awaiting the US Department of Education ruling on the waiver request, Texas also introduced a new testing program (State of Texas Assessment of Academic Readiness – STAAR) and a new state accountability system.

In complying with the 2012-2013 school improvement requirements, the Texas Education Agency (TEA) released the 2012 AYP results to identify campuses and districts as Meets AYP or Missed AYP. These designations are determined through a comparison with scores on state assessments compared to federal performance standards.

Recent decisions (see Nov 1st *To the Administrator Addressed* letter posted on the TEA webpage) by the US Department of Education granted Texas a conditional waiver from some of the provisions of the Elementary and Secondary Education Act of 1965 (ESEA) and NCLB (2001). The waiver will be granted without conditions after the state submits guidelines regarding teacher and principal evaluation and support systems in the spring of 2014.

Along with general program changes, and Highly Qualified requirements, there is a new method of federal accountability that enables more flexibility at the state level in identifying schools in need of intervention activities. Beginning with the 2013-2014 school year, AYP will be superseded by this more flexible approach.

Both the federal and the state accountability systems for Texas address similar system safeguards:

- Performance rates
- Participation rates
- Graduation rates
- Limited use of Alternative Assessments

A key difference in the two safeguard systems is the number of student groups evaluated for performance, participation, and graduation. They are:

Federal System Safeguards evaluated	State System Safeguards evaluated
All Students	All Students
Three Racial/Ethnic Groups: African American, Hispanic, White	Seven Racial/Ethnic Groups: African American, Hispanic, White, American Indian, Asian, Pacific Islander, Two or More Races
Economically Disadvantaged	Economically Disadvantaged
Students receiving Special Education services	Students receiving Special Education services
English Language Learners (ELLs)	English Language Learners (ELLs)

Texas campuses and districts will meet federally approved annual measurable objectives (AMOs) for each student group evaluated in performance, participation, graduation, and limits on the use of alternative assessments. The federal accountability system will only evaluate disaggregated performance rates for reading/English language arts and math. For 2012-2013 the federal performance rate targets were set at 75% for each student group evaluated in reading and math and at 70% for the graduation rate. The targets for reading and math in 2014 are 75%, and the graduation rate is 78%.

There will be two designations for Title I campuses in need of improvement:

Priority Schools – identifies 5% of Title I campuses including School Improvement Grant-Texas Title I Priority Schools (SIG-TTIPS), high schools with less than 60% graduation rates, and lowest-performing schools based upon statewide reading and math assessments.

Focus Schools – identifies 10% of Title I campuses, with the widest gaps between student performance and federal targets of 75% (known as system safeguards).

Federal Accountability

What do administrators need to know about Annual Measurable Achievement Objectives (AMAOs)?

The AMAOs are the objectives that are in place at the district level for Title III federal accountability. Any district receiving Title III funds must be held accountable for the English language acquisition and academic achievement of ELLs. Texas uses TELPAS and STAAR to gather the data that is used to determine if a district has met or has not met the standards set by the TEA. Based upon meeting or not meeting AMAOs, districts must engage in certain required activities and reporting.

AMAO 1 – Progress: Using the current year's TELPAS composite rating, ELLs are expected to make progress of at least one level of proficiency level per year. This AMAO measures how many of the total ELLs in the district have achieved this expectation.

AMAO 2 – Attainment: Once an ELL attains a composite rating in TELPAS of Advanced High, that student is counted as proficient in English. This AMAO measures how many of the total ELLs have attained this level of proficiency for the current year.

AMAO 3 – ELL Accountability (System Safeguards): This AMAO has changed in 2013. This AMAO measures how many of a district's ELLs meet the performance and participation targets for reading/ELA and math set by the state in student academic achievement standards. For 2013, the performance target is 75% of the ELL student group is counted as proficient on both reading/ELA and math tests. The participation target is 95% of the ELL student group enrolled on the test date participating for both reading/ELA and math. You can find the most current guidance for AMAOs in the 2013 AMAOs Guide on the Annual Measurable Achievement Objectives webpage at TEA as well as the 2013 Accountability Manual on the TEA website

What were the main features of the previous federal accountability system in Texas?

As previously authorized, the federal accountability system evaluated reading and math content areas. It measured the percentage of students who are proficient as well as the percentage of students participating in the assessments for reading and math. Grades 3-8 and grade 10 are evaluated. The No Child Left Behind Act of 2001 set 2014 as the year that 100% of students would meet the standard for proficiency. STAAR, STAAR L, STAAR Modified, STAAR Alternate tests are all included in federal accountability measures for Adequate Yearly Progress (AYP).

As new information develops, administrators may find the following information helpful as background information. In 2012, students to be evaluated included every student in the accountability subset (students enrolled on Snapshot Day and on testing day) on a campus. This group is called the All Students Group. The following student groups were included (as long as the group meets minimum size requirements):

- African American
- Hispanic
- White
- Economically Disadvantaged
- Special Education
- Limited English Proficient (LEP) – aka ELLs

Minimum Size Requirement (MSR) was based upon the following: 50/10%/200

If a student group has less than fifty students, it is too small to be evaluated as a separate group. If a student group has more than 200 students, it is large enough to be evaluated separately. If a student group has between 50-200 students, it must be at least 10% of the All Student Group to be evaluated separately. For the participation rate, student groups must meet the Minimum Size Requirement and the All Student Group must have at least 40 students.

In addition to achievement on reading and math tests, two other indicators were also measured: graduation rate (high schools and districts with 12th grade) and attendance rate (elementary and middle schools and districts without 12th grade). For example, some charter schools operate K-grade 8 only. The standard for the graduation rate was 70% and the standard for attendance rate was 90%.

What roles do the Division of Program Monitoring and Interventions, Performance-Based Monitoring, and the Performance-Based Monitoring Analysis System play in determining interventions based upon federal accountability for ELLs?

At TEA, the Division of Program Monitoring and Interventions (PMI) is responsible for:

- both state and federal accountability monitoring and interventions.
- monitoring and interventions for four program areas, including bilingual/ESL programs.
- data validation monitoring.

Using Performance-Based Monitoring (PBM) strategies to assign stages of intervention to districts, this division oversees district implementation of required integrated or single-program intervention activities. Annually, the Performance-Based Monitoring Analysis System (PBMAS) publishes a PBMAS Manual which explains the indicators used in the PBM process and the required activities for each stage.

In 2013, the change to the bilingual/ESL indicators in PBMAS is on Indicator 9 – TELPAS Reading/Beginning Proficiency Level Rate. Indicator 9 measures the percentage of ELLs tested over two years who performed at the Beginning proficiency level on the TELPAS Reading assessment in the current year. This indicator has moved from Report Only to an indicator with performance level assignments.

Federal Accountability

How can administrators keep current about decisions regarding interventions required by the federal accountability system?

The changes in federal accountability for the state of Texas will result in changes in many programs and activities that support ELLs. In order to keep up with the most current rules and guidelines, administrators should do the following:

- Join TEA listservs that address federal accountability (Bilingual/ESL Education, Grants Administration and Federal Program Compliance, No Child Left Behind, Performance Based Monitoring, Program Monitoring and Interventions, SBEC Rules, Student Assessment, and *To the Administrator Addressed*). Administrators can subscribe to these listservs on the Mailing List Administration webpage at TEA.
- Attend meetings via the Texas Education Telecommunication Network (TETN). TETN is open to district administrators, and it addresses federal accountability, such as ESEA, Title III, PMI, and Bilingual/ESL. Work with your local technology department to get access to the TETNs or call Distance Learning at 512-919-5444 for assistance.

How does membership in a Title III, Part A, Shared Services Arrangement (SSA) affect accountability?

The US Department of Education distributes Title III, Part A funds to districts based on the number of ELLs enrolled in the district. According to the statute, the state may not award funds of less than $10,000 to a district. If a district is scheduled to receive less than $10,000 they are required to join a Shared Services Agreement (SSA) in order to receive funding. SSAs for Title III are fiscally managed by the Education Service Centers (ESCs) in Texas.

If a district is a member of a Title III SSA, this may impact their accountability determination. Under the AMAOs, if a district did not meet Minimum Size Requirement (MSR) for AMAO 1 or 2, they could meet the AMAO requirement based upon their own student numbers, OR they could meet the requirement using SSA-level results. With the changes occurring in the federal accountability system, this option may be amended.

How will the new ELL Progress Measure result in individual ELL Progress Measure Plans?

The STAAR assessment system is built upon the concept of progress, similar to TELPAS. Using performance expectations and standards, the state provides a score for each student for each test taken, and this can be placed upon a continuum of scores. The student and parent/guardian can easily gauge the progress a student is making towards various goals; meeting the level II standard, achieving level III standard, and demonstrating college readiness. Campuses and districts can easily identify gaps in achievement through the four performance indexes of the state accountability system and see the progress they make in closing those gaps.

In much the same way, the new Texas English Language Learner (ELL) Progress Measure provides year-to-year performance expectations and specifies the number of years it should take for a student to reach proficiency or to meet the level II performance standards on STAAR tests.

The initial composite proficiency level for ELLs on TELPAS combined with the number of years they have been in the US determines the plan that will apply for each ELL.

For a more complete explanation of the progress measure plans, visit the Student Assessment Division webpage at TEA and locate the 10/22/13 ELL Progress Measure document under the *What's New in Student Assessment* section.

State Accountability

The state of Texas has developed a new Texas Accountability and Intervention System (TAIS) that is intended to encompass all state-level required interventions due to staging in campus/district ratings and through system safeguards such as Program Monitoring and Interventions (PMI), Performance-Based Monitoring (PBM), and Performance-Based Monitoring Analysis System (PBMAS).

LEGAL LINEAGE

- Elementary and Secondary Education Act of 1965, Title I, Part A , Sec. 1111 (b)(2)
- Elementary and Secondary Education Act of 1965, Title I, Part A , Sec. 1116 (a)(1), (b)(1)
- Elementary and Secondary Education Act of 1965, Title III, Part A , Subpart 2, Sec. 3121 (d)
- TEC, Title 2, Subtitle F, Chapter 7, Subchapter A, Sec. 7.028 (b)
- TEC Title 2, Subtitle F, Chapter 28, Subchapter B, Sec. 28.0211, Sec. 28.0212, Sec. 28.0213
- *(Added by HB5) TEC Title 2, Subtitle F, Chapter 28, Subchapter B, Sec. 28.0212, Sec. 28.0217*
- TEC Title 2, Subtitle F, Chapter 29, Subchapter B, Sec. 29.051 – Sec. 29.066
- *(Amended by HB5) TEC Title 2, Subtitle F, Chapter 29, Subchapter C, Sec. 28.081*
- TEC Title 2, Subtitle F, Chapter 39, Subchapter B, Sec. 39.052, Sec. 39.053
- TEC Title 2, Subtitle F, Chapter 39, Subchapter E
- TAC Title 19, Part II, Chapter 74, Subchapter A, §74.4
- TAC Title 19, Part II, Chapter 101, Subchapter AA, §101.1007

JUST ENOUGH INFORMATION

★ Need to Know

- SSI Math and Reading Requirements for 5th and 8th grade ELLs
- Data Collection requirements
- New - Texas ELL Progress Measure

★ Need to Do

- Ensure that all stakeholders are aware of all accountability ratings and interventions that are required for ELLs in the district or on the campus
- Ensure that LPACs and district/campus testing coordinators know which data collection applies to ELLs
- Ensure that appropriate SSI interventions are implemented to benefit ELLs

QUESTIONS

1. How will House Bill 5 (HB5) impact the new state accountability system?
2. What do administrators need to know about ELLs in the new state accountability system?
3. What are the System Safeguards?
4. What accommodations regarding test participation will be in place for recent immigrants, and how will they be represented in the new accountability reporting system?
5. Will STAAR L results be reported in the accountability ratings?
6. What are the Student Success Initiative requirements for ELLs in grades 5 and 8?
7. How will the Texas ELL Progress Measure provide measures of growth and academic attainment for ELLs under the new state accountability system? How is the new Texas ELL Progress Measure different from the STAAR Growth Measure?

FOR MORE INFORMATION (FMI)

- 2013-2014 Fall ELL Assessment Update – TEA PPT presentation
- 2014 District and Campus Coordinator Manual – TEA webpage
- Dropout Prevention and Recovery Resources – TEA webpage
- HB5
- Performance-Based Monitoring Manual – Performance-Based Monitoring TEA webpage
- *Student Attendance Accounting Handbook*, Section 6
- TELPAS Rater Manual – TEA webpage
- TELPAS Reading Test Administrator Manual – on TEA webpage
- TELPAS Resources – TEA webpage
- Texas Accountability and Intervention System (TAIS) – TEA webpage

State Accountability

How will House Bill 5 (HB5) impact the new state accountability system?

The performance index framework, built prior to the passage of HB5, will not be significantly changed in response to the new legislation. Since each of the four performance indexes have built-in flexibility to add, modify, or change indicators or calculations, the system can accommodate any changes brought about under HB5. For example, reducing the number of tests required for graduation does not change the indexes or the performance targets, but it may require some adjustments to the calculations.

What do administrators need to know about ELLs in the new state accountability system?

With the launch of the new accountability system in Texas, ELL performance and participation data is now more visible in campus and district reports. The benefit of this increased visibility is obvious. The progress and performance of ELLs at the student level and as a population will bring welcome scrutiny at all levels of services, i.e., classrooms, campuses, and districts. The emphasis is on the positive – how can state, regional, and local support providers assist in developing effective interventions to address very specific, disaggregated findings in the rating and reporting systems?

Each of the four indexes has a distinct purpose in the accountability system.

- Index 1 provides an overview of overall performance across subject areas tested. ELLs are included in the All Students groups and the ELLs subgroup, as well as any other subgroups to which they might belong.
- Index 2 focuses on actual student growth for certain subgroups, including ELLs.
- Index 3 looks at the academic achievement of economically disadvantaged students, plus the two lowest performing race/ethnicity groups. ELLs and students served by Special Education are specifically not included as potential lowest performing groups. However, ELLs may fall into one of the calculations based upon economic status or race/ethnicity.
- Index 4 focuses on all aspects of postsecondary readiness, not just college-ready measures. ELLs are included as a subgroup in this index.

The rating labels used in 2013, i.e., Met Standard, Met Alternative Standard (for Alternative Education Campus, AEC), or Improvement Required, will be continued in 2014.

District and Campus level Targets by Index

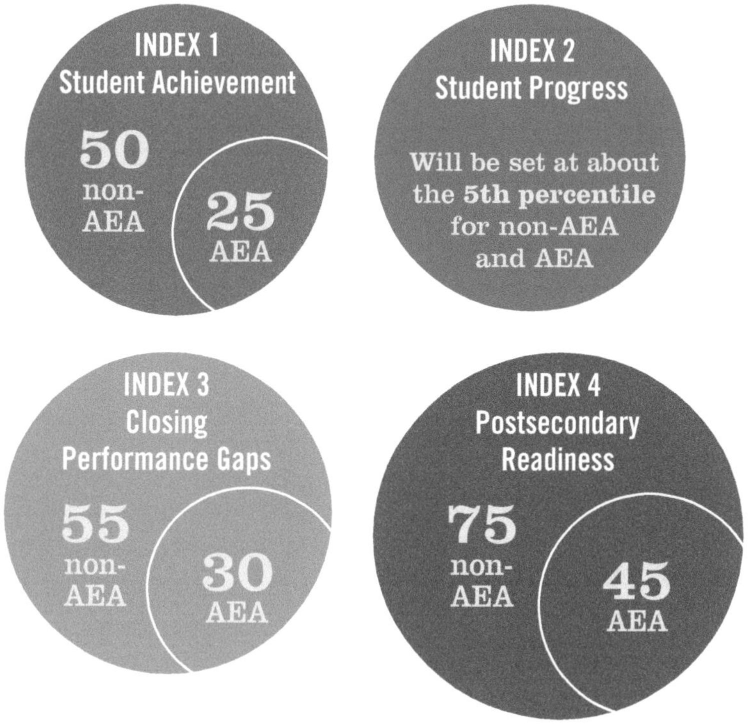

What are the System Safeguards?

In addition to Index 3, which specifically addresses the lowest performing student groups, the System Safeguards are developed to ensure that no student group results can be masked by inclusion in a larger rating group. Poor performance in one area or subject is not masked in the performance index score.

The new state accountability incorporates System Safeguards that disaggregate data by student group, performance level, subject area, and grade. The goal is to prevent any group data from being masked by inclusion in the performance rating of a larger group. System Safeguards ensure that districts and campuses attend directly to the gaps in performance in all subgroups as reported by the state accountability rating system. Disaggregating results from each index also meets federal requirements, i.e., student performance in reading/math, participation rates for testing, graduation rates, improvement calculations, and the 1% / 2% limitations on the use of alternative assessments, which was the state's rationale for applying for the AYP waiver from the US Department of Education in February 2013. Texas will use the System Safeguards to replace the federal AYP evaluation system.

For any indicator that meets accountability minimum size requirements (25 for student groups- including ALL Students group – evaluated under System Safeguards), results will be reported. No small numbers analysis will be done for groups with fewer than 25 results. If any result in the System Safeguards do not meet the target, that indicator must be directly addressed in the campus and district improvement plans, as applicable. System Safeguards will be included in the Texas Accountability Intervention System (TAIS).

What accommodations regarding test participation will be in place for recent immigrants, and how will they be represented in the accountability reporting system?

Recent immigrants will test in the STAAR program using the test that the LPAC deems to be the most appropriate for them. The only exception to this policy applies to asylees and refuges in grades 3-8. The LPAC can offer them a one-time exemption from testing in their first year in US schools.

Will STAAR L results be reported in the accountability ratings?

In 2014, STAAR L results for ELLs will be included in the performance index calculations. More information about the rating calculations will be forthcoming from TEA in the spring of 2014.

For administrators, it is important to understand that there will be very little data that is masked, either through the evaluated groups in each of the four indexes or through the System Safeguards. Campus and district improvement plans should address the cognitive, affective, and linguistic needs of ELLs in strategic and explicit ways. Monitoring of accommodations for ELLs in instruction and local assessments needs to be ongoing.

What are the Student Success Initiative (SSI) requirements for ELLs in grades 5 and 8?

Beginning in 2013, ELLs in grades 5 and 8 – who are not successful on either the reading or math STAAR tests – will be included in the services provided under SSI and will be subject to the same requirements as non-ELLs. This includes ELLs who take the STAAR L test in math. Clearly, these students may require different services and support to prepare them for retesting. Districts and campus leaders should designate staff and design SSI programming accordingly, using the funds allocated for SSI.

How will the Texas ELL Progress Measure provide measures of growth and academic attainment for ELLs under the new state accountability system? How is the Texas ELL Progress Measure different from the STAAR Growth Measure?

Since the data for participation and performance of ELLs will be more visible in the new reporting system of indexes, it will be helpful for districts and campuses to be able to evaluate the actual year-to-year progress and achievement of ELLs within a framework built around progress (expected growth), TELPAS composite score, and time in US schools. This is called the Texas ELL Progress Measure. It has also been referred to as the STAAR ELL Progress Measure.

The ELL Progress Measure considers two factors: the time ELLs need to acquire English and the time they need to demonstrate mastery of academic knowledge and skills for their grade level or course.

ELLs who are eligible for the ELL Progress Measure meet three criteria:

- They are classified as ELLs.
- They take English versions of STAAR (STAAR, STAAR L).
- They are not coded as parent denials in PEIMS.

ELLs who meet these criteria will be assigned to a plan that will combine information about the number of years they have been in US schools (1-4 years, with up to 5 years for eligible asylee/refugee ELLs) with their initial TELPAS composite rating (Beginning, Intermediate, Advanced, Advanced High).

ELLs will receive credit for making progress on their year-to-year expectation. In the final year of their plan, ELLs are expected to meet Level II: Satisfactory Academic Performance standards.

The ELL Progress Measure will be reported on the Confidential Student Reports (CSRs) of eligible ELLs. Beginning with the spring 2014 administration of STAAR, this measure will be used for campus and district accountability.

The STAAR Growth Measure will be calculated for students in certain grades and subjects, including ELLs who take STAAR Spanish tests. Therefore, ELLs who take STAAR Spanish tests will NOT have a Texas ELL Measure developed to track their individual progress and performance.

For a more complete explanation of the Texas ELL Progress Measure, go to the Student Assessment Division webpage at TEA and locate the 10/22/13 ELL Progress Measure document under the *What's New In Student Assessment* section.

Dropout/Personal Graduation Plans (PGP)/ Graduation

Dropout and graduation rates are critical indicators of the success of programs for English language learners.

LEGAL LINEAGE

- TEC Title 2, Subtitle F, Chapter 28, Subchapter B, Sec. 28.0211, Sec. 28.0212, Sec. 28.0213; Sec. 28.025
- TAC Title 19, Part II, Chapter 74, Subchapter G
- HB5
- *TEC Title 2, Subtitle F, Chapter 28, Subchapter B, Sec. 28.02121 – added by HB5*
- *TEC Title 2, Subtitle F, Chapter 28, Subchapter B, Sec. 28.0217 – added by HB5*
- *TEC Title 2, Subtitle F, Chapter 29, Subchapter B, Sec. 29.081 – amended by HB5*

JUST ENOUGH INFORMATION

★ Need to Know

- Graduation/completion requirements
- Definition of a dropout
- PGP requirements
- Coming changes to PGP requirements under HB5
- Data regarding dropout and graduation/ completion rates

★ Need to Do

- Ensure every ELL in middle and high school has a PGP
- Ensure effective dropout prevention activities are implemented for English language learners
- Designate a person to develop and administer PGP's for each English-language learner

QUESTIONS

1. How can administrators support dropout prevention for English language learners?
2. What is a Personal Graduation Plan (PGP), and how does it support ELLs?
3. How do administrators support graduation for ELLs?

FOR MORE INFORMATION (FMI)

- Accountability Interventions System (TAIS) Guidance – TEA webpage
- Accountability Monitoring Intervention Guidance and Resources – TEA webpage
- HB5
- IDRA Power of Student Voices/ Dropout Prevention for Students with Special Needs
- Integrated Intervention Guidance and Resources – TEA webpage
- Performance-Based Monitoring – TEA webpage
- Performance-Based Monitoring Manual – TEA Performance-Based Monitoring webpage
- Program Monitoring and Intervention – TEA webpage
- *Student Attendance Accounting Handbook*, Sec. 6.10 – TEA webpage
- *To the Administrator Addressed* (August 12, 2012) – TEA webpage
- *To the Administrator Addressed* (July 19, 2013) – TEA webpage

How can administrators prevent ELLs from dropping out of school?

The Texas Education Code (TEC) Chapter 29, Sec. 29.081 (d) defines students who are at risk for dropping out of school, and the definition includes students who are identified as English Language Learners (ELLs). House Bill 5 amends the drop-out age from under 21 years of age to under the age of 26. This is a significant change that affects the accelerated instruction provisions (per TEC Sec. 28.0211) for students who fail any EOC test required for graduation. Accelerated instruction must be provided prior to the next test for the course.

ELLs are vulnerable to dropping out of school when they cannot fully participate in classes and are not successful on state and local assessments. Under TAC Chapter 74, §74.4 (b)(4), a strong plan for the acceleration of English acquisition must be provided for ELLs in grades 3-12 who are rated Beginner or Intermediate in English proficiency in TELPAS. According to the statute, "These ELLs require focused, targeted, and systematic second language acquisition instruction to provide them with the foundation of English language vocabulary, grammar, syntax, and English mechanics necessary to support content-based instruction and accelerated learning of English."

ELLs, especially those in their first years in US schools, are often not successful on state and local assessments. Teachers should routinely offer linguistic accommodations on classroom assessments. Local benchmarks should also be linguistically accommodated. Linguistic accommodations to consider would include: extra time, simplified language (similar to that provided to students taking modified assessments), and the use of bilingual or ESL dictionaries. Linguistic accommodations on state assessments are determined by the LPAC.

Teachers of ELLs are required to receive sheltered instruction training, per Section 6.10 of the *Student Attendance Accounting Handbook* (2013-2014). Linguistically accommodated instruction affects not only the acquisition of English language, but it promotes the cognitive and affective development of ELLs. ELLs who feel accepted, welcomed, challenged, and supported are less likely to drop out of school.

ELLs may also drop out of school because they are caring for parents or a younger sibling, working to support a family, or raising children of their own. These obligations complicate an already complex educational program for ELLs. Best practices might include the following:

- assign a counselor dedicated to the ELL population on campus
- advise administrators regarding the impact of disciplinary actions which may be related to cultural or linguistic misunderstandings
- encourage the development of ESL or ELL clubs on campus

For more resources, visit the TEA webpage, Dropout Prevention and Recovery Resources.

Dropout/Personal Graduation Plans/Graduation

What is a Personal Graduation Plan (PGP), and how does it support ELLs?

The High School Completion Initiative, enacted by SB 1108, required personal graduation plans for all students at risk of dropping out of school, and it provided a comprehensive program of intensive instruction to support high school graduation.

Because ELLs are identified as "at-risk" for dropping out of school [TEC Sec. 29.081}, personal graduation plans are required for all middle or high school students who fail a STAAR/EOC test or for any student not likely to graduate before the fifth year of enrollment in high school. Therefore, best practices encourage establishment of personal graduation plans for any student entering ninth grade [TEC Sec. 28.0212].

Under HB5, PGPs will be required for students – effective in the 2013-2014 school year – who meet the criteria listed above.

The elements of a personal graduation plan include:

- education goals for the student
- diagnostic information, appropriate monitoring and intervention, and other evaluation strategies
- an intensive instruction program (described in Section 28.1213)
- participation of the student's parent/guardian, including their expectations for the student
- innovative methods to promote the student's advancement, including flexible scheduling, alternative learning environments, online instruction, and other interventions proven to accelerate the learning process

Personal graduation plans focus on:

- college and workforce readiness
- career placement and advancement
- student transition from secondary to post-secondary education

Under HB5 (Sections 12 and 13), TEA must collaborate with the Workforce Commission and Higher Education Coordinating Board to develop information that explains the advantages of distinguished achievement levels and endorsements, in both Spanish and English. This information must be placed on the district website in both languages. If at least 20% of all students in a grade level speak another language, the information must be provided in that language as well. The principal will designate a counselor or administrator to review each PGP with each entering ninth grader and their parents/guardians. Students and parents/guardians must understand the elements of the distinguished plan, and the options presented to the parents/guardians and student must include that option. The school may not prevent a student and his/her parents/guardians from selecting the distinguished plan of achievement or any endorsement. The PGP must be signed by the parents/guardians and the student by the end of ninth grade. It may be amended by the student later, requiring notification of the student's parents/guardians. These new requirements will go into effect during the 2014-2015 school year.

Much of the LPAC process involves discussion of the very items required in a personal graduation plan. For ELLs, their PGP may include items that relate specifically to their English acquisition levels and mastery of content that may be unfamiliar – due to variations in prior schooling. If the development of PGPs on a campus is handled by the counseling department or other designated individual(s), they need to coordinate with the LPAC to ensure that PGPs for ELLs reflect appropriate strategies and course sequences.

Dropout/Personal Graduation Plans/Graduation

How do administrators support graduation for ELLs?

Under House Bill 5, passed in Spring 2013 (final adoption scheduled for January 2014), the existing three graduation plans (Minimum, Recommended, and Distinguished Achievement) will be replaced by the Foundation High School Program. In addition, five endorsements will be available from which students must choose at least one. They are:

- STEM
- Business and Industry
- Public Services
- Arts and Humanities
- Multi-disciplinary Studies

The State Board of Education has the responsibility of developing curriculum requirements for each endorsement.

To earn the distinguished level of achievement, a student must complete four credits in math (including Algebra II), 4 credits in science, all foundation program requirements, and the requirements for at least one endorsement.

In order to be eligible for automatic college admission under the 10 percent rule, students must earn a distinguished level of achievement by completing four math credits (including Algebra II) plus at least one endorsement.

Of special interest to administrators/teachers of ELLs: students can earn performance acknowledgements for outstanding accomplishments in bilingualism or biliteracy.

As an administrator, it is vital to communicate information about the new graduation requirements and opportunities in HB5 to ELLs and their parents/guardians because the new graduation program is significantly different from the previous one. Parents/guardians and students have many questions about how they will meet the new requirements.

ELLs, especially newcomers, are often scheduled into ESL and content-support classes to acquire sufficient English proficiency that will promote success in state credit-bearing courses. Sometimes this results in an ELL taking five years to complete all state required coursework for graduation. To respond to their questions about graduation, it would be helpful to hold a meeting and include an interpreter to answer parent/guardian/student questions in their native language.

On the other hand, acquiring a second language, while challenging, does not prevent any student from succeeding in upper level classes. Just the fact that a student is classified as an ELL does not prevent them from access to all possible graduation plans, as long as the ELL meets the requirements for the plan they select. Some ELLs are very well-prepared to succeed in advanced academics based upon their prior schooling and educational experiences. They should be encouraged to continue their personal educational advancement. In a meeting about graduation requirements, they and their parents/guadians should receive information about the graduation plan that will best meet their post-secondary aspirations.

With the new graduation requirements, and the unique characteristics of each ELL, the LPAC becomes critically important in ensuring that each ELL class schedule is carefully considered in light of their readiness for advanced coursework – even if linguistic scaffolds and accommodations are necessary to provide the student with access to the subject/course language. In the LPAC meetings where student schedules are discussed, it is a best practice to include a counselor or administrator in charge of the master schedule to provide additional guidance in building the class schedule for each ELL. Careful documentation of these conversations in the LPAC meetings is essential.

For ELLs who arrive at US high schools with interrupted or limited prior schooling, the LPAC must consider all remedies including:

- additional coursework (state, innovative, or local credit courses) to provide necessary background in content area knowledge.
- accelerated acquisition of English to a level that enables the student to function in general education classes with sheltered instruction trained teachers.

All teachers of ELLs must be sheltered instruction trained, per the *Student Attendance Accounting Handbook*, Sec. 6.10 (SAAH, 2013-2014).

ACCOUNTABILITY

School Improvement

As a group, ELLs are required to be included in campus and district improvement plans. Based upon state and federal accountability and safeguard systems, ELLs may be included in school improvement and monitoring activities.

LEGAL LINEAGE

*Elementary and Secondary Education Act (ESEA)/P.L. 107-110 No Child Left Behind (NCLB) Act of 2001 – pending final approval from USDE to Texas waiver request

*Adequate Yearly Progress (AYP)-related School Improvement Program (SIP) – temporary suspension pending final approval from USDE to Texas waiver request.

- Elementary and Secondary Education Act of 1965, Title I, Part A, Sec. 1111 (b)(2)
- Elementary and Secondary Education Act of 1965, Title I, Part A , Sec. 1112 (b)(1)(a-e)(g)(1-5)
- Elementary and Secondary Education Act of 1965, Title I, Part A , Sec. 1116 (a)(1), (b)(1)
- Elementary and Secondary Education Act of 1965, Title III, Part B, Subpart 1, Sec. 3213
- TEC, Title 2, Subtitle F, Chapter 11, Subchapter A, Sec. 11.253
- TEC, Title 2, Subtitle F, Chapter 29, Subchapter B, Sec. 29.081 (b-1) (d)
- TEC, Title 2, Subtitle F, Chapter 39, Subchapter B, Sec. 39.053; Sec. 39.054
- *Added by HB5 - TEC, Title 2, Subtitle F, Chapter 39, Subchapter B, Sec. 39.0545*
- TEC, Title 2, Subtitle F, Chapter 39, Subchapter B, Sec. 39.105
- TAC Title 19, Part II, Chapter 89, Subchapter BB, §89.1265 (d)

JUST ENOUGH INFORMATION

★ Need to Know

- What school improvement activities are required
- What school improvement activities are based upon accountability and safeguard systems
- How ELLs are represented in campus and district improvement plans

★ Need to Do

- Become familiar with school improvement requirements
- Know the data for your campus/district that drives school improvement activities
- Monitor all school improvement activities
- Ensure that district and campus improvement plans include specific and appropriate goals, strategies, and activities for ELLs

QUESTIONS

1. What do administrators need to know about the Texas Accountability Intervention System (TAIS)?
2. What are the system safeguards?
3. How are Supplemental Educational Services affected by the new accountability system?
4. What ongoing school improvement activities include ELLs?
5. How should campus/district improvement plans (CIP/DIP) address academic performance and progress for ELLs in acquiring English language proficiency?

FOR MORE INFORMATION (FMI)

- Accountability Monitoring Intervention Guidance and Resources – TEA webpage
- Advancing Improvement in Education (AIE) Conference – annual conference sponsored by TEA and ESC, Region 13
- Bilingual Education (BE/ESL) Monitoring – TEA webpage
- Districts with Campuses Required to Engage in the Texas Accountability Interventions - TEA webpage
- ESC Collaborative/Texas Turnaround Center – ESC, Region 13
- TEA School Improvement Process – TEA website
- Texas Accountability Interventions System (TAIS) Guidance – TEA Accountability Monitoring Intervention Guidance and Resources webpage
- Texas Center for District & School Support (TCDSS) – ESC, Region 13

School Improvement

What do administrators need to know about the Texas Accountability Intervention System (TAIS)?

The following ratings are subject to intervention according to the Texas Accountability Intervention System (TAIS):

- Districts and campuses rated Improvement Required (as a result of low performance on one of the four indexes)
- Districts and campuses that miss one or more System Safeguard targets (75% achievement on reading and math tests, 78% on graduation rates)
- Districts staged for Performance Based Monitoring (for single and multiple program staging)

Recent changes to the state accountability system have led to a more aligned and integrated approach to performance based interventions through both the Performance Indexes and the Performance-Based Monitoring Analysis System (PBMAS). This approach contributes to ongoing, focused, and supported school improvement.

In PBMAS, if a district is at stage three or below, they will engage in certain TAIS activities. The more 3s as indicators on the district PBMAS report, the more involved the district will be with the TAIS system. The TAIS system for Program Monitoring and Interventions/Performance Based Monitoring involves:

- Data review
- Intervention/Improvement plans
- Monitoring of efforts

Even if a district does not have a 3 in any indicator, the district and campus intervention team still needs to review data because anything other than a zero indicates potential problems. Much of that work could be considered proactive best practices. If you have a "No Data (ND)", this might indicate a problem. A "ND" in an indicator cell on the spreadsheet for bilingual or ESL program information will most likely result in Data Validation and Verification (DVV) requests from TEA.

Another way to look at the performance data is to disaggregate it by feeder patterns. Sometimes interesting trends or results are evident in this analysis. The Texas Assessment Management System, Eduphoria, and even Pearson have large amounts of data available for local analysis.

Part of the TAIS system involves monitoring intervention/improvement activities and submitting quarterly progress reports. In terms of reporting, the TEA Program Monitoring and Intervention team is not looking for a single, generic plan. Instead, they expect to see each staged indicator (especially 3s) addressed with specific interventions and improvement activities.

For more information about the TAIS system, visit the Texas Accountability Intervention System Guidance document on the TEA webpage, Bilingual Education (BE/ESL) Monitoring.

ACCOUNTABILITY

What are the System Safeguards?

Both the federal accountability system and the state accountability system address similar System Safeguards:

- Performance rates
- Participation rates
- Graduation rates
- Limited use of Alternative Assessments

In addition, the AMAOs are also System Safeguards. The AMAOs are discussed in detail in the Federal Accountability section of the Accountability chapter. (See page 124.)

In addition to Index 3 which specifically addresses the lowest performing student groups, the System Safeguards are developed to ensure that no student group's results are masked by inclusion in a larger rating group. Poor performance in one area or subject is not masked in the performance index score.

The new state accountability incorporates System Safeguards that disaggregate data by student group, performance level, subject area, and grade. The goal is to prevent any group's data from being masked by inclusion in a larger group performance rating. System Safeguards ensure that districts and campuses attend directly to the gaps in performance in all subgroups as reported by the state accountability rating system.

Disaggregating results from each index also meets federal requirements (student performance in reading and math, participation rates for testing, graduation rates and improvement calculations, and the 1%/2% limitations on the use of Alternative Assessments) which was the state's rationale for applying for the AYP waiver from the US Department of Education (Feb. 2013). Texas will use the System Safeguards to replace the federal AYP evaluation system.

For any indicator that meets accountability minimum size requirements (25 for student groups – including ALL Students group – evaluated under System Safeguards), results will be reported. No small numbers analysis will be done for groups with fewer than 25 results. If any result in the System Safeguards do not meet the target, that indicator must be directly addressed in the campus and district improvement plans, as applicable. System Safeguards will be included in the Texas Accountability Intervention System (TAIS).

How are Supplemental Educational Services (SES) affected by the new accountability system?

Both School Choice and Supplemental Educational Services (SES) are gone. They are replaced by System Safeguards, Priority campuses, and Focus campuses.

What ongoing school improvement activities include ELLs?

In Texas, the concept of continuous improvement drives all school improvement. Continuous improvement has three desired outcomes:

- Accelerated Achievement
- Sustainability
- System Transformation

The four areas for action include:

- Data Analysis
- Needs Assessment
- Improvement Plan
- Implement and Monitor

As the school improvement process is implemented, it is supported by three key components:

- District Commitments
  Operational flexibility, clear vision and focus, sense of urgency, high expectations, district-wide ownership, and accountability
- Support Systems
  Organizational structure, processes/procedures, communications, capacity, and resources
- Critical Success Factors
  Academic performance, use of quality data to drive instruction, leadership effectiveness, increased learning time, family/community engagement, school climate, and teacher quality [Source: TEA School Improvement Process]

As administrators review the school improvement components and activities, it is clear that ELLs are to be considered in these plans and need to be integrated into all school improvement discussions, decisions, and actions. For reference, recall the requirement in Chapter 89, §89.1210, that addresses the cognitive, linguistic, and affective needs of ELLs, and align those domains to the components listed above. When addressing each of the three domains within the continuous improvement process, administrators can comprehensively meet the needs of ELLs.

How should District and Campus Improvement Plans (DIP and CIP) address academic performance and progress of ELLs in acquiring English language proficiency?

PBMAS data should guide the development of District and Campus Improvement Plans with respect to bilingual/ESL programs. For each indicator (other than zero), goals, strategies and activities on the plans should address the indicator.

As in the TAIS, a thorough review of all data relevant to ELLs should be performed prior to the development of the District and Campus Improvement Plans each year. This data review can be achieved through various lenses:

- Performance data from Performance Indexes One, Two, and Four
- Program specific data from bilingual and ESL programs
- Elementary vs secondary performance data for ELLs
- ELL data from school feeder patterns
- PBMAS staging data
- AMAOs findings
- TELPAS data
- Data for ELLs served by other programs, e.g., Special Education, Gifted and Talented, CTE, RtI, Dyslexia

Goals, strategies, and activities in the District and Campus Improvement Plans should reflect the review of ELL data. The selected activities should be research-based and relevant to the issue identified in the data review. Teachers and LPAC members can contribute significantly to this process. Best practice would be for the LPAC to receive an overview of the program performance and effectiveness each year along with the LPAC Framework training.

LEGAL RESOURCES ★

Federal Statutory References

Elementary and Secondary Education Act of 1965, Title I, Part A – Improving Basic Programs Operated by Local Education Agencies

Sec. 1111 (State Plans)

Sec. 1112 (Local Education Agency Plans)

Sec. 1116 (Academic Assessment and Local Education Agency and School Improvement)

Elementary and Secondary Education Act of 1965, Title I, Part C – Education of Migratory Children

Sec. 1301 (Program Purpose)

Sec. 1304 (State Applications; Services)

Sec. 1308 (Coordination of Migrant Education Activities)

Sec. 1309 (Definitions)

Elementary and Secondary Education Act (ESEA) of 1965, Title III, Part A – English Language Acquisition, Language Enhancement, and Academic Achievement Act

Sec. 3102 (Purpose)

Subpart 1

Sec. 3111 (Formula Grants to States)

Sec. 3114 (Within-State Allocations)

Sec. 3115 (Subgrants to Eligible Entities)

Sec. 3116 (Local Plans)

Subpart 2

Sec. 3121 (Evaluations)

Sec. 3122 (Achievement Objectives and Accountability)

Elementary and Secondary Education Act (ESEA) of 1965, Title III, Part B – Improving Language Instruction Programs

Subpart 1

Sec. 3213 (Comprehensive School and Systemwide Improvement Activities)

Subpart 3

Sec. 3231 (Professional Development)

Subpart 5

Sec. 3253 (Coordination and Reporting Requirements)

No Child Left Behind Act of 2001
(expiring without reauthorization in 2014-text not included in this resource)

Title I, Part C

SEC. 1301 PROGRAM PURPOSE

It is the purpose of this part to assist States to —

(1) support high-quality and comprehensive educational programs for migratory children to help reduce the educational disruptions and other problems that result from repeated moves;

(2) ensure that migratory children who move among the States are not penalized in any manner by disparities among the States in curriculum, graduation requirements, and State academic content and student academic achievement standards;

(3) ensure that migratory children are provided with appropriate educational services (including supportive services) that address their special needs in a coordinated and efficient manner;

(4) ensure that migratory children receive full and appropriate opportunities to meet the same challenging State academic content and student academic achievement standards that all children are expected to meet;

(5) design programs to help migratory children overcome educational disruption, cultural and language barriers, social isolation, various health-related problems, and other factors that inhibit the ability of such children to do well in school, and to prepare such children to make a successful transition to postsecondary education or employment; and

(6) ensure that migratory children benefit from State and local systemic reforms.

SEC. 1304 STATE APPLICATIONS; SERVICES

(a) APPLICATION REQUIRED– Any State desiring to receive a grant under this part for any fiscal year shall submit an application to the Secretary at such time and in such manner as the Secretary may require.

(b) PROGRAM INFORMATION- Each such application shall include—

(1) a description of how, in planning, implementing, and evaluating programs and projects assisted under this part, the State and its local operating agencies will ensure that the special educational needs of migratory children, including preschool migratory children, are identified and addressed through—

(A) the full range of services that are available for migratory children from appropriate local, State, and Federal educational programs;

(B) joint planning among local, State, and Federal educational programs serving migrant children, including language instruction educational programs under part A or B of title III;

(C) the integration of services available under this part with services provided by those other programs; and

(D) measurable program goals and outcomes;

(2) a description of the steps the State is taking to provide all migratory students with the opportunity to meet the same challenging State academic content standards and challenging State student academic achievement standards that all children are expected to meet;

(3) a description of how the State will use funds received under this part to promote interstate and intrastate coordination of services for migratory children, including how, consistent with procedures the Secretary may require, the State will provide for educational continuity through the timely transfer of pertinent school records, including information on health, when children move from one school to another, whether or not such move occurs during the regular school year;

(4) a description of the State's priorities for the use of funds received under this part, and how such priorities relate to the State's assessment of needs for services in the State;

(5) a description of how the State will determine the amount of any subgrants the State will award to local operating agencies, taking into account the numbers and needs of migratory children, the requirements of subsection (d), and the availability of funds from other Federal, State, and local programs;

(6) such budgetary and other information as the Secretary may require; and

(7) a description of how the State will encourage programs and projects assisted under this part to offer family literacy services if the program or project serves a substantial number of migratory children who have parents who do not have a high school diploma or its recognized equivalent or who have low levels of literacy.

(c) ASSURANCES- Each such application shall also include assurances, satisfactory to the Secretary, that—

(1) funds received under this part will be used only—

(A) for programs and projects, including the acquisition of equipment, in accordance with section 1306; and

(B) to coordinate such programs and projects with similar programs and projects within the State and in other States, as well as with other Federal programs that can benefit migratory children and their families;

(2) such programs and projects will be carried out in a manner consistent with the objectives of section 1114, subsections (b) and (d) of section 1115, subsections (b) and (c) of section 1120A, and part I;

(3) in the planning and operation of programs and projects at both the State and local agency operating level, there is consultation with parent advisory councils for programs of 1 school year in duration, and that all such programs and projects are carried out—

(A) in a manner that provides for the same parental involvement as is required for programs and projects under section 1118, unless extraordinary circumstances make such provision impractical; and

(B) in a format and language understandable to the parents;

(4) in planning and carrying out such programs and projects, there has been, and will be, adequate provision for addressing the unmet education needs of preschool migratory children;

(5) the effectiveness of such programs and projects will be determined, where feasible, using the same approaches and standards that will be used to assess the performance of students, schools, and local educational agencies under part A;

(6) to the extent feasible, such programs and projects will provide for—

(A) advocacy and outreach activities for migratory children and their families, including informing such children and families of, or helping such children and families gain access to, other education, health, nutrition, and social services;

(B) professional development programs, including mentoring, for teachers and other program personnel;

(C) family literacy programs, including such programs that use models developed under Even Start;

(D) the integration of information technology into educational and related programs; and

(E) programs to facilitate the transition of secondary school students to postsecondary education or employment; and

(7) the State will assist the Secretary in determining the number of migratory children under paragraphs (1)(A) and (2)(B)(i) of section 1303(a), through such procedures as the Secretary may require.

(d) PRIORITY FOR SERVICES- In providing services with funds received under this part, each recipient of such funds shall give priority to migratory children who are failing, or most at risk of failing, to meet the State's challenging State academic content standards and challenging State student academic achievement standards, and whose education has been interrupted during the regular school year.

(e) CONTINUATION OF SERVICES- Notwithstanding any other provision of this part—

(1) a child who ceases to be a migratory child during a school term shall be eligible for services until the end of such term;

(2) a child who is no longer a migratory child may continue to receive services for 1 additional school year, but only if comparable services are not available through other programs; and

(3) secondary school students who were eligible for services in secondary school may continue to be served through credit accrual programs until graduation.

SEC. 1308 COORDINATION OF MIGRANT EDUCATION ACTIVITIES

(a) IMPROVEMENT OF COORDINATION-

(1) IN GENERAL- The Secretary, in consultation with the States, may make grants to, or enter into contracts with, State educational agencies, local educational agencies, institutions of higher education, and other public and private nonprofit entities to improve the interstate and intrastate coordination among such agencies' educational programs, including the establishment or improvement of programs for credit accrual and exchange, available to migratory students.

(2) DURATION- Grants under this subsection may be awarded for not more than 5 years.

(b) STUDENT RECORDS-

(1) ASSISTANCE- The Secretary shall assist States in developing effective methods for the electronic transfer of student records and in determining the number of migratory children in each State.

(2) INFORMATION SYSTEM-

(A) IN GENERAL- The Secretary, in consultation with the States, shall ensure the linkage of migrant student record systems for the purpose of electronically exchanging, among the States, health and educational information regarding all migratory students. The Secretary shall ensure such linkage occurs in a cost-effective manner, utilizing systems used by the States prior to, or developed after, the date of enactment of the No Child Left Behind Act of 2001, and shall determine the minimum data elements that each State receiving funds under this part shall collect and maintain. Such elements may include —

(i) immunization records and other health information;

(ii) elementary and secondary academic history (including partial credit), credit accrual, and results from State assessments required under section 1111(b);

(iii) other academic information essential to ensuring that migratory children achieve to high standards; and

(iv) eligibility for services under the Individuals with Disabilities Education Act.

(B) NOTICE AND COMMENT- After consulting with the States under subparagraph (A), the Secretary shall publish a notice in the Federal Register seeking public comment on the proposed data elements that each State receiving funds under this part shall be required to collect for purposes of electronic transfer of migratory student information and the requirements that States shall meet for immediate electronic access to such information. Such publication shall occur not later than 120 days after the date of enactment of the No Child Left Behind Act of 2001.

(3) NO COST FOR CERTAIN TRANSFERS- A State educational agency or local educational agency receiving assistance under this part shall make student records available to another State educational agency or local educational agency that requests the records at no cost to the requesting agency, if the request is made in order to meet the needs of a migratory child.

(4) REPORT TO CONGRESS-

(A) IN GENERAL- Not later than April 30, 2003, the Secretary shall report to the Committee on Health, Education, Labor, and Pensions of the Senate and the Committee on Education and the Workforce of the House of Representatives the Secretary's findings and recommendations regarding the maintenance and transfer of health and educational information for migratory students by the States.

(B) REQUIRED CONTENTS- The Secretary shall include in such report —

(i) a review of the progress of States in developing and linking electronic records transfer systems;

(ii) recommendations for the development and linkage of such systems; and

(iii) recommendations for measures that may be taken to ensure the continuity of services provided for migratory students.

(c) AVAILABILITY OF FUNDS- For the purpose of carrying out this section in any fiscal year, the Secretary shall reserve not more than $10,000,000 of the amount appropriated to carry out this part for such year.

(d) INCENTIVE GRANTS- From the amounts made available to carry out this section for any fiscal year, the Secretary may reserve not more than $3,000,000 to award grants of not more than $250,000 on a competitive basis to State educational agencies that propose a consortium arrangement with another State or other appropriate entity that the Secretary determines, pursuant to criteria that the Secretary shall establish, will improve the delivery of services to migratory children whose education is interrupted.

(e) DATA COLLECTION- The Secretary shall direct the National Center for Education Statistics to collect data on migratory children.

SEC. 1309 DEFINITIONS

As used in this part:

(1) LOCAL OPERATING AGENCY- The term local operating agency' means —

(A) a local educational agency to which a State educational agency makes a subgrant under this part;

(B) a public or nonprofit private agency with which a State educational agency or the Secretary makes an arrangement to carry out a project under this part; or

(C) a State educational agency, if the State educational agency operates the State's migrant education program or projects directly.

(2) MIGRATORY CHILD- The term migratory child' means a child who is, or whose parent or spouse is, a migratory agricultural worker, including a migratory dairy worker, or a migratory fisher, and who, in the preceding 36 months, in order to obtain, or accompany such parent or spouse, in order to obtain, temporary or seasonal employment in agricultural or fishing work —

(A) has moved from one school district to another;

(B) in a State that is comprised of a single school district, has moved from one administrative area to another within such district; or

(C) resides in a school district of more than 15,000 square miles, and migrates a distance of 20 miles or more to a temporary residence to engage in a fishing activity.

Title III — Language Instruction for Limited English Proficient and Immigrant Students

Part A — English Language Acquisition, Language Enhancement, and Academic Achievement Act

SEC. 3102. PURPOSES.

The purposes of this part are —

(1) to help ensure that children who are limited English proficient, including immigrant children and youth, attain English proficiency, develop high levels of academic attainment in English, and meet the same challenging State academic content and student academic achievement standards as all children are expected to meet;

(2) to assist all limited English proficient children, including immigrant children and youth, to achieve at high levels in the core academic subjects so that those children can meet the same challenging State academic content and student academic achievement standards as all children are expected to meet, consistent with section 1111(b)(1);

(3) to develop high-quality language instruction educational programs designed to assist State educational agencies, local educational agencies, and schools in teaching limited English proficient children and serving immigrant children and youth;

(4) to assist State educational agencies and local educational agencies to develop and enhance their capacity to provide high-quality instructional programs designed to prepare limited English proficient children, including immigrant children and youth, to enter all-English instruction settings;

(5) to assist State educational agencies, local educational agencies, and schools to build their capacity to establish, implement, and sustain language instruction educational programs and programs of English language development for limited English proficient children;

(6) to promote parental and community participation in language instruction educational programs for the parents and communities of limited English proficient children;

(7) to streamline language instruction educational programs into a program carried out through formula grants to State educational agencies and local educational agencies to help limited English proficient children, including immigrant children and youth, develop proficiency in English, while meeting challenging State academic content and student academic achievement standards;

(8) to hold State educational agencies, local educational agencies, and schools accountable for increases in English proficiency and core academic content knowledge of limited English proficient children by requiring —

(A) demonstrated improvements in the English proficiency of limited English proficient children each fiscal year; and

(B) adequate yearly progress for limited English proficient children, including immigrant children and youth, as described in section 1111(b)(2)(B); and

(9) to provide State educational agencies and local educational agencies with the flexibility to implement language instruction educational programs, based on scientifically based research on teaching limited English proficient children, that the agencies believe to be the most effective for teaching English.

Subpart 1 — Grants and Subgrants for English Language Acquisition and Language Enhancement

SEC. 3111. FORMULA GRANTS TO STATES.

(b) USE OF FUNDS-

(2) STATE ACTIVITIES- Subject to paragraph (3), each State educational agency receiving a grant under subsection (a) may reserve not more than 5 percent of the agency's allotment under subsection (c) to carry out one or more of the following activities:

(A) Professional development activities, and other activities, that assist personnel in meeting State and local certification and licensing requirements for teaching limited English proficient children.

(B) Planning, evaluation, administration, and interagency coordination related to the subgrants referred to in paragraph (1).

(C) Providing technical assistance and other forms of assistance to eligible entities that are receiving subgrants from a State educational agency under this subpart, including assistance in —

(i) identifying and implementing language instruction educational programs and curricula that are based on scientifically based research on teaching limited English proficient children;

(ii) helping limited English proficient children meet the same challenging State academic content and student academic achievement standards as all children are expected to meet;

(iii) identifying or developing, and implementing, measures of English proficiency;

SEC. 3114. WITHIN-STATE ALLOCATIONS.

(a) IN GENERAL- After making the reservation required under subsection (d)(1), each State educational agency receiving a grant under section 3111(c)(3) shall award subgrants for a fiscal year by allocating to each eligible entity in the State having a plan approved under section 3116 an amount that bears the same relationship to the amount received under the grant and remaining after making such reservation as the population of limited English proficient children in schools served by the eligible entity bears to the population of limited English proficient children in schools served by all eligible entities in the State.

(b) LIMITATION- A State educational agency shall not award a subgrant from an allocation made under subsection (a) if the amount of such subgrant would be less than $10,000.

(c) REALLOCATION- Whenever a State educational agency determines that an amount from an allocation made to an eligible entity under subsection (a) for a fiscal year will not be used by the entity for the purpose for which the allocation was made, the agency shall, in accordance with such rules as it determines to be appropriate, reallocate such amount, consistent with such subsection, to other eligible entities in the State that the agency determines will use the amount to carry out that purpose.

(d) REQUIRED RESERVATION- A State educational agency receiving a grant under this subpart for a fiscal year —

(1) shall reserve not more than 15 percent of the agency's allotment under section 3111(c)(3) to award subgrants to eligible entities in the State that have experienced a significant increase, as compared to the average of the 2 preceding fiscal years, in the percentage or number of immigrant children and youth, who have enrolled, during the fiscal year preceding the fiscal year for which the subgrant is made, in public and nonpublic elementary schools and secondary schools in the geographic areas under the jurisdiction of, or served by, such entities; and

(2) in awarding subgrants under paragraph (1) —

(A) shall equally consider eligible entities that satisfy the requirement of such paragraph but have limited or no experience in serving immigrant children and youth; and

(B) shall consider the quality of each local plan under section 3116 and ensure that each subgrant is of sufficient size and scope to meet the purposes of this part.

SEC. 3115. SUBGRANTS TO ELIGIBLE ENTITIES.

(a) PURPOSES OF SUBGRANTS- A State educational agency may make a subgrant to an eligible entity from funds received by the agency under this subpart only if the entity agrees to expend the funds to improve the education of limited English proficient children, by assisting the children to learn English and meet challenging State academic content and student academic achievement standards. In carrying out activities with such funds, the entity shall use approaches and methodologies based on scientifically based research on teaching limited English proficient children and immigrant children and youth for the following purposes:

(1) Developing and implementing new language instruction educational programs and academic content instruction programs for such children, and such children and youth, including programs of early childhood education, elementary school programs, and secondary school programs.

(2) Carrying out highly focused, innovative, locally designed activities to expand or enhance existing language instruction educational programs and academic content instruction programs for such children, and such children and youth.

(3) Implementing, within an individual school, schoolwide programs for restructuring, reforming, and upgrading all relevant programs, activities, and operations relating to language instruction educational programs and academic content instruction for such children, and such children and youth.

(4) Implementing, within the entire jurisdiction of a local educational agency, agencywide programs for restructuring, reforming, and upgrading all relevant programs, activities, and operations relating to language instruction educational programs and academic content instruction for such children, and such children and youth.

(b) ADMINISTRATIVE EXPENSES- Each eligible entity receiving funds under section 3114(a) for a fiscal year may use not more than 2 percent of such funds for the cost of administering this subpart.

(c) REQUIRED SUBGRANTEE ACTIVITIES- An eligible entity receiving funds under section 3114(a) shall use the funds —

(1) to increase the English proficiency of limited English proficient children by providing high-quality language instruction educational programs that are based on scientifically based research demonstrating the effectiveness of the programs in increasing —

(A) English proficiency; and

(B) student academic achievement in the core academic subjects; and

(2) to provide high-quality professional development to classroom teachers (including teachers in classroom settings that are not the settings of language instruction educational programs), principals, administrators, and other school or community-based organizational personnel, that is —

(A) designed to improve the instruction and assessment of limited English proficient children;

(B) designed to enhance the ability of such teachers to understand and use curricula, assessment measures, and instruction strategies for limited English proficient children;

(C) based on scientifically based research demonstrating the effectiveness of the professional development in increasing children's English proficiency or substantially increasing the subject matter knowledge, teaching knowledge, and teaching skills of such teachers; and

(D) of sufficient intensity and duration (which shall not include activities such as one-day or short-term workshops and conferences) to have a positive and lasting impact on the teachers' performance in the classroom, except that this subparagraph shall not apply to an activity that is one component of a long-term, comprehensive professional development plan established by a teacher and the teacher's supervisor based on an assessment of the needs of the teacher, the supervisor, the students of the teacher, and any local educational agency employing the teacher.

(d) AUTHORIZED SUBGRANTEE ACTIVITIES- Subject to subsection (c), an eligible entity receiving funds under section 3114(a) may use the funds to achieve one of the purposes described in subsection (a) by undertaking one or more of the following activities:

(1) Upgrading program objectives and effective instruction strategies.

(2) Improving the instruction program for limited English proficient children by identifying, acquiring, and upgrading curricula, instruction materials, educational software, and assessment procedures.

(3) Providing —

(A) tutorials and academic or vocational education for limited English proficient children; and

(B) intensified instruction.

(4) Developing and implementing elementary school or secondary school language instruction educational programs that are coordinated with other relevant programs and services.

(5) Improving the English proficiency and academic achievement of limited English proficient children.

(6) Providing community participation programs, family literacy services, and parent outreach and training activities to limited English proficient children and their families —

(A) to improve the English language skills of limited English proficient children; and

(B) to assist parents in helping their children to improve their academic achievement and becoming active participants in the education of their children.

(7) Improving the instruction of limited English proficient children by providing for —

(A) the acquisition or development of educational technology or instructional materials;

(B) access to, and participation in, electronic networks for materials, training, and communication; and

(C) incorporation of the resources described in subparagraphs (A) and (B) into curricula and programs, such as those funded under this subpart.

(8) Carrying out other activities that are consistent with the purposes of this section.

(e) ACTIVITIES BY AGENCIES EXPERIENCING SUBSTANTIAL INCREASES IN IMMIGRANT CHILDREN AND YOUTH-

(1) IN GENERAL- An eligible entity receiving funds under section 3114(d)(1) shall use the funds to pay for activities that provide enhanced instructional opportunities for immigrant children and youth, which may include —

(A) family literacy, parent outreach, and training activities designed to assist parents to become active participants in the education of their children;

(B) support for personnel, including teacher aides who have been specifically trained, or are being trained, to provide services to immigrant children and youth;

(C) provision of tutorials, mentoring, and academic or career counseling for immigrant children and youth;

(D) identification and acquisition of curricular materials, educational software, and technologies to be used in the program carried out with funds;

(E) basic instruction services that are directly attributable to the presence in the school district involved of immigrant children and youth, including the payment of costs of providing additional classroom supplies, costs of transportation, or such other costs as are directly attributable to such additional basic instruction services;

(F) other instruction services that are designed to assist immigrant children and youth to achieve in elementary schools and secondary schools in the United States, such as programs of introduction to the educational system and civics education; and

(G) activities, coordinated with community-based organizations, institutions of higher education, private sector entities, or other entities with expertise in working with immigrants, to assist parents of immigrant children and youth by offering comprehensive community services.

(2) DURATION OF SUBGRANTS- The duration of a subgrant made by a State educational agency under section 3114(d)(1) shall be determined by the agency in its discretion.

(f) SELECTION OF METHOD OF INSTRUCTION-

(1) IN GENERAL- To receive a subgrant from a State educational agency under this subpart, an eligible entity shall select one or more methods or forms of instruction to be used in the programs and activities undertaken by the entity to assist limited English proficient children to attain English proficiency and meet challenging State academic content and student academic achievement standards.

(2) CONSISTENCY- Such selection shall be consistent with sections 3125 through 3127.

(g) SUPPLEMENT, NOT SUPPLANT- Federal funds made available under this subpart shall be used so as to supplement the level of Federal, State, and local public funds that, in the absence of such availability, would have been expended for programs for limited English proficient children and immigrant children and youth and in no case to supplant such Federal, State, and local public funds.

SEC. 3116. LOCAL PLANS.

(a) PLAN REQUIRED- Each eligible entity desiring a subgrant from the State educational agency under section 3114 shall submit a plan to the State educational agency at such time, in such manner, and containing such information as the State educational agency may require.

(b) CONTENTS- Each plan submitted under subsection (a) shall —

(1) describe the programs and activities proposed to be developed, implemented, and administered under the subgrant;

(2) describe how the eligible entity will use the subgrant funds to meet all annual measurable achievement objectives described in section 3122;

(3) describe how the eligible entity will hold elementary schools and secondary schools receiving funds under this subpart accountable for —

(A) meeting the annual measurable achievement objectives described in section 3122;

(B) making adequate yearly progress for limited English proficient children, as described in section 1111(b)(2)(B); and

(C) annually measuring the English proficiency of limited English proficient children, so that such children served by the programs carried out under this part develop proficiency in English while meeting State academic content and student academic achievement standards as required by section 1111(b)(1);

(4) describe how the eligible entity will promote parental and community participation in programs for limited English proficient children;

(5) contain an assurance that the eligible entity consulted with teachers, researchers, school administrators, and parents, and, if appropriate, with education-related community groups and nonprofit organizations, and institutions of higher education, in developing such plan; and

(6) describe how language instruction educational programs carried out under the subgrant will ensure that limited English proficient children being served by the programs develop English proficiency.

(c) TEACHER ENGLISH FLUENCY- Each eligible entity receiving a subgrant under section 3114 shall include in its plan a certification that all teachers in any language instruction educational program for limited English proficient children that is, or will be, funded under this part are fluent in English and any other language used for instruction, including having written and oral communications skills.

(d) OTHER REQUIREMENTS FOR APPROVAL- Each local plan shall also contain assurances that —

(1) each local educational agency that is included in the eligible entity is complying with section 3302 prior to, and throughout, each school year;

(2) the eligible entity annually will assess the English proficiency of all children with limited English proficiency participating in programs funded under this part;

(3) the eligible entity has based its proposed plan on scientifically based research on teaching limited English proficient children;

(4) the eligible entity will ensure that the programs will enable children to speak, read, write, and comprehend the English language and meet challenging State academic content and student academic achievement standards; and

(5) the eligible entity is not in violation of any State law, including State constitutional law, regarding the education of limited English proficient children, consistent with sections 3126 and 3127.

Subpart 2 — Accountability and Administration

SEC. 3121. EVALUATIONS.

(a) IN GENERAL- Each eligible entity that receives a subgrant from a State educational agency under subpart 1 shall provide such agency, at the conclusion of every second fiscal year during which the subgrant is received, with an evaluation, in a form prescribed by the agency, that includes —

(1) a description of the programs and activities conducted by the entity with funds received under subpart 1 during the two immediately preceding fiscal years;

(2) a description of the progress made by children in learning the English language and meeting challenging State academic content and student academic achievement standards;

(3) the number and percentage of children in the programs and activities attaining English proficiency by the end of each school year, as determined by a valid and reliable assessment of English proficiency; and

(4) a description of the progress made by children in meeting challenging State academic content and student academic achievement standards for each of the 2 years after such children are no longer receiving services under this part.

(b) USE OF EVALUATION- An evaluation provided by an eligible entity under subsection (a) shall be used by the entity and the State educational agency —

(1) for improvement of programs and activities;

(2) to determine the effectiveness of programs and activities in assisting children who are limited English proficient to attain English proficiency (as measured consistent with subsection (d)) and meet challenging State academic content and student academic achievement standards; and

(3) in determining whether or not to continue funding for specific programs or activities.

(c) EVALUATION COMPONENTS- An evaluation provided by an eligible entity under subsection (a) shall —

(1) provide an evaluation of children enrolled in a program or activity conducted by the entity using funds under subpart 1 (including the percentage of children) who —

(A) are making progress in attaining English proficiency, including the percentage of children who have achieved English proficiency;

(B) have transitioned into classrooms not tailored to limited English proficient children, and have a sufficient level of English proficiency to permit them to achieve in English and transition into classrooms not tailored to limited English proficient children;

(C) are meeting the same challenging State academic content and student academic achievement standards as all children are expected to meet; and

(D) are not receiving waivers for the reading or language arts assessments under section 1111(b)(3)(C); and

(2) include such other information as the State educational agency may require.

(d) EVALUATION MEASURES- A State shall approve evaluation measures for use under subsection (c) that are designed to assess —

(1) the progress of children in attaining English proficiency, including a child's level of comprehension, speaking, listening, reading, and writing skills in English;

(2) student attainment of challenging State student academic achievement standards o n assessments described in section 1111 (b)(3); and

(3) progress in meeting the annual measurable achievement objectives described in section 3122.

(e) SPECIAL RULE FOR SPECIALLY QUALIFIED AGENCIES- Each specially qualified agency receiving a grant under this part shall provide the evaluations described in subsection (a) to the Secretary subject to the same requirements as apply to eligible entities providing such evaluations to State educational agencies under such subsection.

SEC. 3122. ACHIEVEMENT OBJECTIVES AND ACCOUNTABILITY.

(a) ACHIEVEMENT OBJECTIVES-

(1) IN GENERAL- Each State educational agency or specially qualified agency receiving a grant under subpart 1 shall develop annual measurable achievement objectives for limited English proficient children served under this part that relate to such children's development and attainment of English proficiency while meeting challenging State academic content and student academic achievement standards as required by section 1111(b)(1).

(2) DEVELOPMENT OF OBJECTIVES- Such annual measurable achievement objectives shall be developed in a manner that —

(A) reflects the amount of time an individual child has been enrolled in a language instruction educational program; and

(B) uses consistent methods and measurements to reflect the increases described in subparagraphs (A)(i), (A)(ii), and (B) of paragraph (3).

(3) CONTENTS- Such annual measurable achievement objectives —

(A) shall include —

(i) at a minimum, annual increases in the number or percentage of children making progress in learning English;

(ii) at a minimum, annual increases in the number or percentage of children attaining English proficiency by the end of each school year, as determined by a valid and reliable assessment of English proficiency consistent with section 1111(b)(7); and

(iii) making adequate yearly progress for limited English proficient children as described in section 1111(b)(2)(B); and

(B) at the discretion of the agency, may include the number or percentage of children not receiving waivers for reading or language arts assessments under section 1111(b)(3)(C), but this achievement objective shall not be applied to an eligible entity that, in a given school year —

(i) has experienced a large increase in limited English proficient children or immigrant children and youth;

(ii) enrolls a statistically significant number of immigrant children and youth from countries where such children and youth had little or no access to formal education; or

(iii) has a statistically significant number of immigrant children and youth who have fled from war or natural disaster.

(b) ACCOUNTABILITY-

(1) FOR STATES- Each State educational agency receiving a grant under subpart 1 shall hold eligible entities receiving a subgrant under such subpart accountable for meeting the annual measurable achievement objectives under subsection (a), including making adequate yearly progress for limited English proficient children.

(2) IMPROVEMENT PLAN- If a State educational agency determines, based on the annual measurable achievement objectives described in subsection (a), that an eligible entity has failed to make progress toward meeting such objectives for 2 consecutive years, the agency shall require the entity to develop an improvement plan that will ensure that the entity meets such objectives. The improvement plan shall specifically address the factors that prevented the entity from achieving such objectives.

(3) TECHNICAL ASSISTANCE- During the development of the improvement plan described in paragraph (2), and throughout its implementation, the State educational agency shall —

(A) provide technical assistance to the eligible entity;

(B) provide technical assistance, if applicable, to schools served by such entity under subpart 1 that need assistance to enable the schools to meet the annual measurable achievement objectives described in subsection (a);

(C) develop, in consultation with the entity, professional development strategies and activities, based on scientifically based research, that the agency will use to meet such objectives;

(D) require such entity to utilize such strategies and activities; and

(E) develop, in consultation with the entity, a plan to incorporate strategies and methodologies, based on scientifically based research, to improve the specific program or method of instruction provided to limited English proficient children.

(4) ACCOUNTABILITY- If a State educational agency determines that an eligible entity has failed to meet the annual measurable achievement objectives described in subsection (a) for 4 consecutive years, the agency shall —

(A)require such entity to modify the entity's curriculum, program, and method of instruction; or

(B)(i) make a determination whether the entity shall continue to receive funds related to the entity's failure to meet such objectives; and

(ii) require such entity to replace educational personnel relevant to the entity's failure to meet such objectives.

(c) SPECIAL RULE FOR SPECIALLY QUALIFIED AGENCIES- The Secretary shall hold specially qualified agencies receiving a grant under this subpart accountable for meeting the annual measurable achievement objectives described in subsection (a) in the same manner as State educational agencies hold eligible entities accountable under subsection (b).

SEC. 3125. RULES OF CONSTRUCTION.

Nothing in this part shall be construed —

(1) to prohibit a local educational agency from serving limited English proficient children simultaneously with children with similar educational needs, in the same educational settings where appropriate;

(2) to require a State or a local educational agency to establish, continue, or eliminate any particular type of instructional program for limited English proficient children; or

(3) to limit the preservation or use of Native American languages.

SEC. 3126. LEGAL AUTHORITY UNDER STATE LAW.

Nothing in this part shall be construed to negate or supersede State law, or the legal authority under State law of any State agency, State entity, or State public official, over programs that are under the jurisdiction of the State agency, entity, or official.

SEC. 3127. CIVIL RIGHTS.

Nothing in this part shall be construed in a manner inconsistent with any Federal law guaranteeing a civil right.

SEC. 3128. PROGRAMS FOR NATIVE AMERICANS AND PUERTO RICO.

Notwithstanding any other provision of this part, programs authorized under this part that serve Native American (including Native American Pacific Islander) children and children in the Commonwealth of Puerto Rico may include programs of instruction, teacher training, curriculum development, evaluation, and assessment designed for Native American children learning and studying Native American languages and children of limited Spanish proficiency, except that an outcome of programs serving such children shall be increased English proficiency among such children.

SEC. 3129. PROHIBITION.

In carrying out this part, the Secretary shall neither mandate nor preclude the use of a particular curricular or pedagogical approach to educating limited English proficient children.

Subpart 4 — Definitions

SEC. 3141. ELIGIBLE ENTITY.

In this part, the term 'eligible entity' means —

(1) one or more local educational agencies; or

(2) one or more local educational agencies, in collaboration with an institution of higher education, community-based organization, or State educational agency.

Subpart 5 – Administration

SEC. 3253. COORDINATION AND REPORTING REQUIREMENTS.

(a) COORDINATION WITH RELATED PROGRAMS- In order to maximize Federal efforts aimed at serving the educational needs of children and youth of limited English proficiency, the Secretary shall coordinate and ensure close cooperation with other programs serving language-minority and limited English proficient children that are administered by the Department and other agencies. The Secretary shall consult with the Secretary of Labor, the Secretary of Health and Human Services, the Secretary of Agriculture, the Attorney General, and the heads of other relevant agencies to identify and eliminate barriers to appropriate coordination of programs that affect language-minority and limited English proficient children and their families. The Secretary shall provide for continuing consultation and collaboration, between the Office of English Language Acquisition, Language Enhancement, and Academic Achievement for Limited English Proficient Students and relevant programs operated by the Department, including programs under this part and other programs under this Act, in planning, contracts, providing joint technical assistance, providing joint field monitoring activities and in other relevant activities to ensure effective program coordination to provide high-quality educational opportunities to all language-minority and limited English proficient children.

(b) DATA- The Secretary shall, to the extent feasible, ensure that all data collected by the Department shall include the collection and reporting of data on limited English proficient children.

(c) PUBLICATION OF PROPOSALS- The Secretary shall publish and disseminate all requests for proposals for programs funded under this part.

(d) REPORT- The Director shall prepare and, not later than February 1 of every other year, shall submit to the Secretary, the Committee on Education and the Workforce of the House of Representatives, and the Committee on Health, Education, Labor, and Pensions of the Senate a report —

(1) on programs and activities carried out to serve limited English proficient children under this part, and the effectiveness of such programs and activities in improving the academic achievement and English proficiency of children who are limited English proficient;

(2) containing a critical synthesis of data reported by States under section 3224, when applicable;

(3) containing an estimate of the number of certified or licensed teachers working in language instruction educational programs and educating limited English proficient children, and an estimate of the number of

such teachers that will be needed for the succeeding 5 fiscal years;

(4) containing the major findings of scientifically based research carried out under this part; and

(5) containing other information gathered from the reports submitted to the Secretary under this title when applicable.

Title III, Part B, Subpart 3, Sec. 3121 (a-c) — Professional Development

SEC. 3231. PROFESSIONAL DEVELOPMENT GRANTS.

(a) PURPOSE- The purpose of this section is to provide assistance to prepare educators to improve educational services for limited English proficient children by —

(1) supporting professional development programs and activities to prepare teachers, pupil service personnel, administrators, and other educational personnel working in language instruction educational programs to provide effective services to limited English proficient children;

(2) incorporating curricula and resources concerning appropriate and effective instruction and assessment methodologies specific to limited English proficient children into preservice and inservice professional development programs;

(3) upgrading the qualifications and skills of non-certified educational personnel, including paraprofessionals, to enable such personnel to meet high professional standards for educating limited English proficient children;

(4) improving the quality of professional development programs in schools or departments of education at institutions of higher education, for educational personnel serving, or preparing to serve, limited English proficient children; and

(5) supporting the recruitment and training of prospective educational personnel to serve limited English proficient children by providing fellowships for undergraduate,

graduate, doctoral, and post-doctoral study related to the instruction of such children.

(b) AUTHORIZATION-

(1) IN GENERAL- The Secretary is authorized to award grants under this section to —

(A) State educational agencies;

(B) local educational agencies;

(C) institutions of higher education; or

(D) consortia of one or more local educational agencies, State educational agencies, institutions of higher education, for-profit organizations, or nonprofit organizations.

(2) DURATION- Each grant awarded under this section shall be awarded for a period of not more than 4 years.

(c) AUTHORIZED ACTIVITIES- Grants awarded under this section shall be used to conduct high-quality professional development programs and effective activities to improve the quality of instruction and services provided to limited English proficient children, including —

(1) implementing preservice and inservice professional development programs for teachers who serve limited English proficient children, administrators, and other educational personnel who are preparing to provide educational services for limited English proficient children, including professional development programs that assist limited English proficient children to attain English proficiency;

(2) implementing school-based collaborative efforts among teachers to improve instruction in core academic subjects, especially reading, for limited English proficient children;

(3) developing and implementing programs to assist beginning teachers who serve limited English proficient children with transitioning to the teaching profession, including programs that provide mentoring and team teaching with trained and experienced teachers;

(4) implementing programs that support effective teacher use of education technologies to improve instruction and assessment;

(5) developing curricular materials and assessments for teachers that are appropriate to the needs of limited English proficient children, and that are aligned with challenging State academic content and student academic achievement standards, including materials and assessments that ensure limited English proficient children attain English proficiency;

(6) integrating and coordinating activities with entities carrying out other programs consistent with the purpose of this section and supported under this Act, or other Acts as appropriate;

(7) developing and implementing career ladder programs to upgrade the qualifications and skills of non-certified educational personnel working in, or preparing to work in, language instruction educational programs to enable such personnel to meet high professional standards, including standards for certification and licensure as teachers;

(8) developing and implementing activities to help recruit and train secondary school

students as teachers who serve limited English proficient children;

(9) providing fellowships and assistance for costs related to enrollment in a course of study at an institution of higher education that addresses the instruction of limited English proficient children in such areas as teacher training, program administration, research, evaluation, and curriculum development, and for the support of dissertation research related to such study, except that any person receiving such a fellowship or assistance shall agree to —

(A) work in an activity related to improving the educational services for limited English proficient children authorized under this subpart, including work as a teacher that serves limited English proficient children, for a period of time equivalent to the period of time during which such person receives assistance under this paragraph; or

(B) repay such assistance; and

(10) carrying out such other activities as are consistent with the purpose of this section.

State Statutory References

House Bill 5 (HB5)

Section 12 and 13 – amend Subchapter B, Chapter 28 (TEC) by amending section 28.0212 heading to read Junior High or Middle School Personal Graduation Plan. (eff. 2014-2015)

Section 14 – amends Subchapter B, Chapter 28 (TEC) to adding section 28.02121-High School Personal Graduation Plan (eff. 2014-2015)

Section 15 – amends Subchapter B, Chapter 28 (TEC) by adding section 28.0217-Accelerated Instruction for High School Students

Section 16 – amends Subchapter B, Chapter 28 (TEC) by amending subsections and adding subsections to section 28.025 – description of the foundations school program, endorsements, and performance acknowledgement for biliteracy and bilingualism (eff. 2014-2015 for all students except those in their fourth year of high school; then eff. 2013-2014)

Section 20 – amends Subchapter B, Chapter 29 (TEC) by amending subsections and adding subsections to section 29.081 – providing additional accelerated instruction for any student who does not perform satisfactorily on any EOC required for graduation; amends age for definition of "student at risk of dropping out of school"

Sections 31, 32, 34, and 37 – amend Subchapter B, Chapter 39 (TEC) regarding the new assessment program requirements and benchmarking limitations.

Section 38 – amends Sec. 39.027 (TEC) by adding Subsection (a-2) that states unless a student is enrolled in a US school for at least 60 consecutive days during a year, they may not be considered to be enrolled for a year. (eff. 2013-2014)

Texas Education Code (TEC), Title 2, Subtitle F

Chapter 4
TEC Sec. 4.002 (Public Education Goals)

Chapter 7, Subchapter A
TEC Sec. 7.028 (Limitation on Compliance Monitoring)

Chapter 7, Subchapter D
Sec. 7.102 (State Board of Education Powers and Duties)

Chapter 11, Subchapter A
TEC Sec. 11.251 (Planning and Decision-Making Process)

TEC Sec. 11.252 (District-Level Planning and Decision-Making)

TEC Sec. 11.253 (Campus Planning and Site-Based Decision Making)

Chapter 28, Subchapter A
TEC Sec. 28.002 (Required Curriculum)

TEC Sec. 28.005 (Language of Instruction)

TEC Sec. 28.0051 (Dual Language Immersion Program)

Chapter 28, Subchapter B
TEC Sec. 28.0211 (Satisfactory Performance on State Assessment Instruments Required; Accelerated Instruction)

TEC Sec. 28.0212 (Personal Graduation Plan) – renamed to (Junior High or Middle School Personal Graduation Plan) by HB5

TEC Sec. 28.02121 – added by HB5 (High School Personal Graduation Plan)

TEC Sec. 28.0213 (Intensive Instruction Program)

TEC Sec. 28.0217 – added by HB5 (Accelerated Instruction for High School Students)

TEC Sec. 28.025 (High School Diploma and Certificate; Academic Achievement Record)

Texas Education Code (TEC), Title 2, Subtitle F, continued

Chapter 29, Subchapter B

TEC Sec. 29.051 (State Policy)

TEC Sec. 29.052 (Definitions)

TEC Sec. 29.053 (Establishment of Bilingual and Special Language Programs)

TEC Sec. 29.054 (Exception)

TEC Sec. 29.055 (Program Content; Method of Instruction)

TEC 29.056 (Enrollment of Students in Program)

TEC Sec. 29.0561 (Evaluation of Transferred Students; Reenrollment)

TEC Sec. 29.057 (Facilities; Classes)

TEC Sec. 29.058 (Enrollment of Students Who Do Not Have Limited English Proficiency)

TEC Sec. 29.059 (Cooperation among Districts)

TEC Sec. 29.060 (Preschool, Summer School, and Extended Time Programs)

TEC Sec. 29.061 (Bilingual Education and Special Language Program Teachers)

TEC Sec. 29.062 (Compliance)

TEC Sec. 29.063 (Language Proficiency Assessment Committees)

TEC Sec. 29.064 (Appeals)

TEC Sec. 20.066 (PEIMS Reporting Requirements)

Chapter 29, Subchapter C (amended by HB5, Sec. 20)

TEC Sec. 29.081 – (Compensatory, Intensive, and Accelerated Instruction)

Chapter 29, Subchapter E

TEC 29.153 (Free Prekindergarten for Certain Children)

Chapter 39, Subchapter B (many sections amended by HB5, Sec. 31, 32, 34, 37, and 38)

TEC Sec. 39.021 (Essential Skills and Knowledge)

TEC Sec. 39.022 (Assessment Program)

TEC Sec. 39.023 (Adoption and Administration of Instruments)

TEC Sec. 39.027 (Exemption)

Chapter 39, Subchapter C (sections amended by HB5, Sec. 42, and 46)

TEC Sec. 39.052 (Determination of Accreditation Status or Performance Rating)

TEC Sec. 39.053 (Performance Indicators: Student Achievement)

TEC Sec. 39.0545 (added by HB5)

Chapter 39, Subchapter E

TEC Sec. 39.105 (Campus Improvement Plan)

TEC Sec. 39.106 (Campus Intervention Team Duties)

Chapter 42, Subchapter A

TEC Sec. 42.001 (State Policy)

TEC Sec. 42.002 (Purposes of Foundation School Program)

TEC Sec. 42.003 (Student Eligibility)

Chapter 42, Subchapter B

TEC Sec. 42.152 (Compensatory Education Allotment)

TEC Chapter 4

Sec. 4.002. PUBLIC EDUCATION ACADEMIC GOALS.

To serve as a foundation for a well-balanced and appropriate education:

GOAL 1: The students in the public education system will demonstrate exemplary performance in the reading and writing of the English language.

GOAL 2: The students in the public education system will demonstrate exemplary performance in the understanding of mathematics.

GOAL 3: The students in the public education system will demonstrate exemplary performance in the understanding of science.

GOAL 4: The students in the public education system will demonstrate exemplary performance in the understanding of social studies.

TEC Chapter 7

Subchapter A

Sec. 7.028. LIMITATION ON COMPLIANCE MONITORING.

(a) Except as provided by Section 29.001(5), 29.010(a), 39.056, or 39.057, the agency may monitor compliance with requirements applicable to a process or program provided by a school district, campus, program, or school granted charters under Chapter 12, including the process described by Subchapter F, Chapter 11, or a program described by Subchapter B, C, D, E, F, H, or I, Chapter 29, Subchapter A, Chapter 37, or Section 38.003, and the use of funds provided for such a program under Subchapter C, Chapter 42, only as necessary to ensure:

(1) compliance with federal law and regulations;

(2) financial accountability, including compliance with grant requirements; and

(3) data integrity for purposes of:

(A) the Public Education Information Management System (PEIMS); and

(B) accountability under Chapter 39.

(b) The board of trustees of a school district or the governing body of an open-enrollment charter school has primary responsibility for ensuring that the district or school complies with all applicable requirements of state educational programs.

Subchapter D

Sec. 7.102. STATE BOARD OF EDUCATION POWERS AND DUTIES.

(a) The board may perform only those duties relating to school districts or regional education service centers assigned to the board by the constitution of this state or by this subchapter or another provision of this code.

(b) The board has the powers and duties provided by Subsection (c), which shall be carried out with the advice and assistance of the commissioner.

(c)(1) The board shall develop and update a long-range plan for public education.

(2) The board may enter into contracts relating to or accept grants for the improvement of educational programs specifically authorized by statute.

(3) The board may accept a gift, donation, or other contribution on behalf of the public school system or agency and, unless otherwise specified by the donor, may use the contribution in the manner the board determines.

(4) The board shall establish curriculum and graduation requirements.

TEC Chapter 11

Subchapter F

Sec. 11.251 (Planning and Decision-Making Process)

(d) The board shall also ensure that an administrative procedure is provided to clearly define the respective roles and responsibilities of the superintendent, central office staff, principals, teachers, district-level committee members, and campus-level committee members in the areas of planning, budgeting, curriculum, staffing patterns, staff development, and school organization. The board shall ensure that the district-level planning and decision-making committee will be actively involved in establishing the administrative procedure that defines the respective roles and responsibilities pertaining to planning and decision-making at the district and campus levels.

Sec. 11.252. DISTRICT-LEVEL PLANNING AND DECISION-MAKING.

(a) Each school district shall have a district improvement plan that is developed, evaluated, and revised annually, in accordance with district policy, by the superintendent with the assistance of the district-level committee established under Section 11.251. The purpose of the district improvement plan is to guide district and campus staff in the improvement of student performance for all student groups in order to attain state standards in respect to the student achievement indicators adopted under Section 39.053. The district improvement plan must include provisions for:

(1) a comprehensive needs assessment addressing district student performance on

the student achievement indicators, and other appropriate measures of performance, that are disaggregated by all student groups served by the district, including categories of ethnicity, socioeconomic status, sex, and populations served by special programs, including students in special education programs under Subchapter A, Chapter 29;

(2) measurable district performance objectives for all appropriate student achievement indicators for all student populations, including students in special education programs under Subchapter A, Chapter 29, and other measures of student performance that may be identified through the comprehensive needs assessment;

(3) strategies for improvement of student performance that include:

(A) instructional methods for addressing the needs of student groups not achieving their full potential;

(B) methods for addressing the needs of students for special programs, including:

(i) suicide prevention programs, in accordance with Subchapter O-1, Chapter 161, Health and Safety Code, which includes a parental or guardian notification procedure;

(ii) conflict resolution programs;

(iii) violence prevention programs; and

(iv) dyslexia treatment programs;

(C) dropout reduction;

(D) integration of technology in instructional and administrative programs;

(E) discipline management;

(F) staff development for professional staff of the district;

(G) career education to assist students in developing the knowledge, skills, and competencies necessary for a broad range of career opportunities; and

(H) accelerated education;

Sec. 11.253. CAMPUS PLANNING AND SITE-BASED DECISION-MAKING.

(a) Each school district shall maintain current policies and procedures to ensure that effective planning and site-based decision-making occur at each campus to direct and support the improvement of student performance for all students.

(b) Each district's policy and procedures shall establish campus-level planning and decision-making committees as provided for through the procedures provided by Sections 11.251(b)-(e).

(c) Each school year, the principal of each school campus, with the assistance of the campus-level committee, shall develop, review, and revise the campus improvement plan for the purpose of improving student performance for all student populations, including students in special education programs under Subchapter A, Chapter 29, with respect to the student achievement indicators adopted under Section 39.053 and any other appropriate performance measures for special needs populations.

(d) Each campus improvement plan must:

(1) assess the academic achievement for each student in the school using the student achievement indicator system as described by Section 39.053;

(2) set the campus performance objectives based on the student achievement indicator system, including objectives for special needs populations, including students in special education programs under Subchapter A, Chapter 29;

(3) identify how the campus goals will be met for each student;

(4) determine the resources needed to implement the plan;

(5) identify staff needed to implement the plan;

(6) set timelines for reaching the goals;

(7) measure progress toward the performance objectives periodically to ensure that the plan is resulting in academic improvement;

(8) include goals and methods for violence prevention and intervention on campus;

(9) provide for a program to encourage parental involvement at the campus; and

(10) if the campus is an elementary, middle, or junior high school, set goals and objectives for the coordinated health program at the campus based on:

(A) student fitness assessment data, including any data from research-based assessments such as the school health index assessment and planning tool created by the federal Centers for Disease Control and Prevention;

(B) student academic performance data;

(C) student attendance rates;

(D) the percentage of students who are educationally disadvantaged;

(E) the use and success of any method to ensure that students participate in moderate to vigorous physical activity as required by Section 28.002(l); and

(F) any other indicator recommended by the local school health advisory council.

(e) In accordance with the administrative procedures established under Section 11.251(b), the campus-level committee shall be involved in decisions in the areas of planning, budgeting, curriculum, staffing patterns, staff development, and school organization. The campus-level committee must approve the portions of the campus plan addressing campus staff development needs.

(f) This section does not create a new cause of action or require collective bargaining.

(g) Each campus-level committee shall hold at least one public meeting per year. The required meeting shall be held after receipt of the annual campus rating from the agency to discuss the performance of the campus and the campus performance objectives. District policy and campus procedures must be established to ensure that systematic communications measures are in place to periodically obtain broad-based community, parent, and staff input, and to provide information to those persons regarding the recommendations of the campus-level committees.

(h) A principal shall regularly consult the campus-level committee in the planning, operation, supervision, and evaluation of the campus educational program.

TEC Chapter 28

Subchapter A (these sections subject to change under HB5, Sections 14-16)

Sec. 28.002. REQUIRED CURRICULUM.

(a) Each school district that offers kindergarten through grade 12 shall offer, as a required curriculum:

(1) a foundation curriculum that includes:

(A) English language arts;

(B) mathematics;

(C) science; and

(D) social studies, consisting of Texas, United States, and world history, government, economics, with emphasis on the free enterprise system and its benefits, and geography; and

(2) an enrichment curriculum that includes:

(A) to the extent possible, languages other than English;

(B) health, with emphasis on the importance of proper nutrition and exercise;

(C) physical education;

(D) fine arts;

(E) career and technology education;

(F) technology applications; and

(G) religious literature, including the Hebrew Scriptures (Old Testament) and New Testament, and its impact on history and literature.

(b) The State Board of Education by rule shall designate subjects constituting a well-balanced curriculum to be offered by a school district that does not offer kindergarten through grade 12.

(c) The State Board of Education, with the direct participation of educators, parents, business and industry representatives, and employers shall by rule identify the essential knowledge and skills of each subject of the required curriculum that all students should be able to demonstrate and that will be used in evaluating instructional materials under Chapter 31 and addressed on the assessment instruments required under Subchapter B, Chapter 39. As a condition of accreditation, the board shall require each district to provide instruction in the essential knowledge and skills at appropriate grade levels.

(c-1) The State Board of Education shall adopt rules requiring students enrolled in grade levels six, seven, and eight to complete at least one fine arts course during those grade levels as part of a district's fine arts curriculum.

(c-2) Each time the Texas Higher Education Coordinating Board revises the Internet database of the coordinating board's official statewide inventory of workforce education courses, the State Board of Education shall by rule revise the essential knowledge and skills of any corresponding career and technology education curriculum as provided by Subsection (c).

(d) The physical education curriculum required under Subsection (a)(2)(C) must be sequential, developmentally appropriate, and designed, implemented, and evaluated to enable students to develop the motor, self-management, and other skills, knowledge, attitudes, and confidence necessary to participate in physical activity throughout life. Each school district shall establish specific objectives and goals the district intends to accomplish through the physical education curriculum. In identifying the essential knowledge and skills of physical education, the State Board of Education shall ensure that the curriculum:

(1) emphasizes the knowledge and skills capable of being used during a lifetime of regular physical activity;

(2) is consistent with national physical education standards for:

(A) the information that students should learn about physical activity; and

(B) the physical activities that students should be able to perform;

(3) requires that, on a weekly basis, at least 50 percent of the physical education class be used for actual student physical activity and that the activity be, to the extent practicable, at a moderate or vigorous level;

(4) offers students an opportunity to choose among many types of physical activity in which to participate;

(5) offers students both cooperative and competitive games;

(6) meets the needs of students of all physical ability levels, including students who have a disability, chronic health problem, or other special need that precludes the student from participating in regular physical education instruction but who might be able to participate in physical education that is suitably adapted and, if applicable, included in the student's individualized education program;

(7) takes into account the effect that gender and cultural differences might have on the degree of student interest in physical activity or on the types of physical activity in which a student is interested;

(8) teaches self-management and movement skills;

(9) teaches cooperation, fair play, and responsible participation in physical activity;

(10) promotes student participation in physical activity outside of school; and

(11) allows physical education classes to be an enjoyable experience for students.

(e) American Sign Language is a language for purposes of Subsection (a)(2)(A). A public school may offer an elective course in the language.

(f) A school district may offer courses for local credit in addition to those in the required curriculum. The State Board of Education shall be flexible in approving a course for credit for high school graduation under this subsection.

(g) A local instructional plan may draw on state curriculum frameworks and program standards as appropriate. Each district is encouraged to exceed minimum requirements of law and State Board of Education rule. Each district shall ensure that all children in the district participate actively in a balanced curriculum designed to meet individual needs.

(h) The State Board of Education and each school district shall foster the continuation of the tradition of teaching United States and Texas history and the free enterprise system in regular subject matter and in reading courses and in the adoption of instructional materials. A primary purpose of the public school curriculum is to prepare thoughtful, active citizens who understand the importance of patriotism and can function productively in a free enterprise society with appreciation for the basic democratic values of our state and national heritage.

(i) The State Board of Education shall adopt rules for the implementation of this subchapter. Except as provided by Subsection (j), the board may not adopt rules that designate the methodology used by a teacher or the time spent by a teacher or a student on a particular task or subject.

(j) The State Board of Education by rule may require laboratory instruction in secondary science courses and may require a specific amount or percentage of time in a secondary science course that must be laboratory instruction.

(k) The State Board of Education, in consultation with the Department of State Health Services and the Texas Diabetes Council, shall develop a diabetes education program that a school district may use in the health curriculum under Subsection (a)(2)(B).

(l) A school district shall require a student enrolled in full-day prekindergarten, in kindergarten, or in a grade level below grade six to participate in moderate or vigorous daily physical activity for at least 30 minutes throughout the school year as part of the district's physical education curriculum or through structured activity during a school campus's daily recess. To the extent practicable, a school district shall require a student enrolled in prekindergarten on less than a full-day basis to participate in the same type and amount of physical activity as a student enrolled in full-day prekindergarten. A school district shall require students enrolled in grade levels six, seven, and eight to participate in moderate or vigorous daily physical activity for at least 30 minutes for at least four semesters during those grade levels as part of the district's physical education curriculum. If a school district determines, for any particular grade level below grade six, that requiring moderate or vigorous daily physical activity is impractical due to scheduling concerns or other factors, the district may as an alternative require a student in that grade level to participate in moderate or vigorous physical activity for at least 135 minutes during each school week. Additionally, a school district may as an alternative require a student enrolled in a grade level for which the district uses block scheduling to participate in moderate or vigorous physical activity for at least 225 minutes during each period of two school weeks. A school district must provide for an exemption for:

(1) any student who is unable to participate in the required physical activity because of illness or disability; and

(2) a middle school or junior high school student who participates in an extracurricular activity with a moderate or vigorous physical activity component that is considered a structured activity under rules adopted by the commissioner.

(l-1) In adopting rules relating to an activity described by Subsection (l)(2), the commissioner may permit an exemption for a student who participates in a school-related activity or an activity sponsored by a private league or club only if the student provides proof of participation in the activity.

(l-2) To encourage school districts to promote physical activity for children through classroom curricula for health and physical education, the agency, in consultation with the Department of State Health Services, shall designate nationally recognized health and physical education program guidelines that a school district may use in the health curriculum under Subsection (a)(2)(B) or the physical education curriculum under Subsection (a)(2)(C).

(l-3)(1) This subsection may be cited as "Lauren's Law."

(2) The State Board of Education, the Department of State Health Services, or a school district may not adopt any rule, policy, or program under Subsections (a), (k), (l), (l-1), or (l-2) that would prohibit a parent or grandparent of a student from providing any food product of the parent's or grandparent's choice to:

(A) children in the classroom of the child of the parent or grandparent on the occasion of the child's birthday; or

(B) children at a school-designated function.

(m) Section 2001.039, Government Code, as added by Chapter 1499, Acts of the 76th Legislature, Regular Session, 1999, does not apply to a rule adopted by the State Board of Education under Subsection (c) or (d).

(n) The State Board of Education may by rule develop and implement a plan designed to incorporate foundation curriculum requirements into the career and technology education curriculum under Subsection (a)(2)(E).

(p) The State Board of Education, in conjunction with the office of the attorney general, shall develop a parenting and paternity awareness program that a school district shall use in the district's high school health curriculum. A school district may use the program developed under this subsection in the district's middle or junior high school curriculum. At the discretion of the district, a teacher may modify the suggested sequence and pace of the program at any grade level. The program must:

(1) address parenting skills and responsibilities, including child support and other legal rights and responsibilities that come with parenthood;

(2) address relationship skills, including money management, communication skills, and marriage preparation; and

(3) in district middle, junior high, or high schools that do not have a family violence prevention program, address skills relating to the prevention of family violence.

(p-2) A school district may develop or adopt research-based programs and curriculum materials for use in conjunction with the program developed under Subsection (p). The programs and curriculum materials may provide instruction in:

(1) child development;

(2) parenting skills, including child abuse and neglect prevention; and

(3) assertiveness skills to prevent teenage pregnancy, abusive relationships, and family violence.

(p-3) The agency shall evaluate programs and curriculum materials developed under Subsection (p-2) and distribute to other school districts information regarding those programs and materials.

(p-4) A student under 14 years of age may not participate in a program developed under Subsection (p) without the permission of the student's parent or person standing in parental relation to the student.

(q) Notwithstanding any other provision of this title, a school district may not vary the curriculum for a course in the required curriculum under Subsection (a) based on whether a student is enrolled in the minimum, recognized, or advanced high school program.

(r) In adopting the essential knowledge and skills for the health curriculum under Subsection (a)(2)(B), the State Board of Education shall adopt essential knowledge and skills that address the dangers, causes, consequences, signs, symptoms, and treatment of binge drinking and alcohol poisoning. The agency shall compile a list of evidence-based alcohol awareness programs from which a school district shall choose a program to use in the district's middle school, junior high school, and high school health curriculum. In this subsection, "evidence-based alcohol awareness program" means a program, practice, or strategy that has been proven to effectively prevent or delay alcohol use among students, as determined by evaluations that use valid and reliable measures and that are published in peer-reviewed journals.
(s) In this subsection, "bullying" has the meaning assigned by Section 37.0832 and "harassment" has the meaning assigned by Section 37.001. In addition to any other essential knowledge and skills the State Board of Education adopts for the health curriculum under Subsection (a)(2)(B), the board shall adopt for the health curriculum, in consultation with the Texas School Safety Center, essential knowledge and skills that include evidence-based practices that will effectively address awareness, prevention, identification, self-defense in response to, and resolution of and intervention in bullying and harassment.

Sec. 28.005. LANGUAGE OF INSTRUCTION.

(a) Except as provided by this section, English shall be the basic language of instruction in public schools.

(b) It is the policy of this state to ensure the mastery of English by all students, except that bilingual instruction may be offered or permitted in situations in which bilingual instruction is necessary to ensure students' reasonable proficiency in the English language and ability to achieve academic success.

(c) A school district may adopt a dual language immersion program for students enrolled in elementary school grades as provided by Section 28.0051.

Sec. 28.0051. DUAL LANGUAGE IMMERSION PROGRAM.

(a) A dual language immersion program should be designed to produce students with a demonstrated mastery, in both English and one other language, of the required curriculum under Section 28.002(a).

(b) The commissioner by rule shall adopt:

(1) minimum requirements for a dual language immersion program implemented by a school district;

(2) standards for evaluating:

(A) the success of a dual language immersion program; and

(B) the performance of schools that implement a dual language immersion program; and

(3) standards for recognizing:

(A) schools that offer an exceptional dual language immersion program; and

(B) students who successfully complete a dual language immersion program.

(c) A school district may implement a dual language immersion program in a manner and at elementary grade levels consistent with rules adopted by the commissioner under this section.

Subchapter B

Sec. 28.0211. SATISFACTORY PERFORMANCE ON ASSESSMENT INSTRUMENTS REQUIRED; ACCELERATED INSTRUCTION.

(a) Except as provided by Subsection (b) or (e), a student may not be promoted to:

(1) the sixth grade program to which the student would otherwise be assigned if the student does not perform satisfactorily on the fifth grade mathematics and reading assessment instruments under Section 39.023; or

(2) the ninth grade program to which the student would otherwise be assigned if the student does not perform satisfactorily on the eighth grade mathematics and reading assessment instruments under Section 39.023.

(a-1) Each time a student fails to perform satisfactorily on an assessment instrument administered under Section 39.023(a) in the third, fourth, fifth, sixth, seventh, or eighth grade, the school district in which the student attends school shall provide to the student accelerated instruction in the applicable subject area. Accelerated instruction may require participation of the student before or after normal school hours and may include participation at times of the year outside normal school operations.

(a-2) A student who fails to perform satisfactorily on an assessment instrument specified under Subsection (a) and who is promoted to the next grade level must complete accelerated instruction required under Subsection (a-1) before placement in the next grade level. A student who fails to complete required accelerated instruction may not be promoted.

(a-3) The commissioner shall provide guidelines to districts on research-based best practices and effective strategies that a district may use in developing an accelerated instruction program.

(b) A school district shall provide to a student who initially fails to perform satisfactorily on an assessment instrument specified under Subsection (a) at least two additional opportunities to take the assessment instrument. A school district may administer an alternate assessment instrument to a student who has failed an assessment instrument specified under Subsection (a) on the previous two opportunities. Notwithstanding any other provision of this section, a student may be promoted if the student performs at grade level on an alternate assessment instrument under this subsection that is appropriate for the student's grade level and approved by the commissioner.

(c) Each time a student fails to perform satisfactorily on an assessment instrument specified under Subsection (a), the school district in which the student attends school shall provide to the student accelerated instruction in the applicable subject area, including reading instruction for a student who fails to perform satisfactorily on a reading assessment instrument. After a student fails to perform satisfactorily on an assessment instrument a second time, a grade placement committee shall be established to prescribe the accelerated instruction the district shall provide to the student before the student is administered the assessment instrument the third time. The grade placement committee shall be composed of the principal or the principal's designee, the student's parent or guardian, and the teacher of the subject of an assessment instrument on which the student failed to perform satisfactorily. The district shall notify the parent or guardian of the time and place for convening the grade placement committee and the purpose of the committee. An accelerated instruction group administered by a school district under this section may not have a ratio of more than 10 students for each teacher.

(d) In addition to providing accelerated instruction to a student under Subsection (c), the district shall notify the student's parent or guardian of:

(1) the student's failure to perform satisfactorily on the assessment instrument;

(2) the accelerated instruction program to which the student is assigned; and

(3) the possibility that the student might be retained at the same grade level for the next school year.

(e) A student who, after at least three attempts, fails to perform satisfactorily on an assessment instrument specified under Subsection (a) shall be retained at the same grade level for the next school year in accordance with Subsection (a). The student's parent or guardian may appeal the student's retention by submitting a request to the grade placement committee established under Subsection (c). The school district shall give the parent or guardian written notice of the opportunity to appeal. The grade placement committee may decide in favor of a student's promotion only if the committee concludes, using standards adopted by the board of trustees, that if promoted and given accelerated instruction, the student is likely to perform at grade level. A student may not be promoted on the basis of the grade placement committee's decision unless that decision is unanimous. The commissioner by rule shall establish a time line for making the placement determination. This subsection does not create a property interest in promotion. The decision of the grade placement committee is final and may not be appealed.

(f) A school district shall provide to a student who, after three attempts, has failed to perform satisfactorily on an assessment instrument specified under Subsection (a) accelerated instruction during the next school year as prescribed by an educational plan developed for the student by the student's grade placement committee established under Subsection (c). The district shall provide that accelerated instruction regardless of whether the student has been promoted or retained. The educational plan must be designed to enable the student to perform at the appropriate grade level by the conclusion of the school year. During the school year, the student shall be monitored to ensure that the student is progressing in accordance with the plan. The district shall administer to the student the assessment instrument for the grade level in which the student is placed at the time the district regularly administers the assessment instruments for that school year.

(g) This section does not preclude the retention at a grade level, in accordance with state law or school district policy, of a student who performs satisfactorily on an assessment instrument specified under Subsection (a).

(h) In each instance under this section in which a school district is specifically required to provide notice to a parent or guardian of a student, the district shall make a good faith effort to ensure that such notice is provided either in person or by regular mail and that the notice is clear and easy to understand and is written in English or the parent or guardian's native language.

(i) The admission, review, and dismissal committee of a student who participates in a district's special education program under Subchapter B, Chapter 29, and who does not perform satisfactorily on an assessment instrument specified under Subsection (a) and administered under Section 39.023(a) or (b) shall determine:

(1) the manner in which the student will participate in an accelerated instruction program under this section; and

(2) whether the student will be promoted or retained under this section.

(j) A school district or open-enrollment charter school shall provide students required to attend accelerated programs under this section with transportation to those programs if the programs occur outside of regular school hours.

(k) The commissioner shall adopt rules as necessary to implement this section, including rules concerning when school districts shall administer assessment instruments required under this section and which administration of the assessment instruments will be used for purposes of Section 39.054.

(l) Repealed by Acts 2007, 80th Leg., R.S., Ch. 1058, Sec. 17, eff. June 15, 2007.

(l-1) The commissioner may adopt rules requiring a school district that receives federal funding under Title I of the Elementary and Secondary Education Act of 1965 (20 U.S.C. Section 6301 et seq.) to use that funding to provide supplemental educational services under 20 U.S.C. Section 6316 in conjunction with the accelerated instruction provided under this section, provided that the rules may not conflict with federal law governing the use of that funding.

(m) The commissioner shall certify, not later than July 1 of each school year or as soon as practicable thereafter, whether sufficient funds have been appropriated statewide for the purposes of this section. A determination by the commissioner is final and may not be appealed. For purposes of certification, the commissioner may not consider Foundation School Program funds. This section may be implemented only if the commissioner certifies that sufficient funds have been appropriated during a school year for administering the accelerated instruction programs specified under this section, including teacher training for that purpose.

(n) A student who is promoted by a grade placement committee under this section must be assigned in each subject in which the student failed to perform satisfactorily on an assessment instrument specified under Subsection (a) to a teacher who meets all state and federal qualifications to teach that subject and grade.

(o) This section does not require the administration of a fifth or eighth grade assessment instrument in a subject under Section 39.023(a) to a student enrolled in the fifth or eighth grade, as applicable, if the student:

(1) is enrolled in a course in the subject intended for students above the student's grade level and will be administered an assessment instrument adopted or developed under Section 39.023(a) that aligns with the curriculum for the course in which the student is enrolled; or

(2) is enrolled in a course in the subject for which the student will receive high school academic credit and will be administered an end-of-course assessment instrument adopted under Section 39.023(c) for the course.

(p) Notwithstanding any other provision of this section, a student described by Subsection (o) may not be denied promotion on the basis of failure to perform satisfactorily on an assessment instrument not required to be administered to the student in accordance with that subsection.

Sec. 28.0212. PERSONAL GRADUATION PLAN.

(a) A principal shall designate a guidance counselor, teacher, or other appropriate individual to develop and administer a personal graduation plan for each student enrolled in a junior high, middle, or high school who:

(1) does not perform satisfactorily on an assessment instrument administered under Subchapter B, Chapter 39; or

(2) is not likely to receive a high school diploma before the fifth school year following the student's enrollment in grade level nine, as determined by the district.

(b) A personal graduation plan must:

(1) identify educational goals for the student;

(2) include diagnostic information, appropriate monitoring and intervention, and other evaluation strategies;

(3) include an intensive instruction program described by Section 28.0213;

(4) address participation of the student's parent or guardian, including consideration of the parent's or guardian's educational expectations for the student; and

(5) provide innovative methods to promote the student's advancement, including flexible scheduling, alternative learning environments, on-line instruction, and other interventions that are proven to accelerate the learning process and have been scientifically validated to improve learning and cognitive ability.

(c) Notwithstanding Subsection (b), a student's individualized education program developed under Section 29.005 may be used as the student's personal graduation plan under this section.

(d) The agency shall establish minimum standards for a personal graduation plan under this section.

(e) Each school district is encouraged to establish for each student entering grade nine a personal graduation plan that identifies a course of study that:

(1) promotes:

(A) college and workforce readiness; and

(B) career placement and advancement; and

(2) facilitates the student's transition from secondary to postsecondary education.

(g) Each school district is encouraged to establish for each student entering grade nine a personal graduation plan that identifies a course of study that:

(1) promotes:

(A) college and workforce readiness; and

(B) career placement and advancement; and

(2) facilitates the student's transition from secondary to postsecondary education.

Sec. 28.0213. INTENSIVE PROGRAM OF INSTRUCTION.

(a) A school district shall offer an intensive program of instruction to a student who does not perform satisfactorily on an assessment instrument administered under Subchapter B, Chapter 39.

(b) A school district shall design the intensive program of instruction described by Subsection (a) to:

(1) enable the student to:

(A) to the extent practicable, perform at the student's grade level at the conclusion of the next regular school term; or

(B) attain a standard of annual growth specified by the school district and reported by the district to the agency; and

(2) if applicable, carry out the purposes of Section 28.0211.

(c) A school district shall use funds appropriated by the legislature for an intensive program of instruction to plan and implement intensive instruction and other activities aimed at helping a student satisfy state and local high school graduation requirements. The commissioner shall distribute funds to districts that implement a program under this section based on the number of students identified by the district who:

(1) do not perform satisfactorily on an assessment instrument administered under Subchapter B, Chapter 39; or

(2) are not likely to receive a high school diploma before the fifth school year following the student's enrollment in grade nine, as determined by the district.

(d) A school district's determination of the appropriateness of a program for a student under this section is final and does not create a cause of action.

(e) For a student in a special education program under Subchapter A, Chapter 29, who does not perform satisfactorily on an assessment instrument administered under Section 39.023(a), (b), or (c), the student's admission, review, and dismissal committee shall design the program to:

(1) enable the student to attain a standard of annual growth on the basis of the student's individualized education program; and
(2) if applicable, carry out the purposes of Section 28.0211.

(Added by HB5)
Sec. 28.0217. ACCELERATED INSTRUCTION FOR HIGH SCHOOL

STUDENTS. Each time a student fails to perform satisfactorily on an assessment instrument administered under Section 39.023(c), the school district in which the student attends school shall provide to the student accelerated instruction in the applicable subject area, using funds appropriated for accelerated instruction under Section 28.0211.

Accelerated instruction may require participation of the student before or after normal school hours and may include participation at times of the year outside normal school operations.

Sec. 28.025. HIGH SCHOOL DIPLOMA AND CERTIFICATE; ACADEMIC ACHIEVEMENT RECORD.

(This section is changing significantly. See Section 16 of HB5 for amended and added language for this section)

TEC Chapter 29

Subchapter B – Bilingual Education and Special Language Programs

Sec. 29.051. STATE POLICY.

English is the basic language of this state. Public schools are responsible for providing a full opportunity for all students to become competent in speaking, reading, writing, and comprehending the English language. Large numbers of students in the state come from environments in which the primary language is other than English. Experience has shown that public school classes in which instruction is given only in English are often inadequate for the education of those students. The mastery of basic English language skills is a prerequisite for effective participation in the state's educational program. Bilingual education and special language programs can meet the needs of those students and facilitate their integration into the regular school curriculum. Therefore, in accordance with the policy of the state to ensure equal educational opportunity to every student, and in recognition of the educational needs of students of limited English proficiency, this subchapter provides for the establishment of bilingual education and special language programs in the public schools and provides supplemental financial assistance to help school districts meet the extra costs of the programs.

Sec. 29.052. DEFINITIONS.

In this subchapter:

(1) "Student of limited English proficiency" means a student whose primary language is other than English and whose English language skills are such that the student has difficulty performing ordinary classwork in English.

(2) "Parent" includes a legal guardian of a student.

Sec. 29.053. ESTABLISHMENT OF BILINGUAL EDUCATION AND SPECIAL LANGUAGE PROGRAMS.

(a) The agency shall establish a procedure for identifying school districts that are required to offer bilingual education and special language programs in accordance with this subchapter.

(b) Within the first four weeks following the first day of school, the language proficiency assessment committee established under Section 29.063 shall determine and report to the board of trustees of the district the number of students of limited English proficiency on each campus and shall classify each student according to the language in which the student possesses primary proficiency. The board shall report that information to the agency before November 1 each year.

(c) Each district with an enrollment of 20 or more students of limited English proficiency in any language classification in the same grade level shall offer a bilingual education or special language program.

(d) Each district that is required to offer bilingual education and special language programs under this section shall offer the following for students of limited English proficiency:

(1) bilingual education in kindergarten through the elementary grades;

(2) bilingual education, instruction in English as a second language, or other transitional language instruction approved by the agency in post-elementary grades through grade 8; and

(3) instruction in English as a second language in grades 9 through 12.

Sec. 29.054. EXCEPTION.

(a) If a program other than bilingual education must be used in kindergarten through the elementary grades, documentation for the exception must be filed with and approved by the agency.

(b) An application for an exception may be filed with the agency when a district is unable to hire a sufficient number of teachers with teaching certificates appropriate for bilingual education instruction to staff the required program. The application must be accompanied by:

(1) documentation showing that the district has taken all reasonable affirmative steps to secure teachers with teaching certificates appropriate for bilingual education instruction and has failed;

(2) documentation showing that the district has affirmative hiring policies and procedures consistent with the need to serve limited English proficiency students;

(3) documentation showing that, on the basis of district records, no teacher having a teaching certificate appropriate for bilingual instruction or emergency credentials has been unjustifiably denied employment by the district within the past 12 months; and

(4) a plan detailing specific measures to be used by the district to eliminate the conditions that created the need for an exception.

(c) An exception shall be granted under this section on an individual district basis and is valid for only one year. Application for an exception for a second or succeeding year must be accompanied by the documentation prescribed by Subsection (b).

(d) During the period for which a district is granted an exception under this section, the district must use alternative methods approved by the agency to meet the needs of its students of limited English proficiency, including hiring teaching personnel under a bilingual emergency permit.

Sec. 29.055. PROGRAM CONTENT; METHOD OF INSTRUCTION.

(a) A bilingual education program established by a school district shall be a full-time program of dual-language instruction that provides for learning basic skills in the primary language of the students enrolled in the program and for carefully structured and sequenced mastery of English language skills. A program of instruction in English as a second language established by a school district shall be a program of intensive instruction in English from teachers trained in recognizing and dealing with language differences.

(b) A program of bilingual education or of instruction in English as a second language shall be designed to consider the students' learning experiences and shall incorporate the cultural aspects of the students' backgrounds.

(c) In subjects such as art, music, and physical education, students of limited English proficiency shall participate fully with English-speaking students in regular classes provided in the subjects.

(d) Elective courses included in the curriculum may be taught in a language other than English.

(e) Each school district shall provide students enrolled in the program a meaningful opportunity to participate fully with other students in all extracurricular activities.

(f) If money is appropriated for the purpose, the agency shall establish a limited number of pilot programs for the purpose of examining alternative methods of instruction in bilingual education and special language programs.

Sec. 29.056. ENROLLMENT OF STUDENTS IN PROGRAM.

(a) The agency shall establish standardized criteria for the identification, assessment, and classification of students of limited English proficiency eligible for entry into the program or exit from the program. The student's parent must approve a student's entry into the program, exit from the program, or placement in the program. The school district or parent may appeal the decision under Section 29.064. The criteria for identification, assessment, and classification may include:

(1) results of a home language survey conducted within four weeks of each student's enrollment to determine the language normally used in the home and the language normally used by the student, conducted in English and the home language, signed by the student's parents if the student is in kindergarten through grade 8 or by the student if the student is in grades 9 through 12, and kept in the student's permanent folder by the language proficiency assessment committee;

(2) the results of an agency-approved English language proficiency test administered to all students identified through the home survey as normally speaking a language other than English to determine the level of English language proficiency, with students in kindergarten or grade 1 being administered an oral English proficiency test and students in grades 2 through 12 being administered an oral and written English proficiency test; and

(3) the results of an agency-approved proficiency test in the primary language administered to all students identified under

Subdivision (2) as being of limited English proficiency to determine the level of primary language proficiency, with students in kindergarten or grade 1 being administered an oral primary language proficiency test and students in grades 2 through 12 being administered an oral and written primary language proficiency test.

(b) Tests under Subsection (a) shall be administered by professionals or paraprofessionals with the appropriate English and primary language skills and the training required by the test publisher.

(c) The language proficiency assessment committee may classify a student as limited English proficiency if:

(1) the student's ability in English is so limited or the student's disabilities are so severe that assessment procedures cannot be administered;

(2) the student's score or relative degree of achievement on the agency-approved English proficiency test is below the levels established by the agency as indicative of reasonable proficiency;

(3) the student's primary language proficiency score as measured by an agency-approved test is greater than the student's proficiency in English; or

(4) the language proficiency assessment committee determines, based on other information, including a teacher evaluation, parental viewpoint, or student interview, that the student's primary language proficiency is greater than the student's proficiency in English or that the student is not reasonably proficient in English.

(d) Not later than the 10th day after the date of the student's classification as a student of limited English proficiency, the language proficiency assessment committee shall give written notice of the classification to the student's parent. The notice must be in English and the parent's primary language. The parents of students eligible to participate in the required bilingual education program shall be informed of the benefits of the bilingual education or special language program and that it is an integral part of the school program.

(e) The language proficiency assessment committee may retain, for documentation purposes, all records obtained under this section.

(f) The district may not refuse to provide instruction in a language other than English to a student solely because the student has a disability.

(g) A district may transfer a student of limited English proficiency out of a bilingual education or special language program for the first time or a subsequent time if the student is able to participate equally in a regular all-English instructional program as determined by:

(1) agency-approved tests administered at the end of each school year to determine the extent to which the student has developed oral and written language proficiency and specific language skills in English;

(2) satisfactory performance on the reading assessment instrument under Section 39.023(a) or an English language arts assessment instrument under Section 39.023(c), as applicable, with the

assessment instrument administered in English, or, if the student is enrolled in the first or second grade, an achievement score at or above the 40th percentile in the reading and language arts sections of an English standardized test approved by the agency; and

(3) agency-approved criterion-referenced tests and the results of a subjective teacher evaluation.

(h) If later evidence suggests that a student who has been transferred out of a bilingual education or special language program has inadequate English proficiency and achievement, the language proficiency assessment committee may reenroll the student in the program. Classification of students for reenrollment must be based on the criteria required by this section.

Sec. 29.0561. EVALUATION OF TRANSFERRED STUDENTS; REENROLLMENT.

(a) The language proficiency assessment committee shall reevaluate a student who is transferred out of a bilingual education or special language program under Section 29.056(g) if the student earns a failing grade in a subject in the foundation curriculum under Section 28.002(a)(1) during any grading period in the first two school years after the student is transferred to determine whether the student should be reenrolled in a bilingual education or special language program.

(b) During the first two school years after a student is transferred out of a bilingual education or special language program under Section 29.056(g), the language proficiency assessment committee shall review the student's performance and consider:

(1) the total amount of time the student was enrolled in a bilingual education or special language program;

(2) the student's grades each grading period in each subject in the foundation curriculum under Section 28.002(a)(1);

(3) the student's performance on each assessment instrument administered under Section 39.023(a) or (c);

(4) the number of credits the student has earned toward high school graduation, if applicable; and

(5) any disciplinary actions taken against the student under Subchapter A, Chapter 37.

(c) After an evaluation under this section, the language proficiency assessment committee may require intensive instruction for the student or reenroll the student in a bilingual education or special language program.

Sec. 29.057. FACILITIES; CLASSES.

(a) Bilingual education and special language programs must be located in the regular public schools of the district rather than in separate facilities.

(b) Students enrolled in bilingual education or a special language program shall be placed in classes with other students of approximately the same age and level of educational attainment. The school district shall ensure that the instruction given each student is appropriate to the student's level of educational attainment, and the district shall keep adequate records of the educational level and progress of each student enrolled in the program.

(c) The maximum student-teacher ratio shall be set by the agency and shall reflect the special educational needs of students enrolled in the programs.

Sec. 29.058. ENROLLMENT OF STUDENTS WHO DO NOT HAVE LIMITED ENGLISH PROFICIENCY.

With the approval of the school district and a student's parents, a student who does not have limited English proficiency may also participate in a bilingual education program. The number of participating students who do not have limited English proficiency may not exceed 40 percent of the number of students enrolled in the program.

Sec. 29.059. COOPERATION AMONG DISTRICTS.

(a) A school district may join with one or more other districts to provide the bilingual education and special language programs required by this subchapter. The availability of the programs shall be publicized throughout the districts involved.

(b) A school district may allow a nonresident student of limited English proficiency to enroll in or attend its bilingual education or special language programs if the student's district of residence does not provide an appropriate program. The tuition for the student shall be paid by the district in which the student resides.

Sec. 29.060. PRESCHOOL, SUMMER SCHOOL, AND EXTENDED TIME PROGRAMS.

(a) Each school district that is required to offer a bilingual education or special language program shall offer a voluntary program for children of limited English proficiency who will be eligible for admission to kindergarten or the first grade at the beginning of the next school year. A school that operates on a system permitted by this code other than a semester system shall offer 120 hours of instruction on a schedule the board of trustees of the district establishes. A school that operates on a semester system shall offer the program:

(1) during the period school is recessed for the summer; and

(2) for one-half day for eight weeks or on a similar schedule approved by the board of trustees.

(b) Enrollment of a child in the program is optional with the parent of the child.

(c) The program must be an intensive bilingual education or special language program that meets standards established by the agency. The student/teacher ratio for the program may not exceed 18/1.

(d) A school district may establish on a full- or part-time basis other summer school, extended day, or extended week bilingual education or special language programs for students of limited English proficiency and may join with other districts in establishing the programs.

(e) The programs required or authorized by this section may not be a substitute for programs required to be provided during the regular school year.

(f) The legislature may appropriate money from the foundation school fund for support of a program under Subsection (a).

Sec. 29.061. BILINGUAL EDUCATION AND SPECIAL LANGUAGE PROGRAM TEACHERS.

(a) The State Board for Educator Certification shall provide for the issuance of teaching certificates appropriate for bilingual education instruction to teachers who possess a speaking, reading, and writing ability in a language other than English in which bilingual education programs are offered and who meet the general requirements of Chapter 21. The board shall also provide for the issuance of teaching certificates appropriate for teaching English as a second language. The board may issue emergency endorsements in bilingual education and in teaching English as a second language.

(b) A teacher assigned to a bilingual education program must be appropriately certified for bilingual education by the board.

(c) A teacher assigned to an English as a second language or other special language program must be appropriately certified for English as a second language by the board.

(d) A school district may compensate a bilingual education or special language teacher for participating in a continuing education program that is in addition to the teacher's regular contract. The continuing education program must be designed to provide advanced bilingual education or special language program endorsement or skills.

(e) The State Board for Educator Certification and the Texas Higher Education Coordinating Board shall develop a comprehensive plan for meeting the teacher supply needs created by the programs outlined in this subchapter.

Sec. 29.062. COMPLIANCE.

(a) The legislature recognizes that compliance with this subchapter is an imperative public necessity. Therefore, in accordance with the policy of the state, the agency shall evaluate the effectiveness of programs under this subchapter based on the student achievement indicators adopted under Section 39.053, including the results of assessment instruments. The agency may combine evaluations under this section with federal accountability measures concerning students of limited English proficiency.

(b) The areas to be monitored shall include:

(1) program content and design;

(2) program coverage;

(3) identification procedures;

(4) classification procedures;

(5) staffing;

(6) learning materials;

(7) testing materials;

(8) reclassification of students for either entry into regular classes conducted exclusively in English or reentry into a bilingual education or special education program; and

(9) activities of the language proficiency assessment committees.

(c) Not later than the 30th day after the date of an on-site monitoring inspection, the agency shall report its findings to the school district or open-enrollment charter school and to the division of accreditation.

(d) The agency shall notify a school district or open-enrollment charter school found in noncompliance in writing, not later than the 30th day after the date of the on-site monitoring. The district or open-enrollment charter school shall take immediate corrective action.

(e) If a school district or open-enrollment charter school fails to satisfy appropriate standards adopted by the commissioner for purposes of Subsection (a), the agency shall apply sanctions, which may include the removal of accreditation, loss of foundation school funds, or both.

Sec. 29.063. LANGUAGE PROFICIENCY ASSESSMENT COMMITTEES.

(a) Each school district that is required to offer bilingual education and special language programs shall establish a language proficiency assessment committee.

(b) Each committee shall include a professional bilingual educator, a professional transitional language educator, a parent of a limited English proficiency student, and a campus administrator.

(c) The language proficiency assessment committee shall:

(1) review all pertinent information on limited English proficiency students, including the home language survey, the language proficiency tests in English and the primary language, each student's achievement in content areas, and each student's emotional and social attainment;

(2) make recommendations concerning the most appropriate placement for the educational advancement of the limited English proficiency student after the elementary grades;

(3) review each limited English proficiency student's progress at the end of the school year in order to determine future appropriate placement;

(4) monitor the progress of students formerly classified as limited English proficiency who have transferred out of the bilingual education or special language program and, based on the information, designate the most appropriate placement for such students; and

(5) determine the appropriateness of a program that extends beyond the regular school year based on the needs of each limited English proficiency student.

(d) The agency may prescribe additional duties for language proficiency assessment committees.

Sec. 29.064. APPEALS.

A parent of a student enrolled in a school district offering bilingual education or special language programs may appeal to the commissioner if the district fails to comply with the requirements established by law or by the agency as authorized by this subchapter. If the parent disagrees with the placement of the student in the program, the parent may appeal that decision to the board of trustees. Appeals shall be conducted in accordance with procedures adopted by the commissioner.

Sec. 29.066. PEIMS REPORTING REQUIREMENTS.

(a) A school district that is required to offer bilingual education or special language programs shall include the following information in the district's Public Education Information Management System (PEIMS) report:

(1) demographic information, as determined by the commissioner, on students enrolled in district bilingual education or special language programs;

(2) the number and percentage of students enrolled in each instructional model of a bilingual education or special language program offered by the district; and

(3) the number and percentage of students identified as students of limited English proficiency who do not receive specialized instruction.

(b) For purposes of this section, the commissioner shall adopt rules to classify programs under this section as follows:

(1) if the program is a bilingual education program, the program must be classified under the Public Education Information Management System (PEIMS) report as:

(A) transitional bilingual/early exit: a bilingual program that serves students identified as students of limited English proficiency in both English and Spanish and transfers a student to English-only instruction not earlier than two or later than five years after the student enrolls in school;

(B) transitional bilingual/late exit: a bilingual program that serves students identified as students of limited English proficiency in both English and Spanish and transfers a student to English-only instruction not earlier than six or later than seven years after the student enrolls in school;

(C) dual language immersion/two-way: a biliteracy program that integrates students proficient in English and students identified as students of limited English proficiency in both English and Spanish and transfers a student identified as a student of limited English proficiency to English-only instruction not earlier than six or later than seven years after the student enrolls in school; or

(D) dual language immersion/one-way: a biliteracy program that serves only students identified as students of limited English proficiency in both English and Spanish and transfers a student to English-only instruction not earlier than six or later than seven years after the student enrolls in school; and

(2) if the program is a special language program, the program must be classified under the Public Education Information Management System (PEIMS) report as:

(A) English as a second language/content-based: an English program that serves students identified as students of limited English proficiency in English only by providing a full-time teacher certified under Section 29.061(c) to provide supplementary instruction for all content area instruction; or

(B) English as a second language/pull-out: an English program that serves students identified as students of limited English proficiency in English only by providing a part-time teacher certified under Section 29.061(c) to provide English language arts instruction exclusively, while the student remains in a mainstream instructional arrangement in the remaining content areas.

(c) If the school district has received a waiver and is not required to offer a bilingual education or special language program in a student's native language or if the student's parents have refused to approve the student's entry into a program as provided by Section 29.056, the program must be classified under the Public Education Information Management System (PEIMS) report as: no bilingual education or special language services provided.

Subchapter C. Compensatory Education Programs

Sec. 29.081. COMPENSATORY, INTENSIVE, AND ACCELERATED INSTRUCTION.

(a) Each school district shall use the student performance data resulting from the basic skills assessment instruments and achievement tests administered under Subchapter B, Chapter 39, to design and implement appropriate compensatory, intensive, or accelerated instructional services for students in the district's schools that enable the students to be performing at grade level at the conclusion of the next regular school term.

(b) Each district shall provide accelerated instruction to a student enrolled in the district who has taken an end-of-course assessment instrument administered under Section 39.023(c) and has not performed satisfactorily on the assessment instrument or who is at risk of dropping out of school.

(c) Each school district shall evaluate and document the effectiveness of the accelerated instruction in reducing any disparity in performance on assessment instruments administered under Subchapter B, Chapter 39, or disparity in the rates of high school completion between students at risk of dropping out of school and all other district students.

(d) For purposes of this section, "student at risk of dropping out of school" includes each student who is under 21 years of age and who:

(1) was not advanced from one grade level to the next for one or more school years;

(2) if the student is in grade 7, 8, 9, 10, 11, or 12, did not maintain an average equivalent to 70 on a scale of 100 in two or more subjects in the foundation curriculum during a semester in the preceding or current school year or is not maintaining such an average in two or more subjects in the foundation curriculum in the current semester;

(3) did not perform satisfactorily on an assessment instrument administered to the student under Subchapter B, Chapter 39, and who has not in the previous or current school year subsequently performed on that instrument or another appropriate instrument at a level equal to at least 110 percent of the level of satisfactory performance on that instrument;

(4) if the student is in prekindergarten, kindergarten, or grade 1, 2, or 3, did not perform satisfactorily on a readiness test or assessment instrument administered during the current school year;

(5) is pregnant or is a parent;

(6) has been placed in an alternative education program in accordance with Section 37.006 during the preceding or current school year;

(7) has been expelled in accordance with Section 37.007 during the preceding or current school year;

(8) is currently on parole, probation, deferred prosecution, or other conditional release;

(9) was previously reported through the Public Education Information Management System (PEIMS) to have dropped out of school;

(10) is a student of limited English proficiency, as defined by Section 29.052;

(11) is in the custody or care of the Department of Protective and Regulatory Services or has, during the current school year, been referred to the department by a school official, officer of the juvenile court, or law enforcement official;

(12) is homeless, as defined by 42 U.S.C. Section 11302, and its subsequent amendments; or

(13) resided in the preceding school year or resides in the current school year in a residential placement facility in the district, including a detention facility, substance abuse treatment facility, emergency shelter, psychiatric hospital, halfway house, or foster group home.

(d-1) Notwithstanding Subsection (d)(1), a student is not considered a student at risk of dropping out of school if the student did not advance from prekindergarten or kindergarten to the next grade level only as the result of the request of the student's parent.

(e) A school district may use a private or public community-based dropout recovery education program to provide alternative education programs for students at risk of dropping out of school. The programs must:

(1) provide not less than four hours of instructional time per day;

(2) employ as faculty and administrators persons with baccalaureate or advanced degrees;

(3) provide at least one instructor for each 28 students;

(4) perform satisfactorily according to performance indicators and accountability standards adopted for alternative education programs by the commissioner; and

(5) comply with this title and rules adopted under this title except as otherwise provided by this subsection.

(f) The commissioner shall include students in attendance in a program under Subsection (e) in the computation of the district's average daily attendance for funding purposes.

(g) In addition to students described by Subsection (d), a student who satisfies local eligibility criteria adopted by the board of trustees of a school district may receive instructional services under this section. The number of students receiving services under this subsection during a school year may not exceed 10 percent of the number of students described by Subsection (d) who received services from the district during the preceding school year.

Subchapter E. Kindergarten and Prekindergarten Programs

Sec. 29.153. FREE PREKINDERGARTEN FOR CERTAIN CHILDREN.

(a) In this section:

(1) "Child" includes a stepchild.

(2) "Parent" includes a stepparent.

(a-1) A district shall offer prekindergarten classes if the district identifies 15 or more children who are eligible under Subsection (b) and are at least four years of age. A school district may offer prekindergarten classes if the district identifies 15 or more eligible children who are at least three years of age. A district may not charge tuition for a prekindergarten class offered under this section.

(b) A child is eligible for enrollment in a prekindergarten class under this section if the child is at least three years of age and:

(1) is unable to speak and comprehend the English language;

(2) is educationally disadvantaged;

(3) is a homeless child, as defined by 42 U.S.C. Section 11434a, regardless of the residence of the child, of either parent of the child, or of the child's guardian or other person having lawful control of the child;

(4) is the child of an active duty member of the armed forces of the United States, including the state military forces or a reserve component of the armed forces, who is ordered to active duty by proper authority;

(5) is the child of a member of the armed forces of the United States, including the state military forces or a reserve component

of the armed forces, who was injured or killed while serving on active duty; or

(6) is or ever has been in the conservatorship of the Department of Family and Protective Services following an adversary hearing held as provided by Section 262.201, Family Code.

(c) A prekindergarten class under this section shall be operated on a half-day basis. A district is not required to provide transportation for a prekindergarten class, but transportation, if provided, is included for funding purposes as part of the regular transportation system.

(d) On application of a district, the commissioner may exempt a district from the application of this section if the district would be required to construct classroom facilities in order to provide prekindergarten classes.

(e) Each school district shall develop a system to notify the population in the district with children who are eligible for enrollment in a prekindergarten class under this section of the availability of the class. The system must include public notices issued in English and Spanish.

(f) A child who is eligible for enrollment in a prekindergarten class under Subsection (b)(4) or (5) remains eligible for enrollment if the child's parent leaves the armed forces, or is no longer on active duty, after the child begins a prekindergarten class.

TEC CHAPTER 39. PUBLIC SCHOOL SYSTEM ACCOUNTABILITY

Subchapter B. Assessment Of Academic SkilLS

Note: Sec. 39.023 has been extensively amended by HB5 (original text below except where noted)

Sec. 39.021. ESSENTIAL SKILLS AND KNOWLEDGE.

The State Board of Education by rule shall establish the essential skills and knowledge that all students should learn to achieve the goals provided under Section 4.002.

Sec. 39.022. ASSESSMENT PROGRAM.

The State Board of Education by rule shall create and implement a statewide assessment program that is knowledge- and skills-based to ensure school accountability for student achievement that achieves the goals provided under Section 4.002. After adopting rules under this section, the State Board of Education shall consider the importance of maintaining stability in the statewide assessment program when adopting any subsequent modification of the rules.

Sec. 39.023. ADOPTION AND ADMINISTRATION OF INSTRUMENTS.

(l) The State Board of Education shall adopt rules for the administration of the assessment instruments adopted under Subsection (a) in Spanish to students in grades three through five who are of limited English proficiency, as defined by Section 29.052, whose primary language is Spanish, and who are not otherwise exempt from the administration of an assessment instrument under Section 39.027(a)(1) or (2). Each student of limited English proficiency whose primary language is Spanish, other than a student to whom Subsection (b) applies, may be assessed using assessment instruments in Spanish under this subsection for up to three years or assessment instruments in English under Subsection (a). The language proficiency assessment committee established under Section 29.063 shall determine which students are administered assessment instruments in Spanish under this subsection.

(m) The commissioner by rule shall develop procedures under which the language proficiency assessment committee established under Section 29.063 shall determine which students are exempt from the administration of the assessment instruments under Section 39.027(a)(1) or (2). The rules adopted under this subsection shall ensure that the language proficiency assessment committee provides that the exempted students are administered the assessment instruments under Subsections (a) and (c) at the earliest practical date.

Sec. 39.027. EXEMPTION.

(a) A student may be administered an accommodated or alternative assessment instrument or may be granted an exemption from or a postponement of the administration of an assessment instrument under:

(1) Section 39.023(a), (b), (c), or (l) for a period of up to one year after initial enrollment in a school in the United States if the student is of limited English proficiency, as defined by Section 29.052, and has not demonstrated proficiency in English as determined by the assessment system under Subsection (e);

(2) Section 39.023(a), (b), (c), or (l) for a period of up to two years in addition to the exemption period authorized by Subdivision (1) if the student has received an exemption under Subdivision (1) and:

(A) is a recent unschooled immigrant; or

(B) is in a grade for which no assessment instrument in the primary language of the student is available; or

(3) Section 39.023(a), (b), (c), or (l) for a period of up to four years, in addition to the exemption period authorized under Subdivision (1), if the student's initial enrollment in a school in the United States was as an unschooled asylee or refugee.

(4) Expired.

(a-1) For purposes of this section, "unschooled asylee or refugee" means a student who:

(1) initially enrolled in a school in the United States as:

(A) an asylee as defined by 45 C.F.R. Section 400.41; or

(B) a refugee as defined by 8 U.S.C. Section 1101;

(2) has a visa issued by the United States Department of State with a Form I-94 Arrival/Departure record, or a successor document, issued by the United States Citizenship and Immigration Services that is stamped with "Asylee," "Refugee," or "Asylum"; and

(3) as a result of inadequate schooling outside of the United States, lacks the necessary foundation in the essential knowledge and skills of the curriculum prescribed under Section 28.002, as determined by the language proficiency assessment committee established under Section 29.063.

Added by HB5 -

(a-2) Unless a student is enrolled in a school in the United States for a period of at least 60 consecutive days during a year, the student may not be considered to be enrolled in a school in the United States for that year for the purpose of determining a number of years under Subsection (a)(1), (2), or (3).

(b) This section applies beginning with the 2013-2014 school year.

(e) The commissioner shall develop an assessment system that shall be used for evaluating the academic progress, including reading proficiency in English, of all students of limited English proficiency, as defined by Section 29.052. A student who is exempt from the administration of an assessment instrument under Subsection (a)(1) or (2) who achieves reading proficiency in English as determined by the assessment system developed under this subsection shall be administered the assessment instruments described by Sections 39.023(a) and (c). The performance under the assessment system developed under this subsection of students to whom Subsection (a)(1) or (2) applies shall be included in the indicator systems under Section 39.301, as applicable, the performance report under Section 39.306, and the comprehensive annual report under Section 39.332. This information shall be provided in a manner that is disaggregated by the bilingual education or special language program, if any, in which the student is enrolled.

Subchapter C - Accreditation

Sec. 39.052. DETERMINATION OF ACCREDITATION STATUS OR PERFORMANCE RATING.

(a) Each year, the commissioner shall determine the accreditation status of each school district.

(b) In determining the accreditation status of a school district, the commissioner:

(1) shall evaluate and consider:

(A) performance on student achievement indicators described by Section 39.053(c); and

(B) performance under the financial accountability rating system developed under Subchapter D; and

(2) may evaluate and consider:

(A) the district's compliance with statutory requirements and requirements imposed by rule of the commissioner or State Board of Education under specific statutory authority that relate to:

(i) reporting data through the Public Education Information Management System (PEIMS) or other reports required by state or federal law or court order;

(ii) the high school graduation requirements under Section 28.025; or

(iii) an item listed under Sections 7.056(e)(3)(C)-(I) that applies to the district;

(B) the effectiveness of the district's programs for special populations; and

(C) the effectiveness of the district's career and technology program.

(c) Based on a school district's performance under Subsection (b), the commissioner shall:

(1) assign each district an accreditation status; or

(2) revoke the accreditation of the district and order closure of the district.

(d) A school district's accreditation status may be raised or lowered based on the district's performance or may be lowered based on the performance of one or more campuses in the district that is below a standard required under this subchapter.

(e) The commissioner shall notify a school district that receives an accreditation status of accredited-warned or accredited-probation or a campus that performs below a standard required under this subchapter that the performance of the district or campus is below a standard required under this subchapter. The commissioner shall require the district to notify the parents of students enrolled in the district and property owners in the district of the district's accreditation status and the implications of that accreditation status.

(f) A school district that is not accredited may not receive funds from the agency or hold itself out as operating a public school of this state.

(g) This chapter may not be construed to invalidate a diploma awarded, course credit earned, or grade promotion granted by a school district before the commissioner revoked the district's accreditation.

Note: Sec. 39.053 has been extensively amended by HB5 (original text below)

Sec. 39.053. PERFORMANCE INDICATORS: STUDENT ACHIEVEMENT.

(a) The commissioner shall adopt a set of indicators of the quality of learning and student achievement. The commissioner biennially shall review the indicators for the consideration of appropriate revisions.

(b) Performance on the student achievement indicators adopted under this section shall be compared to state-established standards. The indicators must be based on information that is disaggregated by race, ethnicity, and socioeconomic status.

(c) Indicators of student achievement adopted under this section must include:

(1) the results of assessment instruments required under Sections 39.023(a), (c), and (l), including the results of assessment instruments required for graduation retaken by a student, aggregated across grade levels by subject area, including:

(A) for the performance standard determined by the commissioner under Section 39.0241(a):

(i) the percentage of students who performed satisfactorily on the assessment instruments, aggregated across grade levels by subject area; and

(ii) for students who did not perform satisfactorily, the percentage of students who met the standard for annual improvement, as determined by the agency under Section 39.034, on the assessment instruments, aggregated across grade levels by subject area; and

(B) for the college readiness performance standard as determined under Section 39.0241:

(i) the percentage of students who performed satisfactorily on the assessment instruments, aggregated across grade levels by subject area; and

(ii) for students who did not perform satisfactorily, the percentage of students who met the standard for annual improvement, as determined by the agency under Section 39.034, on the assessment instruments, aggregated across grade levels by subject area;

(2) dropout rates, including dropout rates and district completion rates for grade levels 9 through 12, computed in accordance with standards and definitions adopted by the National Center for Education Statistics of the United States Department of Education; and

(3) high school graduation rates, computed in accordance with standards and definitions adopted in compliance with the No Child Left Behind Act of 2001 (20 U.S.C. Section 6301 et seq.).

(d) For purposes of Subsection (c), the commissioner by rule shall determine the period within which a student must retake an assessment instrument for that assessment instrument to be considered in determining the performance rating of the district under Section 39.054.

(d-1) In aggregating results of assessment instruments across grade levels by subject in accordance with Subsection (c)(1), the performance of a student enrolled below the high school level on an assessment instrument required under Section 39.023(c) is included with results relating to other students enrolled at the same grade level.

(e) Performance on the student achievement indicators under Subsections (c)(1) and (2) shall be compared to state standards and required improvement. The state standard shall be established by the commissioner. Required improvement is the progress necessary for the campus or district to meet state standards and, for the student achievement indicator under Subsection (c)(1), for its students to meet each of the performance standards as determined under Section 39.0241.

(f) Annually, the commissioner shall define the state standard for the current school year for each student achievement indicator described by Subsection (c) and shall project the state standards for each indicator for the following two school years. The commissioner shall periodically raise the state standards for the student achievement indicator described by Subsection (c)(1)(B)(i) for accreditation as necessary to reach the goals of achieving, by not later than the 2019-2020 school year:

(1) student performance in this state, disaggregated by race, ethnicity, and socioeconomic status, that ranks nationally in the top 10 states in terms of college readiness; and

(2) student performance, including the percentage of students graduating under the recommended or advanced high school program, with no significant achievement gaps by race, ethnicity, and socioeconomic status.

(g) In defining the required state standard for the indicator described by Subsection (c)(2), the commissioner may not consider as a dropout a student whose failure to attend school results from:

(1) the student's expulsion under Section 37.007; and

(2) as applicable:

(A) adjudication as having engaged in delinquent conduct or conduct indicating a need for supervision, as defined by Section 51.03, Family Code; or

(B) conviction of and sentencing for an offense under the Penal Code.

(g-1) In computing dropout and completion rates under Subsection (c)(2), the commissioner shall exclude:

(1) students who are ordered by a court to attend a high school equivalency certificate program but who have not yet earned a high school equivalency certificate;

(2) students who were previously reported to the state as dropouts;

(3) students in attendance who are not in membership for purposes of average daily attendance;

(4) students whose initial enrollment in a school in the United States in grades 7 through 12 was as unschooled refugees or asylees as defined by Section 39.027(a-1);

(5) students who are in the district exclusively as a function of having been detained at a county detention facility but are otherwise not students of the district in which the facility is located; and

(6) students who are incarcerated in state jails and federal penitentiaries as adults and as persons certified to stand trial as adults.

(h) Each school district shall cooperate with the agency in determining whether a student is a dropout for purposes of accreditation and evaluating performance by school districts and campuses under this chapter.

(i) The commissioner by rule shall adopt accountability measures to be used in assessing the progress of students who have failed to perform satisfactorily as determined by the commissioner under Section 39.0241(a) or under the college readiness standard as determined under Section 39.0241 in the preceding school year on an assessment instrument required under Section 39.023(a), (c), or (l).

Added by HB5 -

Sec. 39.0545. SCHOOL DISTRICT EVALUATION OF PERFORMANCE IN COMMUNITY AND STUDENT ENGAGEMENT; COMPLIANCE.

(a) Each school district shall evaluate the district's performance and the performance of each campus in the district in community and student engagement and in compliance as provided by this section and assign the district and each campus a performance rating of exemplary, recognized, acceptable, or unacceptable for both overal performance and each individual evaluation factor listed under

Subsection (b). Not later than August 8 of each year, the district shall report each performance rating to the agency and make the performance ratings publicly available as provided by commissioner rule.

(b) For purposes of assigning the performance ratings under Subsection (a), a school district must evaluate:

(1) the following programs or specific categories of performance at each campus:

(A) fine arts;

(B) wellness and physical education;

(C) community and parental involvement, such as:

(i) opportunities for parents to assist students in preparing for assessments under Section 39.023;

(ii) tutoring programs that support students taking assessments under Section 39.023; and

(iii) opportunities for students to participate in community service projects;

(D) the 21st Century Workforce Development program;

(E) the second language acquisition program;

(F) the digital learning environment;

(G) dropout prevention strategies; and

(H) educational programs for gifted and talented students; and

(2) the record of the district and each campus regarding compliance with statutory reporting and policy requirements.

(c) A school district shall use criteria developed by a local committee to evaluate:

(1) the performance of the district's campus programs and categories of performance under Subsection (b)(1); and

(2) the record of the district and each campus regarding compliance under Subsection (b)(2).

(b) This section applies beginning with the 2013-2014 school year.

Subchapter E – Accreditation Interventions and Sanctions

Sec. 39.105. CAMPUS IMPROVEMENT PLAN.

(a) This section applies if a campus performance satisfies performance standards under Section 39.054(e) for the current school year but would not satisfy performance standards under Section 39.054(e) if the standards to be used for the following school year were applied to the current school year. On request of the commissioner, the campus-level committee established under Section 11.251 shall revise and submit to the commissioner in an electronic format the portions of the campus improvement plan developed under Section 11.253 that are relevant to those areas for which the campus would not satisfy performance standards.

(b) If the campus to which this section applies is an open-enrollment charter school, the school shall establish a campus-level planning and decision-making committee as provided for through procedures as much as practicable the same as those provided by Sections 11.251(b)-(e) and develop a campus improvement plan as provided by Section 11.253. On request of the commissioner, the school shall submit to the commissioner in an electronic format the portions of the campus improvement plan that are relevant to those areas for which the campus would not satisfy performance standards.

Sec. 39.106. CAMPUS INTERVENTION TEAM DUTIES.

(a) If a campus performance is below any standard under Section 39.054(e), the commissioner shall assign a campus intervention team. A campus intervention team shall:

(1) conduct, with the involvement and advice of the school community partnership team, if applicable:

(A) a targeted on-site needs assessment relevant to an area of insufficient performance of the campus as provided by Subsection (b); or

(B) if the commissioner determines necessary, a comprehensive on-site needs assessment, using the procedures provided by Subsection (b);

(2) recommend appropriate actions as provided by Subsection (c);

(3) assist in the development of a targeted improvement plan;

(4) assist the campus in submitting the targeted improvement plan to the board of trustees for approval and presenting the plan in a public hearing as provided by Subsection (e-1); and

(5) assist the commissioner in monitoring the progress of the campus in implementing the targeted improvement plan.

(b) An on-site needs assessment of the campus under Subsection (a) must determine the contributing education-related and other factors resulting in the campus's low performance and lack of progress. The team shall use all of the following guidelines and procedures relevant to each area of insufficient performance in conducting a targeted on-site needs assessment and shall use each of the following guidelines and procedures in conducting a comprehensive on-site needs assessment:

(1) an assessment of the staff to determine the percentage of certified teachers who are teaching in their field, the percentage of teachers who are fully certified, the number of teachers with more than three years of experience, and teacher retention rates;

(2) compliance with the appropriate class-size rules and number of class-size waivers received;

(3) an assessment of the quality, quantity, and appropriateness of instructional materials, including the availability of technology-based instructional materials;

(4) a report on the parental involvement strategies and the effectiveness of the strategies;

(5) an assessment of the extent and quality of the mentoring program provided for new teachers on the campus and provided for experienced teachers on the campus who have less than two years of teaching experience in the subject or grade level to which the teacher is assigned;

(6) an assessment of the type and quality of the professional development provided to the staff;

(7) a demographic analysis of the student

population, including student demographics, at-risk populations, and special education percentages;

(8) a report of disciplinary incidents and school safety information;

(9) financial and accounting practices;

(10) an assessment of the appropriateness of the curriculum and teaching strategies;

(11) a comparison of the findings from Subdivisions (1) through (10) to other campuses serving the same grade levels within the district or to other campuses within the campus's comparison group if there are no other campuses within the district serving the same grade levels as the campus; and

(12) any other research-based data or information obtained from a data collection process that would assist the campus intervention team in:

(A) recommending an action under Subsection (c); and

(B) executing a targeted improvement plan under Subsection (d-3).

(c) On completing the on-site needs assessment under this section, the campus intervention team shall, with the involvement and advice of the school community partnership team, if applicable, recommend actions relating to any area of insufficient performance, including:

(1) reallocation of resources;

(2) technical assistance;

(3) changes in school procedures or operations;

(4) staff development for instructional and administrative staff;

(5) intervention for individual administrators or teachers;

(6) waivers from state statutes or rules;

(7) teacher recruitment or retention strategies and incentives provided by the district to attract and retain teachers with the characteristics included in Subsection (b)(1); or

(8) other actions the campus intervention team considers appropriate.

(d) The campus intervention team shall assist the campus in submitting the targeted improvement plan to the commissioner for approval.

(d-1) The commissioner may authorize a school community partnership team established under this subchapter to supersede the authority of and satisfy the requirements of establishing and maintaining a campus-level planning and decision-making committee under Subchapter F, Chapter 11.

(d-2) The commissioner may authorize a targeted improvement plan or updated plan developed under this subchapter to supersede the provisions of and satisfy the requirements of developing, reviewing, and revising a campus improvement plan under Subchapter F, Chapter 11.

(d-3) In executing the targeted improvement plan, the campus intervention team shall, if appropriate:

(1) assist the campus in implementing research-based practices for curriculum development and classroom instruction, including bilingual education and special education programs and financial management;

(2) provide research-based technical

assistance, including data analysis, academic deficiency identification, intervention implementation, and budget analysis, to strengthen and improve the instructional programs at the campus; and

(3) require the district to develop a teacher recruitment and retention plan to address the qualifications and retention of the teachers at the campus.

(e) For each year a campus is assigned an unacceptable performance rating, a campus intervention team shall:

(1) continue to work with a campus until:

(A) the campus satisfies all performance standards under Section 39.054(e) for a two-year period; or

(B) the campus satisfies all performance standards under Section 39.054(e) for a one-year period and the commissioner determines that the campus is operating and will continue to operate in a manner that improves student achievement;

(2) assist in updating the targeted improvement plan to identify and analyze areas of growth and areas that require improvement; and

(3) submit each updated plan described by Subdivision (2) to the board of trustees of the school district.

(e-1) After a targeted improvement plan or updated plan is submitted to the board of trustees of the school district, the board:

(1) shall conduct a hearing for the purpose of:

(A) notifying the public of the insufficient performance, the improvements in performance expected by the agency, and the intervention measures or sanctions that may be imposed under this subchapter if the performance does not improve within a designated period; and

(B) soliciting public comment on the targeted improvement plan or any updated plan;

(2) must post the targeted improvement plan on the district's Internet website before the hearing;

(3) may conduct one hearing relating to one or more campuses subject to a targeted improvement plan or an updated plan; and

(4) shall submit the targeted improvement plan or any updated plan to the commissioner for approval.

(f) Notwithstanding any other provision of this subchapter, if the commissioner determines that a campus for which an intervention is ordered under Subsection (a) is not fully implementing the campus intervention team's recommendations or targeted improvement plan or updated plan, the commissioner may order the reconstitution of the campus as provided by Section 39.107.

TEC Chapter 42 Foundation School Program

Subchapter A. General Provisions

Sec. 42.001. STATE POLICY. (a) It is the policy of this state that the provision of public education is a state responsibility and that a thorough and efficient system be provided and substantially financed through state revenue sources so that each student enrolled in the public school system shall have access to programs and services that are appropriate to the student's educational needs and that are substantially equal to those available to any similar student, notwithstanding varying local economic factors.

(b) The public school finance system of this state shall adhere to a standard of neutrality that provides for substantially equal access to similar revenue per student at similar tax effort, considering all state and local tax revenues of districts after acknowledging all legitimate student and district cost differences.

Sec. 42.002. PURPOSES OF FOUNDATION SCHOOL PROGRAM.

(a) The purposes of the Foundation School Program set forth in this chapter are to guarantee that each school district in the state has:

(1) adequate resources to provide each eligible student a basic instructional program and facilities suitable to the student's educational needs; and

(2) access to a substantially equalized program of financing in excess of basic costs for certain services, as provided by this chapter.

(b) The Foundation School Program consists of:

(1) two tiers that in combination provide for:

(A) sufficient financing for all school districts to provide a basic program of education that is rated acceptable or higher under Section 39.054 and meets other applicable legal standards; and

(B) substantially equal access to funds to provide an enriched program; and

(2) a facilities component as provided by Chapter 46.

Sec. 42.003. STUDENT ELIGIBILITY.

(a) A student is entitled to the benefits of the Foundation School Program if, on September 1 of the school year, the student is 5 years of age or older and under 21 years of age and has not graduated from high school, or is at least 21 years of age and under 26 years of age and has been admitted by a school district to complete the requirements for a high school diploma.

(b) A student to whom Subsection (a) does not apply is entitled to the benefits of the Foundation School Program if the student is enrolled in a prekindergarten class under Section 29.153.

(c) A child may be enrolled in the first grade if the child is at least six years of age at the beginning of the school year of the district or has been enrolled in the first grade or has completed kindergarten in the public schools in another state before transferring to a public school in this state.

(d) Notwithstanding Subsection (a), a student younger than five years of age is entitled to the benefits of the Foundation School Program if:

(1) the student performs satisfactorily on the assessment instrument administered under Section 39.023(a) to students in the third grade; and

(2) the district has adopted a policy for admitting students younger than five years of age.

Subchapter B

Sec. 42.152. COMPENSATORY EDUCATION ALLOTMENT.

(a) For each student who is educationally disadvantaged or who is a student who does not have a disability and resides in a residential placement facility in a district in which the student's parent or legal guardian does not reside, a district is entitled to an annual allotment equal to the adjusted basic allotment multiplied by 0.2, and by 2.41 for each full-time equivalent student who is in a remedial and support program under Section 29.081 because the student is pregnant.

(b) For purposes of this section, the number of educationally disadvantaged students is determined:

(1) by averaging the best six months' enrollment in the national school lunch program of free or reduced-price lunches for the preceding school year; or

(2) in the manner provided by commissioner rule, if no campus in the district participated in the national school lunch program of free or reduced-price lunches during the preceding school year.

(c) Funds allocated under this section shall be used to fund supplemental programs and services designed to eliminate any disparity in performance on assessment instruments administered under Subchapter B, Chapter 39, or disparity in the rates of high school completion between students at risk of dropping out of school, as defined by Section 29.081, and all other students. Specifically, the funds, other than an indirect cost allotment established under State Board of Education rule, which may not exceed 45 percent, may be used to meet the costs of providing a compensatory, intensive, or accelerated instruction program under Section 29.081 or a disciplinary alternative education program established under Section 37.008, to pay the costs associated with placing students in a juvenile justice alternative education program established under Section 37.011, or to support a program eligible under Title I of the Elementary and Secondary Education Act of 1965, as provided by Pub. L. No. 103-382 and its subsequent amendments, and by federal regulations implementing that Act, at a campus at which at least 40 percent of the students are educationally disadvantaged. In meeting the costs of providing a compensatory, intensive, or accelerated instruction program under Section 29.081, a district's compensatory education allotment shall be used for costs supplementary to the regular education program, such as costs for program and student evaluation, instructional materials and equipment and other supplies required for quality instruction, supplemental staff expenses, salary for teachers of at-risk students, smaller class size, and individualized instruction. A home-rule school district or an open-enrollment charter school must use funds allocated under Subsection (a) for a purpose authorized in this subsection but is not otherwise subject to Subchapter C, Chapter 29. For purposes of this subsection, a program specifically designed to serve students at risk of dropping out of school, as defined by Section 29.081, is considered to be a program supplemental to the regular education program, and a district may use its compensatory education allotment for such a program.

(c-1) Notwithstanding Subsection (c), funds allocated under this section may be used to fund in proportion to the percentage of students served by the program that meet the criteria in Section 29.081(d) or (g):

(1) an accelerated reading instruction program under Section 28.006(g); or

(2) a program for treatment of students who have dyslexia or a related disorder as required by Section 38.003.

(c-2) Notwithstanding Subsection (c), funds allocated under this section may be used to fund a district's mentoring services program under Section 29.089.

(d) The agency shall evaluate the effectiveness of accelerated instruction and support programs provided under Section 29.081 for students at risk of dropping out of school.

Sec. 42.153. BILINGUAL EDUCATION ALLOTMENT.

(a) For each student in average daily attendance in a bilingual education or special language program under Subchapter B, Chapter 29, a district is entitled to an annual allotment equal to the adjusted basic allotment multiplied by 0.1.

(b) Funds allocated under this section, other than an indirect cost allotment established under State Board of Education rule, must be used in providing bilingual education or special language programs under Subchapter B, Chapter 29, and must be accounted for under existing agency reporting and auditing procedures.

(c) A district's bilingual education or special language allocation may be used only for program and student evaluation, instructional materials and equipment, staff development, supplemental staff expenses, salary supplements for teachers, and other supplies required for quality instruction and smaller class size.

Title 19, Texas Administrative Code (TAC), Part II: Texas Education Agency

Chapter 74, Subchapter A

TAC §74.1 (Essential Knowledge and Skills)

TAC §74.2 (Description of a Required Elementary Curriculum)

TAC §74.3 (Description of a Required Secondary Curriculum)

TAC §74.4 (English Language Proficiency Standards/ Proficiency Level Descriptors – (ELPS/PLDs)

Chapter 89, Subchapter BB

TAC §89.1201 – State Policy

TAC §89.1203 – Definitions

TAC §89.1205 – Required Bilingual and English as a Second Language Programs

TAC §89.1207 – Exceptions and Waivers

TAC §89.1210 – Program Content and Design

TAC §89.1215 – Home Language Survey

TAC §89.1220 – Language Proficiency Assessment Committee

TAC §89.1225 – Testing and Classification of Students

TAC §89.1227 – Minimum Requirements for Dual Language Immersion Program Model

TAC §89.1228 - Dual Language Immersion Program Model Implementation

TAC §89.1230 – Eligible Students with Disabilities

TAC §89.1233 – Participation of English Proficient Students

TAC §89.1235 - Facilities

TAC §89.1240 – Parental Authority and Responsibility

TAC §89.1245 – Staffing and Staff Development

TAC §89.1250 – Required Summer School Program

TAC §89.1265 - Evaluation

TAC §89.1267 – Standards for Evaluation of Dual Language Immersion Program Models

TAC §89.1269 – General Standards for Recognition of Dual Language Program Models

Chapter 97, Subchapter AA

TAC §97.1001 (Accountability System - based upon TEC Chapter 39, amended by House Bill 5)

TAC §97.1004 (Adequate Yearly Progress – will be amended by House Bill 5)

TAC §97.1005 (Performance-Based Monitoring Analysis System – includes indicators that respond to federal requirements included in TELPAS)

Chapter 101, Subchapter AA

TAC §101.1005 (Assessments of Achievement in Academic Content Areas and Courses)

TAC §101.1003 (English Language Proficiency Assessments)

TAC §101.1007 (Assessment Provisions for Graduation)

Chapters 110-115, 118, 126-128, 130

Note: Due to size restrictions, the Texas Essential Knowledge and Skills referred to in these chapters are not included in this book. To view the chapters, visit the Texas Essential Knowledge and Skills webpage at TEA.

Title 19, Texas Administrative Code (TAC), Part VII: State Board for Educator Certification

Note – Due to size restrictions, this statute is not included in this book. For more information about requirements for teaching assignments, visit the State Board for Educator Certification – Administrative Rules webpage at TEA.

Chapter 74. Curriculum Requirements

Subchapter A. Required Curriculum

Statutory Authority: The provisions of this Subchapter A issued under the Texas Education Code, §§7.102, 28.002, 28.023, 28.025, 28.054, and 38.003, unless otherwise noted.

§74.1. Essential Knowledge and Skills.

(a) A school district that offers kindergarten through Grade 12 must offer the following as a required curriculum:

(1) a foundation curriculum that includes:

(A) English language arts;

(B) mathematics;

(C) science; and

(D) social studies, consisting of Texas, United States and world history, government, geography, and economics, with emphasis on the free enterprise system and its benefits; and

(2) an enrichment curriculum that includes:

(A) to the extent possible, languages other than English;

(B) health, with emphasis on the importance of proper nutrition and exercise;

(C) physical education;

(D) fine arts;

(E) career and technical education;

(F) technology applications; and

(G) religious literature, including the Hebrew Scriptures (Old Testament) and New Testament, and its impact on history and literature.

(b) A school district must provide instruction in the essential knowledge and skills of the appropriate grade levels in the foundation and enrichment curriculum as specified in paragraphs (1)-(13) of this subsection. A school district may add elements at its discretion but must not delete or omit instruction in the foundation and enrichment curriculum specified in subsection (a) of this section.

(1) Chapter 110 of this title (relating to Texas Essential Knowledge and Skills for English Language Arts and Reading);

(2) Chapter 111 of this title (relating to Texas Essential Knowledge and Skills for Mathematics);

(3) Chapter 112 of this title (relating to Texas Essential Knowledge and Skills for Science);

(4) Chapter 113 of this title (relating to Texas Essential Knowledge and Skills for Social Studies);

(5) Chapter 114 of this title (relating to Texas Essential Knowledge and Skills for Languages Other Than English);

(6) Chapter 115 of this title (relating to Texas Essential Knowledge and Skills for Health Education);

(7) Chapter 116 of this title (relating to Texas Essential Knowledge and Skills for Physical Education);

(8) Chapter 117 of this title (relating to Texas Essential Knowledge and Skills for Fine Arts);

(9) Chapter 118 of this title (relating to Texas Essential Knowledge and Skills for Economics with Emphasis on the Free Enterprise System and Its Benefits);

(10) Chapter 126 of this title (relating to Texas Essential Knowledge and Skills for Technology Applications);

(11) Chapter 127 of this title (relating to Texas Essential Knowledge and Skills for Career Development);

(12) Chapter 128 of this title (relating to Texas Essential Knowledge and Skills for Spanish Language Arts and English as a Second Language); and

(13) Chapter 130 of this title (relating to Texas Essential Knowledge and Skills for Career and Technical Education).

Source: The provisions of this §74.1 adopted to be effective September 1, 1996, 21 TexReg 4311; amended to be effective September 1, 1998, 23 TexReg 5675; amended to be effective October 3, 2004, 29 TexReg 9185; amended to be effective January 9, 2007, 32 TexReg 80; amended to be effective April 21, 2010, 35 TexReg 3028; amended to be effective May 30, 2012, 37 TexReg 3808.

§74.2. Description of a Required Elementary Curriculum.

A school district that offers kindergarten through Grade 5 must provide instruction in the required curriculum as specified in §74.1 of this title (relating to Essential Knowledge and Skills). The district must ensure that sufficient time is provided for teachers to teach and for students to learn English language arts and reading, mathematics, science, social studies, fine arts, health, physical education, technology applications, and to the extent possible, languages other than English. The school district may provide instruction in a variety of arrangements and settings, including mixed-age programs designed to permit flexible learning arrangements for developmentally appropriate instruction for all student populations to support student attainment of course and grade level standards.

Source: The provisions of this §74.2 adopted to be effective September 1, 1996, 21 TexReg 4311; amended to be effective September 1, 1998, 23 TexReg 5675; amended to be effective January 9, 2007, 32 TexReg 80.

§74.3. Description of a Required Secondary Curriculum.

(a) Middle Grades 6-8.

(1) A school district that offers Grades 6-8 must provide instruction in the required curriculum as specified in §74.1 of this title (relating to Essential Knowledge and Skills). The district must ensure that sufficient time is provided for teachers to teach and for students to learn English language arts, mathematics, science, social studies, fine arts, health, physical education, technology applications, and to the extent possible, languages other than English. The school district may provide instruction in a variety of arrangements and settings, including mixed-age programs designed to permit flexible learning arrangements for developmentally appropriate instruction for all student populations to support student attainment of course and grade level standards.

(2) The school district must ensure that, beginning with students who enter Grade 6 in the 2010-2011 school year, each student completes one Texas essential knowledge and skills-based fine arts course in Grade 6, Grade 7, or Grade 8.

(b) **Secondary Grades 9-12.**

(1) A school district that offers Grades 9-12 must provide instruction in the required curriculum as specified in §74.1 of this title. The district must ensure that sufficient time is provided for teachers to teach and for students to learn the subjects in the required curriculum. The school district may provide instruction in a variety of arrangements and settings, including mixed-age programs designed to permit flexible learning arrangements for developmentally appropriate instruction for all student populations to support student attainment of course and grade level standards.

(2) The school district must offer the courses listed in this paragraph and maintain evidence that students have the opportunity to take these courses:

(A) English language arts--English I, II, III, and IV;

(B) mathematics--Algebra I, Algebra II, Geometry, Precalculus, and Mathematical Models with Applications;

(C) science--Integrated Physics and Chemistry, Biology, Chemistry, Physics, and at least two additional science courses selected from Aquatic Science, Astronomy, Earth and Space Science, Environmental Systems, Advanced Animal Science, Advanced Biotechnology, Advanced Plant and Soil Science, Anatomy and Physiology, Engineering Design and Problem Solving, Food Science, Forensic Science, Medical Microbiology, Pathophysiology, and Scientific Research and Design. The requirement to offer two additional courses may be reduced to one by the commissioner of education upon application of a school district with a total high school enrollment of less than 500 students. Science courses shall include at least 40% hands-on laboratory investigations and field work using appropriate scientific inquiry;

(D) social studies--United States History Studies Since 1877, World History Studies, United States Government, World Geography Studies, and Economics with Emphasis on the Free Enterprise System and Its Benefits;

(E) physical education--at least two courses selected from Foundations of Personal Fitness, Adventure/Outdoor Education, Aerobic Activities, or Team or Individual Sports;

(F) fine arts--courses selected from at least two of the four fine arts areas (art, music, theatre, and dance)--Art I, II, III, IV; Music I, II, III, IV; Theatre I, II, III, IV; or Dance I, II, III, IV;

(G) career and technical education--coherent sequences of courses selected from at least three of the following sixteen career clusters:

(i) Agriculture, Food, and Natural Resources;

(ii) Architecture and Construction;

(iii) Arts, Audio/Video Technology, and Communications;

(iv) Business Management and Administration;

(v) Education and Training;

(vi) Finance;

(vii) Government and Public Administration;

(viii) Health Science;

(ix) Hospitality and Tourism;

(x) Human Services;

(xi) Information Technology;

(xii) Law, Public Safety, Corrections, and Security;

(xiii) Manufacturing;

(xiv) Marketing;

(xv) Science, Technology, Engineering, and Mathematics; and

(xvi) Transportation, Distribution, and Logistics;

(H) languages other than English--Levels I, II, and III or higher of the same language;

(I) technology applications--at least four courses selected from Computer Science I, Computer Science II, Computer Science III, Digital Art and Animation, Digital Communications in the 21st Century, Digital Design and Media Production, Digital Forensics, Digital Video and Audio Design, Discrete Mathematics, Fundamentals of Computer Science, Game Programming and Design, Independent Study in Evolving/Emerging Technologies, Independent Study in Technology Applications, Mobile Application Development, Robotics Programming and Design, 3-D Modeling and Animation, Web Communications, Web Design, and Web Game Development; and

(J) speech--Communication Applications.

(3) Districts may offer additional courses from the complete list of courses approved by the State Board of Education to satisfy graduation requirements as referenced in this chapter.

(4) The school district must provide each student the opportunity to participate in all courses listed in subsection (b)(2) of this section. The district must provide students the opportunity each year to select courses in which they intend to participate from a list that includes all courses required to be offered in subsection (b)(2) of this section. If the school district will not offer the required courses every year, but intends to offer particular courses only every other year, it must notify all enrolled students of that fact. A school district must teach a course that is specifically required for high school graduation at least once in any two consecutive school years. For a subject that has an end-of-course assessment, the district must either teach the course every year or employ options described in Subchapter C of this chapter (relating to Other Provisions) to enable students to earn credit for the course and must maintain evidence that it is employing those options.

(5) For students entering Grade 9 beginning with the 2007-2008 school year, districts must ensure that one or more courses offered in the required curriculum for the recommended and advanced high school programs include a research writing component.

(c) Courses in the foundation and enrichment curriculum in Grades 6-12 must be provided in a manner that allows all grade promotion and high school graduation requirements to be met in a timely manner. Nothing in this chapter shall be construed to require a district to offer a specific course in the foundation and enrichment curriculum except as required by this subsection.

Statutory Authority: The provisions of this §74.3 issued under the Texas Education Code, §§7.102(c)(4), 28.002, and 28.025.

Source: The provisions of this §74.3 adopted to be effective September 1, 1996, 21 TexReg 4311; amended to be effective October 13, 1997, 22 TexReg 10129; amended to be effective September 1, 1998, 23 TexReg 5675; amended to be effective September 1, 2001, 25 TexReg 7691; amended to be effective October 3, 2004, 29 TexReg 9185; amended to be effective January 9, 2007, 32 TexReg 80; amended to be effective December 23, 2009, 34 TexReg 9198; amended to be effective April 21, 2010, 35 TexReg 3028; amended to be effective May 30, 2012, 37 TexReg 3808.

§74.4. English Language Proficiency Standards.

(a) Introduction.

(1) The English language proficiency standards in this section outline English language proficiency level descriptors and student expectations for English language learners (ELLs). School districts shall implement this section as an integral part of each subject in the required curriculum. The English language proficiency standards are to be published along with the Texas Essential Knowledge and Skills (TEKS) for each subject in the required curriculum.

(2) In order for ELLs to be successful, they must acquire both social and academic language proficiency in English. Social language proficiency in English consists of the English needed for daily social interactions. Academic language proficiency consists of the English needed to think critically, understand and learn new concepts, process complex academic material, and interact and communicate in English academic settings.

(3) Classroom instruction that effectively integrates second language acquisition with quality content area instruction ensures that ELLs acquire social and academic language proficiency in English, learn the knowledge and skills in the TEKS, and reach their full academic potential.

(4) Effective instruction in second language acquisition involves giving ELLs opportunities to listen, speak, read, and write at their current levels of English development while gradually increasing the linguistic complexity of the English they read and hear, and are expected to speak and write.

(5) The cross-curricular second language acquisition skills in subsection (c) of this

section apply to ELLs in Kindergarten-Grade 12.

(6) The English language proficiency levels of beginning, intermediate, advanced, and advanced high are not grade-specific. ELLs may exhibit different proficiency levels within the language domains of listening, speaking, reading, and writing. The proficiency level descriptors outlined in subsection (d) of this section show the progression of second language acquisition from one proficiency level to the next and serve as a road map to help content area teachers instruct ELLs commensurate with students' linguistic needs.

(b) School district responsibilities. In fulfilling the requirements of this section, school districts shall:

(1) identify the student's English language proficiency levels in the domains of listening, speaking, reading, and writing in accordance with the proficiency level descriptors for the beginning, intermediate, advanced, and advanced high levels delineated in subsection (d) of this section;

(2) provide instruction in the knowledge and skills of the foundation and enrichment curriculum in a manner that is linguistically accommodated (communicated, sequenced, and scaffolded) commensurate with the student's levels of English language proficiency to ensure that the student learns the knowledge and skills in the required curriculum;

(3) provide content-based instruction including the cross-curricular second language acquisition essential knowledge and skills in subsection (c) of this section in a manner that is linguistically accommodated to help the student acquire English language proficiency; and

(4) provide intensive and ongoing foundational second language acquisition instruction to ELLs in Grade 3 or higher who are at the beginning or intermediate level of English language proficiency in listening, speaking, reading, and/or writing as determined by the state's English language proficiency assessment system. These ELLs require focused, targeted, and systematic second language acquisition instruction to provide them with the foundation of English language vocabulary, grammar, syntax, and English mechanics necessary to support content-based instruction and accelerated learning of English.

(c) Cross-curricular second language acquisition essential knowledge and skills.

(1) Cross-curricular second language acquisition/learning strategies. The ELL uses language learning strategies to develop an awareness of his or her own learning processes in all content areas. In order for the ELL to meet grade-level learning expectations across the foundation and enrichment curriculum, all instruction delivered in English must be linguistically accommodated (communicated, sequenced, and scaffolded) commensurate with the student's level of English language proficiency. The student is expected to:

(A) use prior knowledge and experiences to understand meanings in English;

(B) monitor oral and written language production and employ self-corrective techniques or other resources;

(C) use strategic learning techniques such as concept mapping, drawing, memorizing, comparing, contrasting, and reviewing to acquire basic and grade-level vocabulary;

(D) speak using learning strategies such as requesting assistance, employing non-verbal cues, and using synonyms and circumlocution (conveying ideas by defining or describing when exact English words are not known);

(E) internalize new basic and academic language by using and reusing it in meaningful ways in speaking and writing activities that build concept and language attainment;

(F) use accessible language and learn new and essential language in the process;

(G) demonstrate an increasing ability to distinguish between formal and informal English and an increasing knowledge of when to use each one commensurate with grade-level learning expectations; and

(H) develop and expand repertoire of learning strategies such as reasoning inductively or deductively, looking for patterns in language, and analyzing sayings and expressions commensurate with grade-level learning expectations.

(2) Cross-curricular second language acquisition/listening. The ELL listens to a variety of speakers including teachers, peers, and electronic media to gain an increasing level of comprehension of newly acquired language in all content areas. ELLs may be at the beginning, intermediate, advanced, or advanced high stage of English language acquisition in listening. In order for the ELL to meet grade-level learning expectations across the foundation and enrichment curriculum, all instruction delivered in English must be linguistically accommodated (communicated, sequenced, and scaffolded) commensurate with the student's level of English language proficiency. The student is expected to:

(A) distinguish sounds and intonation patterns of English with increasing ease;

(B) recognize elements of the English sound system in newly acquired vocabulary such as long and short vowels, silent letters, and consonant clusters;

(C) learn new language structures, expressions, and basic and academic vocabulary heard during classroom instruction and interactions;

(D) monitor understanding of spoken language during classroom instruction and interactions and seek clarification as needed;

(E) use visual, contextual, and linguistic support to enhance and confirm understanding of increasingly complex and elaborated spoken language;

(F) listen to and derive meaning from a variety of media such as audio tape, video, DVD, and CD ROM to build and reinforce concept and language attainment;

(G) understand the general meaning, main points, and important details of spoken language ranging from situations in which topics, language, and contexts are familiar to unfamiliar;

(H) understand implicit ideas and information in increasingly complex spoken language commensurate with grade-level learning expectations; and

(I) demonstrate listening comprehension of increasingly complex spoken English by following directions, retelling or summarizing spoken messages, responding to questions and requests, collaborating with peers, and taking notes commensurate with content and grade-level needs.

(3) Cross-curricular second language acquisition/speaking. The ELL speaks in a variety of modes for a variety of purposes with an awareness of different language registers (formal/informal) using vocabulary with increasing fluency and accuracy in language arts and all content areas. ELLs may be at the beginning, intermediate, advanced, or advanced high stage of English language acquisition in speaking. In order for the ELL to meet grade-level learning expectations across the foundation and enrichment curriculum, all instruction delivered in English must be linguistically accommodated (communicated, sequenced, and scaffolded) commensurate with the student's level of English language proficiency. The student is expected to:

(A) practice producing sounds of newly acquired vocabulary such as long and short vowels, silent letters, and consonant clusters to pronounce English words in a manner that is increasingly comprehensible;

(B) expand and internalize initial English vocabulary by learning and using high-frequency English words necessary for identifying and describing people, places, and objects, by retelling simple stories and basic information represented or supported by pictures, and by learning and using routine language needed for classroom communication;

(C) speak using a variety of grammatical structures, sentence lengths, sentence types, and connecting words with increasing accuracy and ease as more English is acquired;

(D) speak using grade-level content area vocabulary in context to internalize new English words and build academic language proficiency;

(E) share information in cooperative learning interactions;

(F) ask and give information ranging from using a very limited bank of high-frequency, high-need, concrete vocabulary, including key words and expressions needed for basic communication in academic and social contexts, to using abstract and content-based vocabulary during extended speaking assignments;

(G) express opinions, ideas, and feelings ranging from communicating single words and short phrases to participating in extended discussions on a variety of social and grade-appropriate academic topics;

(H) narrate, describe, and explain with increasing specificity and detail as more English is acquired;

(I) adapt spoken language appropriately for formal and informal purposes; and

(J) respond orally to information presented in a wide variety of print, electronic, audio, and visual media to build and reinforce concept and language attainment.

(4) Cross-curricular second language acquisition/reading. The ELL reads a variety of texts for a variety of purposes with an increasing level of comprehension in all content areas. ELLs may be at the beginning, intermediate, advanced, or advanced high stage of English language acquisition in reading. In order for the ELL to meet grade-level learning expectations across the foundation and enrichment curriculum, all instruction delivered in English must be

linguistically accommodated (communicated, sequenced, and scaffolded) commensurate with the student's level of English language proficiency. For Kindergarten and Grade 1, certain of these student expectations apply to text read aloud for students not yet at the stage of decoding written text. The student is expected to:

(A) learn relationships between sounds and letters of the English language and decode (sound out) words using a combination of skills such as recognizing sound-letter relationships and identifying cognates, affixes, roots, and base words;

(B) recognize directionality of English reading such as left to right and top to bottom;

(C) develop basic sight vocabulary, derive meaning of environmental print, and comprehend English vocabulary and language structures used routinely in written classroom materials;

(D) use prereading supports such as graphic organizers, illustrations, and pretaught topic-related vocabulary and other prereading activities to enhance comprehension of written text;

(E) read linguistically accommodated content area material with a decreasing need for linguistic accommodations as more English is learned;

(F) use visual and contextual support and support from peers and teachers to read grade-appropriate content area text, enhance and confirm understanding, and develop vocabulary, grasp of language structures, and background knowledge needed to comprehend increasingly challenging language;

(G) demonstrate comprehension of increasingly complex English by participating in shared reading, retelling or summarizing material, responding to questions, and taking notes commensurate with content area and grade level needs;

(H) read silently with increasing ease and comprehension for longer periods;

(I) demonstrate English comprehension and expand reading skills by employing basic reading skills such as demonstrating understanding of supporting ideas and details in text and graphic sources, summarizing text, and distinguishing main ideas from details commensurate with content area needs;

(J) demonstrate English comprehension and expand reading skills by employing inferential skills such as predicting, making connections between ideas, drawing inferences and conclusions from text and graphic sources, and finding supporting text evidence commensurate with content area needs; and

(K) demonstrate English comprehension and expand reading skills by employing analytical skills such as evaluating written information and performing critical analyses commensurate with content area and grade-level needs.

(5) Cross-curricular second language acquisition/writing. The ELL writes in a variety of forms with increasing accuracy to effectively address a specific purpose and audience in all content areas. ELLs may be at the beginning, intermediate, advanced, or advanced high stage of English language acquisition in writing. In order for the ELL to meet grade-level learning expectations across

foundation and enrichment curriculum, all instruction delivered in English must be linguistically accommodated (communicated, sequenced, and scaffolded) commensurate with the student's level of English language proficiency. For Kindergarten and Grade 1, certain of these student expectations do not apply until the student has reached the stage of generating original written text using a standard writing system. The student is expected to:

(A) learn relationships between sounds and letters of the English language to represent sounds when writing in English;

(B) write using newly acquired basic vocabulary and content-based grade-level vocabulary;

(C) spell familiar English words with increasing accuracy, and employ English spelling patterns and rules with increasing accuracy as more English is acquired;

(D) edit writing for standard grammar and usage, including subject-verb agreement, pronoun agreement, and appropriate verb tenses commensurate with grade-level expectations as more English is acquired;

(E) employ increasingly complex grammatical structures in content area writing commensurate with grade-level expectations, such as:

(i) using correct verbs, tenses, and pronouns/antecedents;

(ii) using possessive case (apostrophe s) correctly; and

(iii) using negatives and contractions correctly;

(F) write using a variety of grade-appropriate sentence lengths, patterns, and connecting words to combine phrases, clauses, and sentences in increasingly accurate ways as more English is acquired; and

(G) narrate, describe, and explain with increasing specificity and detail to fulfill content area writing needs as more English is acquired.

(d) **Proficiency level descriptors.**

(1) Listening, Kindergarten-Grade 12. ELLs may be at the beginning, intermediate, advanced, or advanced high stage of English language acquisition in listening. The following proficiency level descriptors for listening are sufficient to describe the overall English language proficiency levels of ELLs in this language domain in order to linguistically accommodate their instruction.

(A) Beginning. Beginning ELLs have little or no ability to understand spoken English in academic and social settings. These students:

(i) struggle to understand simple conversations and simple discussions even when the topics are familiar and the speaker uses linguistic supports such as visuals, slower speech and other verbal cues, and gestures;

(ii) struggle to identify and distinguish individual words and phrases during social and instructional interactions that have not been intentionally modified for ELLs; and

(iii) may not seek clarification in English when failing to comprehend the English they hear; frequently remain silent, watching others for cues.

(B) Intermediate. Intermediate ELLs have the ability to understand simple, high-frequency spoken English used in routine academic and social settings. These students:

(i) usually understand simple or routine directions, as well as short, simple conversations and short, simple discussions on familiar topics; when topics are unfamiliar, require extensive linguistic supports and adaptations such as visuals, slower speech and other verbal cues, simplified language, gestures, and preteaching to preview or build topic-related vocabulary;

(ii) often identify and distinguish key words and phrases necessary to understand the general meaning during social and basic instructional interactions that have not been intentionally modified for ELLs; and

(iii) have the ability to seek clarification in English when failing to comprehend the English they hear by requiring/requesting the speaker to repeat, slow down, or rephrase speech.

(C) Advanced. Advanced ELLs have the ability to understand, with second language acquisition support, grade-appropriate spoken English used in academic and social settings. These students:

(i) usually understand longer, more elaborated directions, conversations, and discussions on familiar and some unfamiliar topics, but sometimes need processing time and sometimes depend on visuals, verbal cues, and gestures to support understanding;

(ii) understand most main points, most important details, and some implicit information during social and basic instructional interactions that have not been intentionally modified for ELLs; and

(iii) occasionally require/request the speaker to repeat, slow down, or rephrase to clarify the meaning of the English they hear.

(D) Advanced high. Advanced high ELLs have the ability to understand, with minimal second language acquisition support, grade-appropriate spoken English used in academic and social settings. These students:

(i) understand longer, elaborated directions, conversations, and discussions on familiar and unfamiliar topics with occasional need for processing time and with little dependence on visuals, verbal cues, and gestures; some exceptions when complex academic or highly specialized language is used;

(ii) understand main points, important details, and implicit information at a level nearly comparable to native English-speaking peers during social and instructional interactions; and

(iii) rarely require/request the speaker to repeat, slow down, or rephrase to clarify the meaning of the English they hear.

(2) Speaking, Kindergarten-Grade 12. ELLs may be at the beginning, intermediate, advanced, or advanced high stage of English language acquisition in speaking. The following proficiency level descriptors for speaking are sufficient to describe the overall English language proficiency levels of ELLs in this language domain in order to linguistically accommodate their instruction.

(A) Beginning. Beginning ELLs have little or no ability to speak English in academic and social settings. These students:

(i) mainly speak using single words

and short phrases consisting of recently practiced, memorized, or highly familiar material to get immediate needs met; may be hesitant to speak and often give up in their attempts to communicate;

(ii) speak using a very limited bank of high-frequency, high-need, concrete vocabulary, including key words and expressions needed for basic communication in academic and social contexts;

(iii) lack the knowledge of English grammar necessary to connect ideas and speak in sentences; can sometimes produce sentences using recently practiced, memorized, or highly familiar material;

(iv) exhibit second language acquisition errors that may hinder overall communication, particularly when trying to convey information beyond memorized, practiced, or highly familiar material; and

(v) typically use pronunciation that significantly inhibits communication.

(B) Intermediate. Intermediate ELLs have the ability to speak in a simple manner using English commonly heard in routine academic and social settings. These students:

(i) are able to express simple, original messages, speak using sentences, and participate in short conversations and classroom interactions; may hesitate frequently and for long periods to think about how to communicate desired meaning;

(ii) speak simply using basic vocabulary needed in everyday social interactions and routine academic contexts; rarely have vocabulary to speak in detail;

(iii) exhibit an emerging awareness of English grammar and speak using mostly simple sentence structures and simple tenses; are most comfortable speaking in present tense;

(iv) exhibit second language acquisition errors that may hinder overall communication when trying to use complex or less familiar English; and

(v) use pronunciation that can usually be understood by people accustomed to interacting with ELLs.

(C) Advanced. Advanced ELLs have the ability to speak using grade-appropriate English, with second language acquisition support, in academic and social settings. These students:

(i) are able to participate comfortably in most conversations and academic discussions on familiar topics, with some pauses to restate, repeat, or search for words and phrases to clarify meaning;

(ii) discuss familiar academic topics using content-based terms and common abstract vocabulary; can usually speak in some detail on familiar topics;

(iii) have a grasp of basic grammar features, including a basic ability to narrate and describe in present, past, and future tenses; have an emerging ability to use complex sentences and complex grammar features;

(iv) make errors that interfere somewhat with communication when using complex grammar structures, long sentences, and less familiar words and expressions; and

(v) may mispronounce words, but use pronunciation that can usually be understood by people not accustomed to interacting with ELLs.

(D) Advanced high. Advanced high ELLs

have the ability to speak using grade-appropriate English, with minimal second language acquisition support, in academic and social settings. These students:

(i) are able to participate in extended discussions on a variety of social and grade-appropriate academic topics with only occasional disruptions, hesitations, or pauses;

(ii) communicate effectively using abstract and content-based vocabulary during classroom instructional tasks, with some exceptions when low-frequency or academically demanding vocabulary is needed; use many of the same idioms and colloquialisms as their native English-speaking peers;

(iii) can use English grammar structures and complex sentences to narrate and describe at a level nearly comparable to native English-speaking peers;

(iv) make few second language acquisition errors that interfere with overall communication; and

(v) may mispronounce words, but rarely use pronunciation that interferes with overall communication.

(3) Reading, Kindergarten-Grade 1. ELLs in Kindergarten and Grade 1 may be at the beginning, intermediate, advanced, or advanced high stage of English language acquisition in reading. The following proficiency level descriptors for reading are sufficient to describe the overall English language proficiency levels of ELLs in this language domain in order to linguistically accommodate their instruction and should take into account developmental stages of emergent readers.

(A) Beginning. Beginning ELLs have little or no ability to use the English language to build foundational reading skills. These students:

(i) derive little or no meaning from grade-appropriate stories read aloud in English, unless the stories are:

(I) read in short "chunks;"

(II) controlled to include the little English they know such as language that is high frequency, concrete, and recently practiced; and

(III) accompanied by ample visual supports such as illustrations, gestures, pantomime, and objects and by linguistic supports such as careful enunciation and slower speech;

(ii) begin to recognize and understand environmental print in English such as signs, labeled items, names of peers, and logos; and

(iii) have difficulty decoding most grade-appropriate English text because they:

(I) understand the meaning of very few words in English; and

(II) struggle significantly with sounds in spoken English words and with sound-symbol relationships due to differences between their primary language and English.

(B) Intermediate. Intermediate ELLs have a limited ability to use the English language to build foundational reading skills. These students:

(i) demonstrate limited comprehension (key words and general meaning) of grade-appropriate stories read aloud in English, unless the stories include:

(I) predictable story lines;

(II) highly familiar topics;

(III) primarily high-frequency, concrete vocabulary;

(IV) short, simple sentences; and

(V) visual and linguistic supports;

(ii) regularly recognize and understand common environmental print in English such as signs, labeled items, names of peers, logos; and

(iii) have difficulty decoding grade-appropriate English text because they:

(I) understand the meaning of only those English words they hear frequently; and

(II) struggle with some sounds in English words and some sound-symbol relationships due to differences between their primary language and English.

(C) Advanced. Advanced ELLs have the ability to use the English language, with second language acquisition support, to build foundational reading skills. These students:

(i) demonstrate comprehension of most main points and most supporting ideas in grade-appropriate stories read aloud in English, although they may still depend on visual and linguistic supports to gain or confirm meaning;

(ii) recognize some basic English vocabulary and high-frequency words in isolated print; and

(iii) with second language acquisition support, are able to decode most grade-appropriate English text because they:

(I) understand the meaning of most grade-appropriate English words; and

(II) have little difficulty with English sounds and sound-symbol relationships that result from differences between their primary language and English.

(D) Advanced high. Advanced high ELLs have the ability to use the English language, with minimal second language acquisition support, to build foundational reading skills. These students:

(i) demonstrate, with minimal second language acquisition support and at a level nearly comparable to native English-speaking peers, comprehension of main points and supporting ideas (explicit and implicit) in grade-appropriate stories read aloud in English;

(ii) with some exceptions, recognize sight vocabulary and high-frequency words to a degree nearly comparable to that of native English-speaking peers; and

(iii) with minimal second language acquisition support, have an ability to decode and understand grade-appropriate English text at a level nearly comparable to native English-speaking peers.

(4) Reading, Grades 2-12. ELLs in Grades 2-12 may be at the beginning, intermediate, advanced, or advanced high stage of English language acquisition in reading. The following proficiency level descriptors for reading are sufficient to describe the overall English language proficiency levels of ELLs in this language domain in order to linguistically accommodate their instruction.

(A) Beginning. Beginning ELLs have little or no ability to read and understand English used in academic and social contexts. These students:

(i) read and understand the very limited

recently practiced, memorized, or highly familiar English they have learned; vocabulary predominantly includes:

(I) environmental print;

(II) some very high-frequency words; and

(III) concrete words that can be represented by pictures;

(ii) read slowly, word by word;

(iii) have a very limited sense of English language structures;

(iv) comprehend predominantly isolated familiar words and phrases; comprehend some sentences in highly routine contexts or recently practiced, highly familiar text;

(v) are highly dependent on visuals and prior knowledge to derive meaning from text in English; and

(vi) are able to apply reading comprehension skills in English only when reading texts written for this level.

(B) Intermediate. Intermediate ELLs have the ability to read and understand simple, high-frequency English used in routine academic and social contexts. These students:

(i) read and understand English vocabulary on a somewhat wider range of topics and with increased depth; vocabulary predominantly includes:

(I) everyday oral language;

(II) literal meanings of common words;

(III) routine academic language and terms; and

(IV) commonly used abstract language such as terms used to describe basic feelings;

(ii) often read slowly and in short phrases; may re-read to clarify meaning;

(iii) have a growing understanding of basic, routinely used English language structures;

(iv) understand simple sentences in short, connected texts, but are dependent on visual cues, topic familiarity, prior knowledge, pretaught topic-related vocabulary, story predictability, and teacher/peer assistance to sustain comprehension;

(v) struggle to independently read and understand grade-level texts; and

(vi) are able to apply basic and some higher-order comprehension skills when reading texts that are linguistically accommodated and/or simplified for this level.

(C) Advanced. Advanced ELLs have the ability to read and understand, with second language acquisition support, grade-appropriate English used in academic and social contexts. These students:

(i) read and understand, with second language acquisition support, a variety of grade-appropriate English vocabulary used in social and academic contexts:

(I) with second language acquisition support, read and understand grade-appropriate concrete and abstract vocabulary, but have difficulty with less commonly encountered words;

(II) demonstrate an emerging ability to understand words and phrases beyond their literal meaning; and

(III) understand multiple meanings of commonly used words;

(ii) read longer phrases and simple sentences from familiar text with appropriate rate and speed;

(iii) are developing skill in using their

growing familiarity with English language structures to construct meaning of grade-appropriate text; and

(iv) are able to apply basic and higher-order comprehension skills when reading grade-appropriate text, but are still occasionally dependent on visuals, teacher/peer assistance, and other linguistically accommodated text features to determine or clarify meaning, particularly with unfamiliar topics.

(D) Advanced high. Advanced high ELLs have the ability to read and understand, with minimal second language acquisition support, grade-appropriate English used in academic and social contexts. These students:

(i) read and understand vocabulary at a level nearly comparable to that of their native English-speaking peers, with some exceptions when low-frequency or specialized vocabulary is used;

(ii) generally read grade-appropriate, familiar text with appropriate rate, speed, intonation, and expression;

(iii) are able to, at a level nearly comparable to native English-speaking peers, use their familiarity with English language structures to construct meaning of grade-appropriate text; and

(iv) are able to apply, with minimal second language acquisition support and at a level nearly comparable to native English-speaking peers, basic and higher-order comprehension skills when reading grade-appropriate text.

(5) Writing, Kindergarten-Grade 1. ELLs in Kindergarten and Grade 1 may be at the beginning, intermediate, advanced, or advanced high stage of English language acquisition in writing. The following proficiency level descriptors for writing are sufficient to describe the overall English language proficiency levels of ELLs in this language domain in order to linguistically accommodate their instruction and should take into account developmental stages of emergent writers.

(A) Beginning. Beginning ELLs have little or no ability to use the English language to build foundational writing skills. These students:

(i) are unable to use English to explain self-generated writing such as stories they have created or other personal expressions, including emergent forms of writing (pictures, letter-like forms, mock words, scribbling, etc.);

(ii) know too little English to participate meaningfully in grade-appropriate shared writing activities using the English language;

(iii) cannot express themselves meaningfully in self-generated, connected written text in English beyond the level of high-frequency, concrete words, phrases, or short sentences that have been recently practiced and/or memorized; and

(iv) may demonstrate little or no awareness of English print conventions.

(B) Intermediate. Intermediate ELLs have a limited ability to use the English language to build foundational writing skills. These students:

(i) know enough English to explain briefly and simply self-generated writing, including emergent forms of writing, as long as the topic is highly familiar and concrete and requires very high-frequency English;

(ii) can participate meaningfully in grade-appropriate shared writing activities using the English language only when the writing topic is highly familiar and concrete and requires very high-frequency English;

(iii) express themselves meaningfully in self-generated, connected written text in English when their writing is limited to short sentences featuring simple, concrete English used frequently in class; and

(iv) frequently exhibit features of their primary language when writing in English such as primary language words, spelling patterns, word order, and literal translating.

(C) Advanced. Advanced ELLs have the ability to use the English language to build, with second language acquisition support, foundational writing skills. These students:

(i) use predominantly grade-appropriate English to explain, in some detail, most self-generated writing, including emergent forms of writing;

(ii) can participate meaningfully, with second language acquisition support, in most grade-appropriate shared writing activities using the English language;

(iii) although second language acquisition support is needed, have an emerging ability to express themselves in self-generated, connected written text in English in a grade-appropriate manner; and

(iv) occasionally exhibit second language acquisition errors when writing in English.

(D) Advanced high. Advanced high ELLs have the ability to use the English language to build, with minimal second language acquisition support, foundational writing skills. These students:

(i) use English at a level of complexity and detail nearly comparable to that of native English-speaking peers when explaining self-generated writing, including emergent forms of writing;

(ii) can participate meaningfully in most grade-appropriate shared writing activities using the English language; and

(iii) although minimal second language acquisition support may be needed, express themselves in self-generated, connected written text in English in a manner nearly comparable to their native English-speaking peers.

(6) Writing, Grades 2-12. ELLs in Grades 2-12 may be at the beginning, intermediate, advanced, or advanced high stage of English language acquisition in writing. The following proficiency level descriptors for writing are sufficient to describe the overall English language proficiency levels of ELLs in this language domain in order to linguistically accommodate their instruction.

(A) Beginning. Beginning ELLs lack the English vocabulary and grasp of English language structures necessary to address grade-appropriate writing tasks meaningfully. These students:

(i) have little or no ability to use the English language to express ideas in writing and engage meaningfully in grade-appropriate writing assignments in content area instruction;

(ii) lack the English necessary to develop or demonstrate elements of grade-appropriate writing such as focus and coherence, conventions, organization, voice, and development of ideas in English; and

(iii) exhibit writing features typical at this level, including:

(I) ability to label, list, and copy;

(II) high-frequency words/phrases and short, simple sentences (or even short paragraphs) based primarily on recently practiced, memorized, or highly familiar material; this type of writing may be quite accurate;

(III) present tense used primarily; and

(IV) frequent primary language features (spelling patterns, word order, literal translations, and words from the student's primary language) and other errors associated with second language acquisition may significantly hinder or prevent understanding, even for individuals accustomed to the writing of ELLs.

(B) Intermediate. Intermediate ELLs have enough English vocabulary and enough grasp of English language structures to address grade-appropriate writing tasks in a limited way. These students:

(i) have a limited ability to use the English language to express ideas in writing and engage meaningfully in grade-appropriate writing assignments in content area instruction;

(ii) are limited in their ability to develop or demonstrate elements of grade-appropriate writing in English; communicate best when topics are highly familiar and concrete, and require simple, high-frequency English; and

(iii) exhibit writing features typical at this level, including:

(I) simple, original messages consisting of short, simple sentences; frequent inaccuracies occur when creating or taking risks beyond familiar English;

(II) high-frequency vocabulary; academic writing often has an oral tone;

(III) loosely connected text with limited use of cohesive devices or repetitive use, which may cause gaps in meaning;

(IV) repetition of ideas due to lack of vocabulary and language structures;

(V) present tense used most accurately; simple future and past tenses, if attempted, are used inconsistently or with frequent inaccuracies;

(VI) undetailed descriptions, explanations, and narrations; difficulty expressing abstract ideas;

(VII) primary language features and errors associated with second language acquisition may be frequent; and

(VIII) some writing may be understood only by individuals accustomed to the writing of ELLs; parts of the writing may be hard to understand even for individuals accustomed to ELL writing.

(C) Advanced. Advanced ELLs have enough English vocabulary and command of English language structures to address grade-appropriate writing tasks, although second language acquisition support is needed. These students:

(i) are able to use the English language, with second language acquisition support, to express ideas in writing and engage meaningfully in grade-appropriate writing assignments in content area instruction;

(ii) know enough English to be able to develop or demonstrate elements of grade-appropriate writing in English, although second language acquisition support is particularly needed when topics are abstract, academically challenging, or unfamiliar; and

(iii) exhibit writing features typical at this level, including:

(I) grasp of basic verbs, tenses, grammar features, and sentence patterns; partial grasp of more complex verbs, tenses, grammar features, and sentence patterns;

(II) emerging grade-appropriate vocabulary; academic writing has a more academic tone;

(III) use of a variety of common cohesive devices, although some redundancy may occur;

(IV) narrations, explanations, and descriptions developed in some detail with emerging clarity; quality or quantity declines when abstract ideas are expressed, academic demands are high, or low-frequency vocabulary is required;

(V) occasional second language acquisition errors; and

(VI) communications are usually understood by individuals not accustomed to the writing of ELLs.

(D) Advanced high. Advanced high ELLs have acquired the English vocabulary and command of English language structures necessary to address grade-appropriate writing tasks with minimal second language acquisition support. These students:

(i) are able to use the English language, with minimal second language acquisition support, to express ideas in writing and engage meaningfully in grade-appropriate writing assignments in content area instruction;

(ii) know enough English to be able to develop or demonstrate, with minimal second language acquisition support, elements of grade-appropriate writing in English; and

(iii) exhibit writing features typical at this level, including:

(I) nearly comparable to writing of native English-speaking peers in clarity and precision with regard to English vocabulary and language structures, with occasional exceptions when writing about academically complex ideas, abstract ideas, or topics requiring low-frequency vocabulary;

(II) occasional difficulty with naturalness of phrasing and expression; and

(III) errors associated with second language acquisition are minor and usually limited to low-frequency words and structures; errors rarely interfere with communication.

(e) **Effective date.** The provisions of this section supersede the ESL standards specified in Chapter 128 of this title (relating to Texas Essential Knowledge and Skills for Spanish Language Arts and English as a Second Language) upon the effective date of this section.

Source: The provisions of this §74.4 adopted to be effective December 25, 2007, 32 TexReg 9615.

Chapter 89. Adaptations for Special Populations

Subchapter BB. Commissioner's Rules Concerning State Plan for Educating English Language Learners

Statutory Authority: The provisions of this Subchapter BB issued under the Texas Education Code, §§29.051, 29.053, 29.054, 29.056, 29.0561, 29.060, and 29.066, unless otherwise noted

§89.1201. Policy.

(a) It is the policy of the state that every student in the state who has a home language other than English and who is identified as an English language learner shall be provided a full opportunity to participate in a bilingual education or English as a second language (ESL) program, as required in the Texas Education Code (TEC), Chapter 29, Subchapter B. To ensure equal educational opportunity, as required in the TEC, §1.002(a), each school district shall:

(1) identify English language learners based on criteria established by the state;

(2) provide bilingual education and ESL programs, as integral parts of the regular program as described in the TEC, §4.002;

(3) seek certified teaching personnel to ensure that English language learners are afforded full opportunity to master the essential knowledge and skills required by the state; and

(4) assess achievement for essential knowledge and skills in accordance with the TEC, Chapter 39, to ensure accountability for English language learners and the schools that serve them.

(b) The goal of bilingual education programs shall be to enable English language learners to become competent in listening, speaking, reading, and writing in the English language through the development of literacy and academic skills in the primary language and English. Such programs shall emphasize the mastery of English language skills, as well as mathematics, science, and social studies, as integral parts of the academic goals for all students to enable English language learners to participate equitably in school.

(c) The goal of ESL programs shall be to enable English language learners to become competent in listening, speaking, reading, and writing in the English language through the integrated use of second language methods. The ESL program shall emphasize the mastery of English language skills, as well as mathematics, science, and social studies, as integral parts of the academic goals for all students to enable English language learners to participate equitably in school.

(d) Bilingual education and ESL programs shall be integral parts of the total school program. Such programs shall use instructional approaches designed to meet the special needs of English language learners. The basic curriculum content of the programs shall be based on the essential knowledge and skills required by the state.

Source: The provisions of this §89.1201 adopted to be effective September 1, 1996, 21 TexReg 5700; amended to be effective May 28, 2012, 37 TexReg 3822.

§89.1203. Definitions.

The following words and terms, when used in this subchapter, shall have the following meanings, unless the context clearly indicates otherwise.

(1) English language learner--A person who is in the process of acquiring English and has another language as the first native language. The terms English language learner and limited English proficient student are used interchangeably.

(2) Dual language immersion--An educational approach in which students learn two languages in an instructional setting that integrates subject content presented in English and another language. Models vary depending on the amount of each language used for instruction at each grade level. The program must be based on instruction that adds to the student's first language. The implementation of a dual language immersion program model is optional.

(3) School district--For the purposes of this subchapter, the definition of a school district includes an open-enrollment charter school.

Source: The provisions of this §89.1203 adopted to be effective May 28, 2012, 37 TexReg 3822.

§89.1205. Required Bilingual Education and English as a Second Language Programs.

(a) Each school district that has an enrollment of 20 or more English language learners in any language classification in the same grade level district-wide shall offer a bilingual education program as described in subsection (b) of this section for the English language learners in prekindergarten through the elementary grades who speak that language. "Elementary grades" shall include at least prekindergarten through Grade 5; sixth grade shall be included when clustered with elementary grades.

(b) A school district shall provide a bilingual education program by offering dual language instruction in prekindergarten through the elementary grades, using one of the four bilingual program models described in §89.1210 of this title (relating to Program Content and Design).

(c) School districts are authorized to establish a bilingual education program at grade levels in which the bilingual education program is not required under subsection (a) of this section.

(d) All English language learners for whom a school district is not required to offer a bilingual education program shall be provided an English as a second language program as described in subsection (e) of this section, regardless of the students' grade levels and home language, and regardless of the number of such students.

(e) A school district shall provide English as a second language instruction by offering an English as a second language program using one of the two models described in §89.1210 of this title.

(f) School districts may join with other school districts to provide bilingual education or English as a second language programs.

Source: The provisions of this §89.1205 adopted to be effective September 1, 1996, 21 TexReg 5700; amended to be effective March 5, 1999, 24 TexReg 1383; amended to be effective April 18, 2002, 27 TexReg 3107; amended to be effective September 17, 2007, 32 TexReg 6311; amended to be effective May 28, 2012, 37 TexReg 3822.

§89.1207. Exceptions and Waivers.

(a) Bilingual education program.

(1) Exceptions. A school district that is unable to provide a bilingual education program as required by §89.1205(a) of this title (relating to Required Bilingual Education and English as a Second Language Programs) shall request from the commissioner of education an exception to the bilingual education program and the approval of an alternative program. The approval of an exception to the bilingual education program shall be valid only during the school year for which it was granted. A request for a bilingual education program exception must be submitted by November 1 and shall include:

(A) a statement of the reasons the school district is unable to offer the bilingual education program with supporting documentation;

(B) a description of the proposed alternative modified bilingual education or intensive English as a second language programs designed to meet the affective, linguistic, and cognitive needs of the English language learners, including the manner through which the students will be given opportunity to master the essential knowledge and skills required by Chapter 74 of this title (relating to Curriculum Requirements);

(C) an acknowledgement that certified teachers available in the school district will be assigned to grade levels beginning at prekindergarten followed successively by subsequent grade levels to ensure that the linguistic and academic needs of the English language learners with beginning levels of English proficiency are served on a priority basis;

(D) a description of the training program the school district will provide to improve the skills of the certified teachers that are assigned to implement the proposed alternative program and an assurance that at least 10% of the bilingual education allotment shall be used to fund this training program; and

(E) a description of the actions the school district will take to ensure that the program required under §89.1205(a) of this title will be provided the subsequent year, including its plans for recruiting and training an adequate number of certified teachers to eliminate the need for subsequent exceptions and measurable targets for the subsequent year.

(2) Approval of exceptions. Bilingual education program exceptions will be granted by the commissioner if the requesting school district:

(A) meets or exceeds the state average for English language learner performance on the required state assessments;

(B) meets the requirements and measurable targets of the action plan described in paragraph (1)(E) of this subsection submitted the previous year and approved by the Texas Education Agency (TEA); or

(C) reduces by 25% the number of teachers under exception for bilingual Spanish programs when compared to the number of exceptions granted the previous year.

(3) Denial of exceptions. A school district denied a bilingual education program exception must submit to the commissioner a detailed action plan for complying with required regulations for the following school year.

(4) Appeals. A school district denied a bilingual education program exception may appeal to the commissioner or the commissioner's designee. The decision of the commissioner or commissioner's designee is final and may not be appealed further.

(5) Special accreditation investigation. The commissioner may authorize a special accreditation investigation under the Texas Education Code (TEC), §39.057, if a school district:

(A) is denied a bilingual education program exception for more than three consecutive years; or

(B) is granted an exception based on meeting or exceeding the state average for English language learner performance on the required state assessments but has excessive numbers of allowable exemptions from the required state assessments.

(6) Sanctions. Based on the results of a special accreditation investigation, the commissioner may take appropriate action under the TEC, §39.102.

(b) English as a second language program.

(1) Waivers. A school district that is unable to provide an English as a second language program as required by §89.1205(d) of this title because of an insufficient number of certified teachers shall request from the commissioner a waiver of the certification requirements for each teacher who will provide instruction in English as a second language for English language learners. The approval of a waiver of certification requirements shall be valid only during the school year for which it was granted. A request for an English as a second language program waiver must be submitted by November 1 and shall include:

(A) a statement of the reasons the school district is unable to provide a sufficient number of certified teachers to offer the English as a second language program;

(B) a description of the manner in which the teachers in the English as a second language program will meet the affective, linguistic, and cognitive needs of the English language learners, including the manner through which the students will be given opportunity to master the essential knowledge and skills required by Chapter 74 of this title;

(C) an assurance that certified teachers available in the school district will be assigned to grade levels beginning at prekindergarten followed successively by subsequent grade levels in the elementary school campus and, if needed, secondary campuses, to ensure that the linguistic and academic needs of the English language learners with the lower levels of English proficiency are served on a priority basis;

(D) the name of each teacher not on

permit who is assigned to implement the English as a second language program and for each teacher under a waiver, the estimated date for the completion of the English as a second language supplemental certification, which must be completed by the end of the school year for which the waiver was requested;

(E) a description of the training program that the school district will provide to improve the skills of the certified teachers that are assigned to implement the proposed English as a second language program and an assurance that at least 10% of the bilingual education allotment shall be used to fund this training; and

(F) a description of the actions the school district will take to ensure that the program required under §89.1205(d) of this title will be provided the subsequent year, including its plans for recruiting and training an adequate number of certified teachers to eliminate the need for subsequent waivers.

(2) Approval of waivers. English as a second language waivers will be granted by the commissioner if the requesting school district:

(A) meets or exceeds the state average for English language learner performance on the required state assessments; or

(B) meets the requirements and measurable targets of the action plan described in paragraph (1)(F) of this subsection submitted the previous year and approved by the TEA.

(3) Denial of waivers. A school district denied an English as a second language program waiver must submit to the commissioner a detailed action plan for complying with required regulations for the following school year.

(4) Appeals. A school district denied an English as a second language waiver may appeal to the commissioner or the commissioner's designee. The decision of the commissioner or commissioner's designee is final and may not be appealed further.

(5) Special accreditation investigation. The commissioner may authorize a special accreditation investigation under the TEC, §39.057, if a school district:

(A) is denied an English as a second language waiver for more than three consecutive years; or

(B) is granted a waiver based on meeting or exceeding the state average for English language learner performance on the required state assessments but has excessive numbers of allowable exemptions from the required state assessments.

(6) Sanctions. Based on the results of a special accreditation investigation, the commissioner may take appropriate action under the TEC, §39.102.

Source: The provisions of this §89.1207 adopted to be effective September 17, 2007, 32 TexReg 6311; amended to be effective May 28, 2012, 37 TexReg 3822.

§89.1210. Program Content and Design.

(a) Each school district required to offer a bilingual education or English as a second language program shall provide each English language learner the opportunity to be enrolled in the required program at his or her grade level. Each student's level of proficiency shall be designated by the language proficiency assessment committee in accordance with §89.1220(g) of this title (relating to Language Proficiency Assessment Committee). The school district shall modify the instruction, pacing, and materials to ensure that English language learners have a full opportunity to master the essential knowledge and skills of the required curriculum. Students participating in the bilingual education program may demonstrate their mastery of the essential knowledge and skills in either their home language or in English for each content area.

(b) The bilingual education program shall be a full-time program of instruction in which both the students' home language and English shall be used for instruction. The amount of instruction in each language within the bilingual education program shall be commensurate with the students' level of proficiency in each language and their level of academic achievement. The students' level of language proficiency and academic achievement shall be designated by the language proficiency assessment committee. The Texas Education Agency (TEA) shall develop program guidelines to ensure that the programs are developmentally appropriate, that the instruction in each language is appropriate, and that the students are challenged to perform at a level commensurate with their linguistic proficiency and academic potential.

(c) The bilingual education program shall be an integral part of the regular educational program required under Chapter 74 of this title (relating to Curriculum Requirements). In bilingual education programs using Spanish and English as languages of instruction, school districts shall use state-adopted English and Spanish instructional materials and supplementary materials as curriculum tools to enhance the learning process; in addition, school districts may use other curriculum adaptations that have been developed. The bilingual education program shall address the affective, linguistic, and cognitive needs of English language learners as follows.

(1) Affective. English language learners shall be provided instruction in their home language to introduce basic concepts of the school environment, and instruction both in their home language and in English, which instills confidence, self-assurance, and a positive identity with their cultural heritages. The program shall address the history and cultural heritage associated with both the students' home language and the United States.

(2) Linguistic. English language learners shall be provided instruction in the skills of listening, speaking, reading, and writing both in their home language and in English. The instruction in both languages shall be structured to ensure that the students master the required essential knowledge and skills and higher-order thinking skills in all subjects.

(3) Cognitive. English language learners shall be provided instruction in language arts, mathematics, science, and social studies both in their home language and in English. The content area instruction in both languages shall be structured to ensure that

the students master the required essential knowledge and skills and higher-order thinking skills in all subjects.

(d) The bilingual education program shall be implemented with consideration for each English language learner's unique readiness level through one of the following program models.

(1) Transitional bilingual/early exit is a bilingual program model that serves a student identified as limited English proficient in both English and Spanish, or another language, and transfers the student to English-only instruction. This model provides instruction in literacy and academic content areas through the medium of the student's first language, along with instruction in English oral and academic language development. Non-academic subjects such as art, music, and physical education may also be taught in English. Exiting of a student to an all-English program of instruction will occur no earlier than the end of Grade 1 or, if the student enrolls in school during or after Grade 1, no earlier than two years or later than five years after the student enrolls in school. A student who has met exit criteria in accordance with §89.1225(h), (j), and (k) of this title (relating to Testing and Classification of Students) may continue receiving services, but the school district will not receive the bilingual education allotment for that student.

(2) Transitional bilingual/late exit is a bilingual program model that serves a student identified as limited English proficient in both English and Spanish, or another language, and transfers the student to English-only instruction. Academic growth is accelerated through cognitively challenging academic work in the student's first language along with meaningful academic content taught through the student's second language, English. The goal is to promote high levels of academic achievement and full academic language proficiency in the student's first language and English. A student enrolled in a transitional bilingual/late exit program is eligible to exit the program no earlier than six years or later than seven years after the student enrolls in school. A student who has met exit criteria in accordance with §89.1225(h), (j), and (k) of this title may continue receiving services, but the school district will not receive the bilingual education allotment for that student.

(3) Dual language immersion/two-way is a biliteracy program model that integrates students proficient in English and students identified as limited English proficient. This model provides instruction in both English and Spanish, or another language, and transfers a student identified as limited English proficient to English-only instruction. Instruction is provided to both native English speakers and native speakers of another language in an instructional setting where language learning is integrated with content instruction. Academic subjects are taught to all students through both English and the other language. Program exit will occur no earlier than six years or later than seven years after the student enrolls in school. A student who has met exit criteria in accordance with §89.1225(h), (j), and (k) of this title may continue receiving services, but the school district will not receive the bilingual education allotment for that student. The primary goals of a dual language immersion program model are:

(A) the development of fluency and literacy in English and another language for all students, with special attention given to English language learners participating in the program;

(B) the integration of English speakers and English language learners for academic instruction, in accordance with the program design and model selected by the school district board of trustees. Whenever possible, 50% of the students in a program should be dominant English speakers and 50% of the students should be native speakers of the other language at the beginning of the program; and

(C) the promotion of bilingualism, biliteracy, cross-cultural awareness, and high academic achievement.

(4) Dual language immersion/one-way is a biliteracy program model that serves only students identified as limited English proficient. This model provides instruction in both English and Spanish, or another language, and transfers a student to English-only instruction. Instruction is provided to English language learners in an instructional setting where language learning is integrated with content instruction. Academic subjects are taught to all students through both English and the other language. Program exit will occur no earlier than six years or later than seven years after the student enrolls in school. A student who has met exit criteria in accordance with §89.1225(h), (j), and (k) of this title may continue receiving services, but the school district will not receive the bilingual education allotment for that student. The primary goals of a dual language immersion program model are:

(A) the development of fluency and literacy in English and another language for all students, with special attention given to English language learners participating in the program;

(B) the integration of English speakers and English language learners for academic instruction, in accordance with the program design and model selected by the school district board of trustees; and

(C) the promotion of bilingualism, biliteracy, cross-cultural awareness, and high academic achievement.

(e) English as a second language programs shall be intensive programs of instruction designed to develop proficiency in listening, speaking, reading, and writing in the English language. Instruction in English as a second language shall be commensurate with the student's level of English proficiency and his or her level of academic achievement. In prekindergarten through Grade 8, instruction in English as a second language may vary from the amount of time accorded to instruction in English language arts in the general education program for English proficient students to a full-time instructional setting using second language methods. In high school, the English as a second language program shall be consistent with graduation requirements under Chapter 74 of this title. The language proficiency assessment committee may recommend appropriate services that may include content courses provided through sheltered instructional approaches by trained teachers, enrollment in English as a second language courses, additional state elective English courses, and special assistance provided through locally determined programs.

(f) The English as a second language program shall be an integral part of the regular educational program required under Chapter 74 of this title. School districts shall use state-adopted English as a second language instructional materials and supplementary materials as curriculum tools. In addition, school districts may use other curriculum adaptations that have been developed. The school district shall provide for ongoing coordination between the English as a second language program and the regular educational program. The English as a second language program shall address the affective, linguistic, and cognitive needs of English language learners as follows.

(1) Affective. English language learners shall be provided instruction using second language methods in English to introduce basic concepts of the school environment, which instills confidence, self-assurance, and a positive identity with their cultural heritages. The program shall address the history and cultural heritage associated with both the students' home language and the United States.

(2) Linguistic. English language learners shall be provided intensive instruction to develop proficiency in listening, speaking, reading, and writing in the English language. The instruction in academic content areas shall be structured to ensure that the students master the required essential knowledge and skills and higher-order thinking skills.

(3) Cognitive. English language learners shall be provided instruction in English in language arts, mathematics, science, and social studies using second language methods. The instruction in academic content areas shall be structured to ensure that the students master the required essential knowledge and skills and higher-order thinking skills.

(g) The English as a second language program shall be implemented with consideration for each English language learner's unique readiness level through one of the following program models.

(1) An English as a second language/content-based program model is an English program that serves only students identified as English language learners by providing a full-time teacher certified under the Texas Education Code (TEC), §29.061(c), to provide supplementary instruction for all content area instruction. The program integrates English as a second language instruction with subject matter instruction that focuses not only on learning a second language, but using that language as a medium to learn mathematics, science, social studies, or other academic subjects. Exiting of a student to an all-English program of instruction without English as a second language support will occur no earlier than the end of Grade 1 or, if the student enrolls in school during or after Grade 1, no earlier than two years or later than five years after the student enrolls in school. At the high school level, the English language learner receives sheltered instruction in all content areas. A student who has met exit criteria in accordance with §89.1225(h), (j), and (k) of this title may continue receiving services, but the school district will not receive the bilingual education allotment for that student.

(2) An English as a second language/pull-out program model is an English program that serves only students identified as English language learners by providing a part-time teacher certified under the TEC, §29.061(c), to provide English language arts instruction exclusively, while the student remains in a mainstream instructional arrangement in the remaining content areas. Instruction may be provided by the English as a second language teacher in a pull-out or inclusionary delivery model. Exiting of a student to an all-English program of instruction without English as a second language support will occur no earlier than the end of Grade 1 or, if the student enrolls in school during or after Grade 1, no earlier than two years or later than five years after the student enrolls in school. At the high school level, the English language learner receives sheltered instruction in all content areas. A student who has met exit criteria in accordance with §89.1225(h), (j), and (k) of this title may continue receiving services, but the school district will not receive the bilingual education allotment for that student.

(h) Except in the courses specified in subsection (i) of this section, English as a second language strategies, which may involve the use of the students' home language, may be provided in any of the courses or electives required for promotion or graduation to assist the English language learners to master the essential knowledge and skills for the required subject(s). The use of English as a second language strategies shall not impede the awarding of credit toward meeting promotion or graduation requirements.

(i) In subjects such as art, music, and physical education, the English language learners shall participate with their English-speaking peers in regular classes provided in the subjects. The school district shall ensure that students enrolled in bilingual education and English as a second language programs have a meaningful opportunity to participate with other students in all extracurricular activities.

(j) The required bilingual education or English as a second language programs shall be provided to every English language learner with parental approval until such time that the student meets exit criteria as described in §89.1225(h) of this title or graduates from high school.

Source: The provisions of this §89.1210 adopted to be effective September 1, 1996, 21 TexReg 5700; amended to be effective March 5, 1999, 24 TexReg 1383; amended to be effective April 18, 2002, 27 TexReg 3107; amended to be effective May 28, 2012, 37 TexReg 3822.

§89.1215. Home Language Survey.

(a) School districts shall conduct only one home language survey of each student. The home language survey shall be administered to each student new to the school district and to students previously enrolled who were not surveyed in the past. School districts shall require that the survey be signed by the student's parent or guardian for each student in prekindergarten through Grade 8, or by the student in Grades 9-12. The original copy of the survey shall be kept in the student's permanent record.

(b) The home language survey shall be administered in English and Spanish; for students of other language groups, the home language survey shall be translated into the home language whenever possible. The home language survey shall contain the following questions.

(1) "What language is spoken in your home most of the time?"

(2) "What language does your child speak most of the time?"

(c) Additional information may be collected by the school district and recorded on the home language survey.

(d) The home language survey shall be used to establish the student's language classification for determining whether the school district is required to provide a bilingual education or English as a second language program. If the response on the home language survey indicates that a language other than English is used, the student shall be tested in accordance with §89.1225 of this title (relating to Testing and Classification of Students).

Source: The provisions of this §89.1215 adopted to be effective September 1, 1996, 21 TexReg 5700; amended to be effective May 28, 2012, 37 TexReg 3822.

§89.1220. Language Proficiency Assessment Committee.

(a) School districts shall by local board policy establish and operate a language proficiency assessment committee. The school district shall have on file policy and procedures for the selection, appointment, and training of members of the language proficiency assessment committee(s).

(b) In school districts required to provide a bilingual education program, the language proficiency assessment committee shall be composed of the membership described in the Texas Education Code (TEC), §29.063. If the school district does not have an individual in one or more of the school job classifications required, the school district shall designate another professional staff member to serve on the language proficiency assessment committee. The school district may add other members to the committee in any of the required categories.

(c) In school districts and grade levels not required to provide a bilingual education program, the language proficiency assessment committee shall be composed of one or more professional personnel, a campus administrator, and a parent of an English language learner participating in the program designated by the school district.

(d) No parent serving on the language proficiency assessment committee shall be an employee of the school district.

(e) A school district shall establish and operate a sufficient number of language proficiency assessment committees to enable them to discharge their duties within 20 school days of the enrollment of English language learners.

(f) All members of the language proficiency assessment committee, including parents, shall be acting for the school district and shall observe all laws and rules governing confidentiality of information concerning individual students. The school district shall be responsible for the orientation and training of all members, including the parents, of the language proficiency assessment committee.

(g) Upon their initial enrollment and at the end of each school year, the language proficiency assessment committee shall review all pertinent information on all English language learners identified in accordance with §89.1225(f) of this title (relating to Testing and Classification of Students), and shall:

(1) designate the language proficiency level of each English language learner in accordance with the guidelines issued pursuant to §89.1210(b) and (e) of this title (relating to Program Content and Design);

(2) designate the level of academic achievement of each English language learner;

(3) designate, subject to parental approval, the initial instructional placement of each English language learner in the required program;

(4) facilitate the participation of English language learners in other special programs for which they are eligible provided by the school district with either state or federal funds; and

(5) classify students as English proficient in accordance with the criteria described in §89.1225(h) of this title, and recommend their exit from the bilingual education or English as a second language program.

(h) Before the administration of the state criterion-referenced test each year, the language proficiency assessment committee shall determine the appropriate assessment option for each English language learner as outlined in Chapter 101, Subchapter AA, of this title (relating to Commissioner's Rules Concerning the Participation of English Language Learners in State Assessments).

(i) The language proficiency assessment committee shall give written notice to the student's parent advising that the student has been classified as an English language learner and requesting approval to place the student in the required bilingual education or English as a second language program. The notice shall include information about the benefits of the bilingual education or English as a second language program for which the student has been recommended and that it is an integral part of the school program.

(j) Pending parent approval of an English language learner's entry into the bilingual education or English as a second language program recommended by the language proficiency assessment committee, the school district shall place the student in the recommended program, but may count only English language learners with parental approval for the bilingual education allotment.

(k) The language proficiency assessment committee shall monitor the academic progress of each student who has exited from a bilingual or English as a second language program during the first two years after exiting in accordance with the TEC, §29.0561.

(l) The student's permanent record shall contain documentation of all actions impacting the English language learner.

(1) Documentation shall include:

(A) the identification of the student as an English language learner;

(B) the designation of the student's level of language proficiency;

(C) the recommendation of program placement;

(D) parental approval of entry or placement into the program;

(E) the dates of entry into, and placement within, the program;

(F) assessment information as outlined in Chapter 101, Subchapter AA, of this title;

(G) additional instructional interventions provided to students to ensure adequate yearly progress;

(H) the date of exit from the program and parental approval; and

(I) the results of monitoring for academic success, including students formerly classified as English language learners, as required under the TEC, §29.063(c)(4).

(2) Current documentation as described in paragraph (1) of this subsection shall be forwarded in the same manner as other student records to another school district in which the student enrolls.

(m) A school district may identify, exit, or place a student in a program without written approval of the student's parent or guardian if:

(1) the student is 18 years of age or has had the disabilities of minority removed;

(2) reasonable attempts to inform and obtain permission from a parent or guardian have been made and documented;

(3) approval is obtained from:

(A) an adult who the school district recognizes as standing in parental relation to the student, including a foster parent or employee of a state or local governmental agency with temporary possession or control of the student; or

(B) the student, if no parent, guardian, or other responsible adult is available; or
(4) a parent or guardian has not objected in writing to the proposed entry, exit, or placement.

Source: The provisions of this §89.1220 adopted to be effective September 1, 1996, 21 TexReg 5700; amended to be effective March 5, 1999, 24 TexReg 1383; amended to be effective April 18, 2002, 27 TexReg 3107; amended to be effective September 17, 2007, 32 TexReg 6311; amended to be effective May 28, 2012, 37 TexReg 3822.

§89.1225. Testing and Classification of Students.

(a) For identifying English language learners, school districts shall administer to each student who has a language other than English as identified on the home language survey:

(1) in prekindergarten through Grade 1, an oral language proficiency test approved by the Texas Education Agency (TEA); and

(2) in Grades 2-12, a TEA-approved oral language proficiency test and the English reading and English language arts sections from a TEA-approved norm-referenced assessment, or another test approved by the TEA, unless the norm-referenced standardized achievement instrument is not valid in accordance with subsection (f)(2)(C) of this section.

(b) School districts that provide a bilingual education program shall administer an oral language proficiency test in the home language of the student who is eligible to be served in the bilingual education program. If the home language of the student is Spanish, the school district shall administer the Spanish version of the TEA-approved oral language proficiency test that was administered in English. If the home language of the student is other than Spanish, the school district shall determine the student's level of proficiency using informal oral language assessment measures.

(c) All the oral language proficiency testing shall be administered by professionals or paraprofessionals who are proficient in the language of the test and trained in language proficiency testing.

(d) The grade levels and the scores on each test that shall identify a student as an English language learner shall be established by the TEA. The commissioner of education shall review the approved list of tests, grade levels, and scores annually and update the list.

(e) Students with a language other than English shall be administered the required oral language proficiency test in prekindergarten through Grade 12 and norm-referenced standardized achievement instrument in Grades 2-12 within 20 school days of their enrollment.

(f) For entry into a bilingual education or English as a second language program, a student shall be identified as an English language learner using the following criteria.

(1) In prekindergarten through Grade 1, the student's score on the English oral language proficiency test is below the level designated for indicating limited English proficiency under subsection (d) of this section.

(2) In Grades 2-12:

(A) the student's score on the English oral language proficiency test is below the level designated for indicating limited English proficiency under subsection (d) of this section;

(B) the student's score on the English reading and/or English language arts sections of the TEA-approved norm-referenced standardized achievement instrument at his or her grade level is below the 40th percentile; or

(C) the student's ability in English is so limited that the administration, at his or her grade level, of the reading and language arts sections of a TEA-approved norm-referenced standardized achievement instrument or other test approved by the TEA is not valid.

(3) In the absence of data required in paragraph (2)(B) of this subsection, evidence that the student is not academically successful as defined in subsection (j) of this section is required.

(4) The admission review and dismissal (ARD) committee in conjunction with the language proficiency assessment committee shall determine an appropriate assessment instrument and designated level of performance for indicating limited English proficiency as required under subsection (d) of this section for students for whom those tests would be inappropriate as part of the individualized education program (IEP). The decision for entry into a bilingual education or English as a second language program shall be determined by the ARD committee in conjunction with the language proficiency assessment committee in accordance with §89.1220(g) of this title (relating to Language Proficiency Assessment Committee).

(g) Within 20 school days of their initial enrollment in the school district, students shall be identified as English language learners and enrolled into the required bilingual education or English as a second language program. Prekindergarten and kindergarten students preregistered in the spring shall be identified as English language learners and enrolled in the required bilingual education or English as a second language program within 20 school days of the start of the school year in the fall.

(h) For exit from a bilingual education or English as a second language program, a student may be classified as English proficient at the end of the school year in which a student would be able to participate equally in a general education, all-English instructional program. This determination shall be based upon all of the following:

(1) TEA-approved tests that measure the extent to which the student has developed oral and written language proficiency and specific language skills in English;

(2) satisfactory performance on the reading assessment instrument under the Texas Education Code (TEC), §39.023(a), or a TEA-approved English language arts assessment instrument administered in English, or a score at or above the 40th percentile on both the English reading and the English language arts sections of a TEA-approved norm-referenced standardized achievement instrument for a student who is enrolled in Grade 1 or 2; and

(3) TEA-approved criterion-referenced written tests when available, or other TEA-approved tests when criterion-referenced tests are not available, and the results of a subjective teacher evaluation.

(i) A student may not be exited from the bilingual education or English as a second language program in prekindergarten or kindergarten. A school district must ensure that English language learners are prepared to meet academic standards required by the TEC, §28.0211.

(j) For determining whether a student who has been exited from a bilingual education or English as a second language program is academically successful, the following criteria shall be used at the end of the school year:

(1) the student meets state performance standards in English on the criterion-referenced assessment instrument required in the TEC, §39.023, for the grade level as applicable; and

(2) the student has passing grades in all subjects and courses taken.

(k) The ARD committee in conjunction with the language proficiency assessment committee shall determine an appropriate assessment instrument and performance standard requirement for exit under subsection (h) of this section for students for whom those tests would be inappropriate as part of the IEP. The decision to exit a student who receives both special education and special language services from the bilingual education or English as a second language program is determined by the ARD committee in conjunction with the language proficiency assessment committee in accordance with applicable provisions of subsection (h) of this section.

(l) Notwithstanding §101.101 of this title (relating to Group-Administered Tests), all tests used for the purpose of identification, exit, and placement of students and approved by the TEA must be re-normed at least every eight years.

Source: The provisions of this §89.1225 adopted to be effective September 1, 1996, 21 TexReg 5700; amended to be effective April 18, 2002, 27 TexReg 3107; amended to be effective September 17, 2007, 32 TexReg 6311; amended to be effective May 28, 2012, 37 TexReg 3822.

§89.1227. Minimum Requirements for Dual Language Immersion Program Model.

(a) A dual language immersion program model must address all curriculum requirements specified in Chapter 74, Subchapter A, of this title (relating to Required Curriculum) to include foundation and enrichment areas, English language proficiency standards, and college and career readiness standards.

(b) A dual language immersion program model shall be a full-time program of academic instruction in English and another language.

(c) A minimum of 50% of instructional time must be provided in the language other than English.

(d) Implementation should:

(1) begin at prekindergarten, kindergarten, or Grade 1, as applicable;

(2) continue without interruption incrementally through the elementary grades whenever possible; and

(3) consider expansion to middle school and high school whenever possible.

(e) A dual language immersion program model shall be developmentally appropriate and based on current best practices research.

Source: The provisions of this §89.1227 adopted to be effective May 28, 2012, 37 TexReg 3822.

§89.1228. Dual Language Immersion Program Model Implementation.

(a) Student enrollment in a dual language immersion program model is optional.

(b) A dual language immersion program model must fully disclose candidate selection criteria and ensure that access to the program is not based on race, creed, color, religious affiliation, age, or disability.

(c) A school district must obtain written parental approval for student participation in the program sequence and model established by the school district.

(d) A school district implementing a dual language immersion program model must develop a policy on enrollment and continuation for students in this program model. The policy must address:

(1) eligibility criteria;

(2) program purpose;

(3) grade levels in which the program will be implemented;

(4) support of program goals as stated in §89.1210 of this title (relating to Program Content and Design); and

(5) expectations for students and parents.

Source: The provisions of this §89.1228 adopted to be effective May 28, 2012, 37 TexReg 3822.

§89.1230. Eligible Students with Disabilities.

(a) School districts shall implement assessment procedures that differentiate between language proficiency and handicapping conditions in accordance with Subchapter AA of this chapter (relating to Commissioner's Rules Concerning Special Education Services) and shall establish placement procedures that ensure that placement in a bilingual education or English as a second language program is not refused solely because the student has a disability.

(b) Admission, review, and dismissal committee members shall meet in conjunction with language proficiency assessment committee members to review the educational needs of each English language learner who qualifies for services in the special education program.

Source: The provisions of this §89.1230 adopted to be effective September 1, 1996, 21 TexReg 5700; amended to be effective March 5, 1999, 24 TexReg 1383; amended to be effective May 28, 2012, 37 TexReg 3822.

§89.1233. Participation of English Proficient Students.

School districts may enroll students who are not English language learners in the bilingual education program in accordance with the Texas Education Code, §29.058.

Source: The provisions of this §89.1233 adopted to be effective March 5, 1999, 24 TexReg 1383amended to be effective May 28, 2012, 37 TexReg 3822.

§89.1235. Facilities.

Bilingual education and English as a second language programs shall be located in the regular public schools of the school district rather than in separate facilities. In order to provide the required bilingual education or English as a second language programs, school districts may concentrate the programs at a limited number of facilities within the school district provided that the enrollment in those facilities shall not exceed 60% English language learners. Recent immigrant English language learners enrolled in newcomer centers shall return to home campuses no later than two years after initial enrollment in a newcomer program.

Source: The provisions of this §89.1235 adopted to be effective September 1, 1996, 21 TexReg 5700; amended to be effective May 28, 2012, 37 TexReg 3822.

§89.1240. Parental Authority and Responsibility.

(a) The parents shall be notified that their child has been classified as an English language learner and recommended for placement in the required bilingual education or English as a second language program. They shall be provided information describing the bilingual education or English as a second language program recommended, its benefits to the student, and its being an integral part of the school program to ensure that the parents understand the purposes and content of the program. The entry or placement of a student in the bilingual education or English as a second language program must be approved in writing by the student's parent. The parent's approval shall be considered valid for the student's continued participation in the required bilingual education or English as a second language program until the student meets the exit criteria described in §89.1225(h) of this title (relating to Testing and Classification of Students), graduates from high school, or the parent requests a change in program placement.

(b) The school district shall notify the student's parent of the student's reclassification as English proficient and his or her exit from the bilingual education or English as a second language program and acquire approval as required under the Texas Education Code, §29.056(a). Students meeting exit requirements may continue in the bilingual education or English as a second language program with parental approval but are not eligible for inclusion in the school district bilingual education allotment.

(c) The parent of a student enrolled in a school district that is required to offer bilingual education or English as a second language programs may appeal to the commissioner of education if the school district fails to comply with the law or the rules. Appeals shall be filed in accordance with Chapter 157 of this title (relating to Hearings and Appeals).

Source: The provisions of this §89.1240 adopted to be effective September 1, 1996, 21 TexReg 5700; amended to be effective April 18, 2002, 27 TexReg 3107; amended to be effective May 28, 2012, 37 TexReg 3822.

§89.1245. Staffing and Staff Development.

(a) School districts shall take all reasonable affirmative steps to assign appropriately certified teachers to the required bilingual education and English as a second language programs in accordance with the Texas Education Code (TEC), §29.061, concerning bilingual education and special language program teachers. School districts that are unable to secure a sufficient number of certified bilingual education and English as a second language teachers to provide the required programs, shall request emergency teaching permits or special assignment permits, as appropriate, in accordance with Chapter 230 of this title (relating to Professional Educator Preparation and Certification).

(b) School districts that are unable to employ a sufficient number of teachers, including part-time teachers, who meet the requirements of subsection (a) of this section for the bilingual education and English as a second language programs shall apply on or before November 1 for an exception to the bilingual education program as provided in §89.1207(a) of this title (relating to Exceptions and Waivers) or a waiver of the certification requirements in the English as a second language program as provided in §89.1207(b) of this title as needed.

(c) Teachers assigned to the bilingual education program and/or English as a second language program may receive salary supplements as authorized by the TEC, §42.153.

(d) School districts may compensate teachers and aides assigned to bilingual education and English as a second language programs for participation in continuing education programs designed to increase their skills or lead to bilingual education or English as a second language certification.

(e) School districts that are unable to staff their bilingual education and English as a second language programs with fully certified teachers shall use at least 10% of their bilingual education allotment for preservice and inservice training to improve the skills of the teachers who provide instruction in the alternative bilingual education program, instruction in English as a second language, and/or content area instruction in special classes for English language learners.

(f) The commissioner of education shall encourage school districts to cooperate with colleges and universities to provide training for teachers assigned to the bilingual education and/or English as a second language programs.

(g) The Texas Education Agency (TEA) shall develop, in collaboration with education service centers (ESCs), bilingual education training guides for implementing bilingual education and English as a second language training programs. The materials shall provide a framework for:

(1) developmentally appropriate bilingual education programs for early childhood through the elementary grades;

(2) affectively appropriate instruction in bilingual education and English as a second language programs in accordance with §89.1210(c)(1) and (f)(1) of this title (relating to Program Content and Design);

(3) linguistically appropriate bilingual education and English as a second language programs in accordance with §89.1210(c)(2) and (f)(2) of this title;

(4) cognitively appropriate programs for English language learners in accordance with §89.1210(c)(3) and (f)(3) of this title; and

(5) developmentally appropriate programs for English language learners identified as gifted and talented and English language learners with disabilities.

Source: The provisions of this §89.1245 adopted to be effective September 1, 1996, 21 TexReg 5700; amended to be effective March 5, 1999, 24 TexReg 1383; amended to be effective April 18, 2002, 27 TexReg 3107; amended to be effective May 28, 2012, 37 TexReg 3822.

§89.1250. Required Summer School Programs.

Summer school programs that are provided under the Texas Education Code (TEC), §29.060, for English language learners who will be eligible for admission to kindergarten or Grade 1 at the beginning of the next school year shall be implemented in accordance with this section.

(1) Purpose of summer school programs.

(A) English language learners shall have an opportunity to receive special instruction designed to prepare them to be successful in kindergarten and Grade 1.

(B) Instruction shall focus on language development and essential knowledge and skills appropriate to the level of the student.

(C) The program shall address the affective, linguistic, and cognitive needs of the English language learners in accordance with §89.1210(c) and (f) of this title (relating to Program Content and Design).

(2) Establishment of, and eligibility for, the program.

(A) Each school district required to offer a bilingual or English as a second language (ESL) program in accordance with the TEC, §29.053, shall offer the summer program.

(B) To be eligible for enrollment:

(i) a student must be eligible for admission to kindergarten or to Grade 1 at the beginning of the next school year and must be an English language learner; and

(ii) a parent or guardian must have approved placement of the English language learner in the required bilingual or ESL program following the procedures described in §89.1220(g) of this title (relating to Language Proficiency Assessment Committee) and §89.1225(a)-(f) of this title (relating to Testing and Classification of Students).

(C) Limited English proficiency shall be determined by evaluating students using an oral language proficiency test approved by the Texas Education Agency.

(3) Operation of the program.

(A) Enrollment is optional.

(B) The program shall be operated on a one-half day basis, a minimum of three hours each day, for eight weeks or the equivalent of 120 hours of instruction.

(C) The student/teacher ratio for the

program district-wide shall not exceed 18 to one.

(D) A school district is not required to provide transportation for the summer program.

(E) Teachers shall possess certification or endorsement as required in the TEC, §29.061, and §89.1245 of this title (relating to Staffing and Staff Development).

(F) Reporting of student progress shall be determined by the board of trustees. A summary of student progress shall be provided to parents at the conclusion of the program. This summary shall be provided to the student's teacher at the beginning of the next regular school term.

(G) A school district may join with other school districts in cooperative efforts to plan and implement programs.

(H) The summer school program shall not substitute for any other program required to be provided during the regular school term, including those required in the TEC, §29.153.

(4) Funding and records for programs.

(A) A school district shall use state and local funds for program purposes. School districts may use federal funds, consistent with requirements for the expenditure of federal funds, for the program.

(i) Available funds appropriated by the legislature for the support of summer school programs provided under the TEC, §29.060, shall be allocated to school districts in accordance with this subsection.

(ii) Funding for the summer school program shall be on a unit basis in such an allocation system to ensure a pupil/teacher ratio of not more than 18 to one. The numbers of students required to earn units shall be established by the commissioner. The allotment per unit shall be determined by the commissioner based on funds available.

(iii) Any school district required to offer the program under paragraph (2)(A) of this subsection that has less than ten students district-wide desiring to participate is not required to operate the program. However, those school districts must demonstrate that they have aggressively attempted to encourage student participation.

(iv) Payment to school districts for summer school programs shall be based on units employed. This information must be submitted in a manner and according to a schedule established by the commissioner in order for a school district to be eligible for funding.

(B) A school district shall maintain records of eligibility, attendance, and progress of students.

Source: The provisions of this §89.1250 adopted to be effective September 1, 1996, 21 TexReg 5700; amended to be effective April 18, 2002, 27 TexReg 3107; amended to be effective February 17, 2005, 30 TexReg 709; amended to be effective September 17, 2007, 32 TexReg 6311; amended to be effective May 28, 2012, 37 TexReg 3822.

§89.1265. Evaluation.

(a) All school districts required to conduct a bilingual education or English as a second language program shall conduct periodic assessment in the languages of instruction to determine program impact and student outcomes in all subject areas.

(b) Annual reports of educational performance shall reflect the academic progress in either language of the English language learners, the extent to which they are becoming proficient in English, the number of students who have been exited from the bilingual education and English as a second language programs, and the number of teachers and aides trained and the frequency, scope, and results of the training. These reports shall be retained at the district level.

(c) School districts shall report to parents the progress of their child as a result of participation in the program offered to English language learners in English and the home language at least annually.

(d) Each school year, the principal of each school campus, with the assistance of the campus level committee, shall develop, review, and revise the campus improvement plan described in the Texas Education Code, §11.253, for the purpose of improving student performance for English language learners.

Source: The provisions of this §89.1265 adopted to be effective September 1, 1996, 21 TexReg 5700; amended to be effective April 18, 2002, 27 TexReg 3107; amended to be effective May 28, 2012, 37 TexReg 3822.

§89.1267. Standards for Evaluation of Dual Language Immersion Program Models.

(a) A school district implementing a dual language immersion program must conduct annual formative and summative evaluations collecting a full range of data to determine program impact on student academic success.

(b) The success of a dual language immersion program is evident by students in the program demonstrating high levels of language proficiency in English and the other language and mastery of the Texas essential knowledge and skills for the foundation and enrichment areas. Indicators of success may include scores on statewide student assessments in English, statewide student assessments in Spanish (if appropriate), norm-referenced standardized achievement tests in both languages, and/or language proficiency tests in both languages.

Source: The provisions of this §89.1267 adopted to be effective May 28, 2012, 37 TexReg 3822.

§89.1269. General Standards for Recognition of Dual Language Immersion Program Models.

(a) School district recognition. An exceptional dual language immersion program model may be recognized by the local school district board of trustees using the following criteria.

(1) A school district must exceed the minimum requirements stated in §89.1227 of this title (relating to Minimum Requirements for Dual Language Immersion Program Model).

(2) A school district must not receive the lowest performance rating in the state accountability system.

(3) A school district must not be identified for any stage of intervention for the district's bilingual and/or English as a second language program under the performance-based monitoring system.

(4) A school district must meet the adequate yearly progress participation and performance criteria in reading and mathematics for the English language learner student group under Elementary and Secondary Education Act (ESEA) regulations.

(b) Student recognition. A student participating in a dual language immersion program model may be recognized by the program and its local school district board of trustees using the following criteria. (1) The student must meet or exceed statewide student assessment passing standards, as required by the Texas Education Code, §39.024, in all subject areas at the appropriate grade level.

(2) The student must meet or exceed expected levels of language proficiency on a recognized language proficiency test from the list of tests approved by the commissioner of education.

Source: The provisions of this §89.1269 adopted to be effective May 28, 2012, 37 TexReg 3822

Chapter 97. Planning and Accountability

Subchapter AA. Accountability and Performance Monitoring

§97.1001. Accountability Rating System.

(a) The rating standards established by the commissioner of education under Texas Education Code (TEC), §§39.052(a) and (b)(1)(A); 39.053, 39.054, 39.201, and 39.203(a) and (c)(1), as those sections existed before amendment by House Bill 5, 83rd Texas Legislature, Regular Session, 2013; §39.055, as that section existed before amendment by Senate Bill 306, 83rd Texas Legislature, Regular Session, 2013; §39.116; and §29.081(e), shall be used to evaluate the performance of districts, campuses, and charter schools. The indicators, standards, and procedures used to determine ratings will be annually published in official Texas Education Agency publications. These publications will be widely disseminated and cover the following procedures:

(1) indicators, standards, and procedures used to determine district ratings;

(2) indicators, standards, and procedures used to determine campus ratings;

(3) indicators, standards, and procedures used to determine Distinction Designations; and

(4) procedures for submitting a rating appeal.

(b) The procedures by which districts, campuses, and charter schools are rated and acknowledged for 2013 are based upon specific criteria and calculations, which are described in excerpted sections of the 2013 Accountability Manual provided in this subsection.

Figure: 19 TAC §97.1001(b)

(c) Ratings may be revised as a result of investigative activities by the commissioner as authorized under TEC, §39.056 and §39.057.

(d) The specific criteria and calculations used in the accountability manual are established annually by the commissioner of education and communicated to all school districts and charter schools.

(e) The specific criteria and calculations used in the annual accountability manual adopted for school years prior to 2013-2014 remain in effect for all purposes, including accountability, data standards, and audits, with respect to those school years.

Statutory Authority: The provisions of this §97.1001 issued under the Texas Education Code, §§39.052(a) and (b)(1)(A); 39.053, 39.054, 39.201, and 39.203(a) and (c)(1), as those sections existed before amendment by House Bill 5, 83rd Texas Legislature, Regular Session, 2013; §39.055, as that section existed before amendment by Senate Bill 306, 83rd Texas Legislature, Regular Session, 2013; §39.116; and §29.081(e).

Source: The provisions of this §97.1001 adopted to be effective June 13, 2000,

25 TexReg 5625; amended to be effective October 3, 2005, 30 TexReg 6265; amended to be effective July 30, 2006, 31 TexReg 5800; amended to be effective July 26, 2007, 32 TexReg 4549; amended to be effective July 31, 2008, 33 TexReg 5923; amended to be effective July 22, 2009, 34 TexReg 4734; amended to be effective July 26, 2010, 35 TexReg 6522; amended to be effective July 28, 2011, 36 TexReg 4657; amended to be effective August 7, 2013, 38 TexReg 4891.

§97.1004. Adequate Yearly Progress.

(a) In accordance with the federal No Child Left Behind Act and Texas Education Code, §§7.055(b)(32), 39.073, and 39.075, as these sections existed before amendment by House Bill 3, 81st Texas Legislature, 2009, all public school campuses, school districts, and the state are evaluated for Adequate Yearly Progress (AYP). Districts, campuses, and the state are required to meet AYP criteria on three measures: reading/English language arts, mathematics, and either graduation rate (for high schools and districts) or attendance rate (for elementary and middle/junior high schools). The performance of a school district, campus, or the state is reported through indicators of AYP status established by the commissioner of education.

(b) The determination of AYP for school districts and charter schools in 2012 is based on specific criteria and calculations, which are described in excerpted sections of the 2012 AYP Guide provided in this subsection.

Figure: 19 TAC §97.1004(b)

(c) The specific criteria and calculations used in AYP are established annually by the commissioner of education and communicated to all school districts and charter schools.

(d) The specific criteria and calculations used in the AYP guide adopted for the school years prior to 2012-2013 remain in effect for all purposes, including accountability, data standards, and audits, with respect to those school years.

Statutory Authority: The provisions of this §97.1004 issued under the Texas Education Code, §§7.055(b)(32) and 39.073 and 39.075(a)(4), as those sections existed before amendment by HB 3, 81st Texas Legislature, 2009.

Source: The provisions of this §97.1004 adopted to be effective July 14, 2005, 30 TexReg 3995; amended to be effective November 3, 2005, 30 TexReg 7036; amended to be effective September 20, 2006, 31 TexReg 7988; amended to be effective August 8, 2007, 32 TexReg 4753; amended to be effective September 30, 2008, 33 TexReg 8167; amended to be effective September 1, 2009, 34 TexReg 5912; amended to be effective October 31, 2010, 35 TexReg 9500; amended to be effective August 2, 2011, 36 TexReg 4799; amended to be effective September 2, 2012, 37 TexReg 6592.

§97.1005. Performance-Based Monitoring Analysis System.

(a) In accordance with Texas Education Code, §7.028(a), the purpose of the Performance-Based Monitoring Analysis System (PBMAS) is to report annually on the performance of school districts and charter schools in selected program areas: bilingual education/English as a Second Language, career and technical education, special education, and certain Title programs under the federal No Child Left Behind Act. The performance of a school district or charter school is reported through indicators of student performance and program effectiveness and corresponding performance levels established by the commissioner of education.

(b) The assignment of performance levels for school districts and charter schools in the 2013 PBMAS is based on specific criteria and calculations, which are described in excerpted sections of the PBMAS 2013 Manual provided in this subsection.

Figure: 19 TAC §97.1005(b)

(c) The specific criteria and calculations used in the PBMAS are established annually by the commissioner of education and communicated to all school districts and charter schools.

(d) The specific criteria and calculations used in the annual PBMAS manual adopted for the school years prior to 2013-2014 remain in effect for all purposes, including accountability and performance monitoring, data standards, and audits, with respect to those school years.

Statutory Authority: The provisions of this §97.1005 issued under the Texas Education Code, §§7.028(a); 29.001(5); 29.010(a); 39.051; 39.052; 39.054 and 39.056, as those sections existed before amendment by House Bill 5, 83rd Texas Legislature, Regular Session, 2013; §39.057, as that section existed before amendment by House Bill 5 and Senate Bill 123, 83rd Texas Legislature, Regular Session, 2013; §39.058; and §§39.102-39.104.

Source: The provisions of this §97.1005 adopted to be effective June 5, 2005, 30 TexReg 3098; amended to be effective November 24, 2005, 30 TexReg 7737; amended to be effective September 20, 2006, 31 TexReg 7989; amended to be effective August 8, 2007, 32 TexReg4754; amended to be effective July 15, 2008, 33 TexReg 5525; amended to be effective August 25, 2009, 34 TexReg 5690; amended to be effective August 4, 2010, 35 TexReg 6651; amended to be effective July 28, 2011, 36 TexReg 4658; amended to be effective August 9, 2012, 37 TexReg 5743; amended to be effective August 22, 2013, 38 TexReg 5257.

Chapter 101. Assessment

Subchapter AA. Commissioner's Rules Concerning the Participation of English Language Learners in State Assessments

Statutory Authority: The provisions of this Subchapter AA issued under the Texas Education Code, §§39.023, 39.025, and 39.027, unless otherwise noted.

Division 1. Assessments of English Language Proficiency and Academic Content for English Language Learners

§101.1001. Scope of Rules.

(a) Except as specified in subsection (b) of this section, the provisions of this division shall apply to all students.

(b) The provisions of §101.1005(b)(1)-(2) of this title (relating to Assessments of Achievement in Academic Content Areas and Courses) and §101.1007 of this title (relating to Assessment Provisions for Graduation) shall apply beginning with students first enrolled in Grade 9 or below in the 2011-2012 school year.

Source: The provisions of this §101.1001 adopted to be effective December 22, 2011, 36 TexReg 8521.

§101.1003. English Language Proficiency Assessments.

(a) In Kindergarten-Grade 12, an English language learner (ELL), as defined by the Texas Education Code (TEC), Chapter 29, Subchapter B, as a student of limited English proficiency, shall be administered state-identified English language proficiency assessments annually in listening, speaking, reading, and writing to fulfill state requirements under the TEC, Chapter 39, Subchapter B, and federal requirements.

(b) In rare cases, the admission, review, and dismissal (ARD) committee in conjunction with the language proficiency assessment committee (LPAC) may determine that it is not appropriate for an ELL who receives special education services to participate in an English language proficiency assessment required by subsection (a) of this section for reasons associated with the student's particular disability. The ARD committee shall document the decisions and justifications in the student's individualized education program, and the LPAC shall document the decisions and justifications in the student's permanent record file.

(c) In the case of an ELL who receives special education services, the ARD committee in conjunction with the LPAC shall determine and document the need for allowable testing accommodations in accordance with administrative procedures established by the Texas Education Agency.

Source: The provisions of this §101.1003 adopted to be effective December 22, 2011, 36 TexReg 8521.

§101.1005. Assessments of Achievement in Academic Content Areas and Courses.

(a) The language proficiency assessment committee (LPAC) shall select the appropriate assessment option for each English language learner (ELL) in accordance with this subchapter. For each ELL who receives special education services, the student's admission, review, and dismissal (ARD) committee in conjunction with the student's LPAC shall select the appropriate assessments. The LPAC shall document the decisions and justifications in the student's permanent record file, and the ARD committee shall document the decisions and justifications in the student's individualized education program. Assessment decisions shall be made on an individual student basis and in accordance with administrative procedures established by the Texas Education Agency (TEA).

(b) Except as provided by subsection (c) of this section, an ELL shall participate in the Grades 3-8 and end-of-course assessments as required by the Texas Education Code (TEC), §39.023(c). Except as specified in paragraphs (1)-(3) of this subsection, an ELL shall be administered the general form of the English-version state assessment.

(1) A Spanish-speaking ELL in Grades 3-5 may be administered the state's Spanish-version assessment if an assessment in Spanish will provide the most appropriate measure of the student's academic progress.

(2) An ELL in Grade 3 or higher may be administered the linguistically accommodated English version of the state's mathematics, science, or social studies assessment if:

(A) a Spanish-version assessment does not exist or is not the most appropriate measure of the student's academic progress;

(B) the student has not yet demonstrated English language proficiency in reading as determined by the assessment under §101.1003 of this title (relating to English Language Proficiency Assessments); and

(C) the student has been enrolled in U.S. schools for three school years or less or qualifies as an unschooled asylee or refugee enrolled in U.S. schools for five school years or less.

(3) In certain cases, an ELL who receives special education services may, as a result of his or her particular disabling condition, qualify to be administered an alternative assessment instrument based on alternative achievement standards.

(c) In accordance with the TEC, §39.027(a), an unschooled asylee or refugee who meets the criteria of paragraphs (1)-(3) of this subsection shall be granted an exemption from an administration of an assessment instrument under the TEC, §39.023(a), (b), or (l). This exemption will only apply during the school year an unschooled asylee or refugee is first enrolled in a U.S. public school. An unschooled asylee or refugee is a student who:

(1) enrolled in a U.S. school as an asylee as defined by 45 Code of Federal Regulations §400.41 or a refugee as defined by 8 United States Code §1101;

(2) has a Form I-94 Arrival/Departure record, or a successor document, issued by the United States Citizenship and Immigration Services that is stamped with "Asylee," "Refugee," or "Asylum"; and

(3) as a result of inadequate schooling outside the United States, lacks the necessary foundation in the essential knowledge and skills of the curriculum prescribed under the TEC, §28.002, as determined by the LPAC.

(d) For purposes of LPAC determinations in subsection (c) of this section, inadequate schooling outside the United States is defined as little or no formal schooling outside the United States such that the asylee or refugee lacked basic literacy in his or her primary language upon enrollment in school in the United States.

(e) The LPAC shall, in conjunction with the ARD committee if the ELL is receiving special education services under the TEC, Chapter 29, Subchapter A, determine and document any allowable testing accommodations for assessments under this section in accordance with administrative procedures established by the TEA.

(f) An ELL whose parent or guardian has declined the services required by the TEC, Chapter 29, Subchapter B, is not eligible for special assessment, accommodation, or accountability provisions made available to ELLs on the basis of limited English proficiency.

(g) School districts may administer the assessment of academic skills in Spanish to a student who is not identified as limited English proficient but who participates in a bilingual program if the LPAC determines the assessment in Spanish to be the most appropriate measure of the student's academic progress.

(h) Policies for including the academic performance of an ELL in state and federal accountability measures, which will take into account the second language acquisition developmental needs of this student population, shall be delineated in the official TEA publications required by Chapter 97 of this title (relating to Planning and Accountability).

Statutory Authority: The provisions of this §101.1005 issued under the Texas Education Code, §39.023 and §39.027.

Source: The provisions of this §101.1005 adopted to be effective December 22, 2011, 36 TexReg 8521; amended to be effective March 27, 2013, 38 TexReg 1972.

§101.1007. Assessment Provisions for Graduation.

(a) Although an English language learner (ELL) shall not be exempt from taking an end-of-course assessment for reasons associated with limited English proficiency or inadequate schooling outside the United States, special provisions under subsection (b) of this section shall apply to an ELL enrolled in an English I or II course or an English for Speakers of Other Languages (ESOL) I or II course if the ELL:

(1) has been enrolled in U.S. schools for three school years or less or qualifies as an unschooled asylee or refugee enrolled in U.S. schools for five school years or less; and

(2) the student has not yet demonstrated English language proficiency in reading as determined by the assessment under §101.1003 of this title (relating to English Language Proficiency Assessments).

(b) Concerning the applicable English I or English II assessment in which the student is enrolled, an ELL who meets the eligibility criteria in subsection (a) of this section shall not be required to:

(1) use the assessment score as part of the cumulative score for graduation;

(2) retake the assessment each time it is administered if the student passes the course but fails to achieve the established minimum score on the assessment; or

(3) have the score on the assessment count for 15% of the student's final grade in the course.

Source: The provisions of this §101.1007 adopted to be effective December 22, 2011, 36 TexReg 8521.

Division 2. Grade 10 and Exit-Level Assessments for Certain English Language Learners

§101.1021. Scope of Rules.

Beginning with the 2011-2012 school year, the provisions of this division shall apply only to students first enrolled in Grade 9 or higher prior to the 2011-2012 school year, or first enrolled in Grade 10 or higher in the 2011-2012 school year.

Source: The provisions of this §101.1021 adopted to be effective December 22, 2011, 36 TexReg 8521.

§101.1023. English Language Learners at the Exit Level.

English language learners (ELLs) are not eligible for an exemption from exit-level testing requirements for graduation on the basis of limited English proficiency. However, ELLs who are recent immigrants may be granted a postponement of the administration of the exit-level assessment during their first 12 months of enrollment in U.S. schools. A postponement is not permitted if a student would otherwise not be afforded the opportunity to take the exit-level assessments at least one time before the student's scheduled graduation date. The language proficiency assessment committee shall document the reason for the postponement in the student's permanent record file.

Source: The provisions of this §101.1023 adopted to be effective December 22, 2011, 36 TexReg 8521.

§101.1025. English Language Learners in Grade 10.

(a) In accordance with paragraphs (1)-(3) of this subsection, certain English language learners (ELLs) who have had inadequate schooling outside the United States may be eligible for a limited English proficiency (LEP) exemption from the assessment of academic skills during a period not to exceed their first three school years of enrollment in U.S. schools.

(1) An ELL who achieves a rating of advanced high on the state-administered English language proficiency assessment in reading under §101.1003 of this title (relating to English Language Proficiency Assessments) during the student's first school year of enrollment in U.S. schools is not eligible for an exemption in the second or third school year of enrollment in U.S. schools. An ELL who achieves a rating of advanced or advanced high on this assessment during the student's second school year of enrollment in U.S. schools is not eligible for an exemption in the third school year of enrollment in U.S. schools.

(2) During the first school year of enrollment in U.S. schools, the student may be granted a LEP exemption if the language proficiency assessment committee (LPAC) determines that the student has not had the schooling outside the United States necessary to provide the foundation of learning that Texas schools require and measure on the assessment, whether the foundation be in knowledge of the English language or specific academic skills and concepts in the subjects assessed.

(3) During the second and third school year of enrollment in U.S. schools, the student whose schooling outside the United States was inadequate may be granted a LEP exemption if the LPAC determines that the student lacks the academic language proficiency in English necessary for an assessment of academic skills in English to measure the student's academic progress in a valid, reliable manner.

(b) The reason for a LEP exemption granted to a student shall be documented by the LPAC in the student's permanent record file.

(c) Students exempted under subsection (a) of this section shall be administered assessments in subjects and grades required by federal law and regulations in accordance with linguistically accommodated testing procedures delineated in the test administration materials.

(d) An ELL whose parent or guardian has declined the services required by the Texas Education Code, Chapter 29, Subchapter B, is not eligible for an exemption under this section or an exit-level test postponement under §101.1023 of this title (relating to English Language Learners at the Exit Level).

Source: The provisions of this §101.1025 adopted to be effective December 22, 2011, 36 TexReg 8521.

APPENDIX ★

ELPS District Implementation Checklist

Goal	We will have met this goal when...	Steps	Person(s) Responsible	Dates/ Deadlines
Administrators and specialists integrate ELPS into ongoing professional development and evaluation.				
Staff understands the importance of TELPAS and other formal assessments to identify language levels of ELLs.				
Staff understands the need for ELLs to develop social and academic English.				
Staff understands methods for providing linguistically accommodated instruction for ELLs.				
Staff understands cross curricular student expectations.				
Staff develops a plan for systematic academic language development for ELLs.				
Teachers include ELPS in lesson plans in core content areas.				

Two Key Questions for Assessing Quality Instruction for ELLs

Do English language learners understand the key content concepts (aligned to TEKS)?	Are English language learners developing their ability to read, write, listen, and speak using academic English about content concepts (in ways described in the ELPS)?

ELPS Aligned Walk-Through Observation

Observer: **Teacher:**

Class: **Date:**

Indicator	Comments/Questions
❍ Content and language objectives posted	
❍ Evidence of explicit vocabulary instruction	
❍ Evidence of teacher use of variety of techniques to make content comprehensible	
❍ Evidence of reading and writing in academic English	
❍ Evidence of student-student interaction focusing on lesson concepts	
❍ Specific instructional interventions for ELLs appropriate to students' language levels, e.g., sentence stems, native language resources, word banks, low risk environment for language production, etc.	

ELPS Aligned Lesson Observation

Indicator	Comments/Questions
❍ Teacher posts and explains clearly defined content objectives aligned to the TEKS.	
❍ Teacher posts and explains clearly defined language objectives aligned to the ELPS.	
❍ Teacher clearly communicates key concepts, words, phrases, and directions for instructional tasks to ELLs (using visuals, gestures, native language resources, etc., as needed).	
❍ Teacher differentiates instruction (alters instruction, language demands, and assessment) to align with the students' language development level.	
❍ Teacher provides verbal and procedural scaffolding for ELLs, e.g., sentence stems, modeling, instruction in strategies etc.	
❍ Teacher provides opportunities for students to read and write using academic English.	
❍ Teacher provides opportunities for ELLs to listen and speak using academic and social English.	
❍ ELLs demonstrate understanding of content and language objectives.	

ELPS Aligned Lesson Observation Coaching Tool

Indicator	Comments/Questions
Teacher posts and explains clearly defined content objectives aligned to the TEKS.	• Are the objectives posted? • Do ELLs understand the objectives? • Are the objectives aligned with the TEKS? • Does the lesson align with the objectives?
Teacher posts and explains clearly defined language objectives aligned to the ELPS .	• Are the objectives posted? • Do ELLs understand the objectives? • Are the objectives aligned with the ELPS? • Does the lesson align with the objectives?
Teacher clearly communicates key concepts, words, phrases, and directions for instructional tasks to English learners using visuals, gestures, native language resources, etc. as needed.	• Do ELLs understand the key concepts? • Does the teacher explicitly teach key concept area vocabulary? • Does the teacher teach ELLs specific words and phrases necessary for instructional tasks? • Do ELLs show a clear understanding of instructional tasks?
Teacher differentiates instruction (alters instruction, language demands, and assessment) to align with the students' language development level.	• Is the teacher aware of the students' language levels? • Are instructions, assignments, and assessments appropriate for the students' level of language development?
Teacher provides verbal and procedural scaffolding for ELLs, e.g., sentence stems, modeling, instruction in strategies etc.	• Does the teacher provide models, examples, and structures that enable ELLs to work toward independence? • Do ELLs use specific strategies when they need clarification about content or language?
Teacher provides opportunities for students to read and write using academic English.	• Do ELLs read academic English during the lesson? • Do ELLs write during the lesson? • Are ELLs supported in finding ways to enable them to read and write during the lesson?
Teacher provides opportunities for ELLs to listen and speak using academic and social English.	• Do ELLs listen and speak using social English? • Do ELLs use content area vocabulary during classroom interactions? • Do ELLs use academic English structures during classroom interactions?
ELLs demonstrate understanding of content and language objectives.	• Are ELLs assessed for understanding of content and language throughout the lesson?

Language Objectives Aligned to Cross Curricular Student Expectations

(subsection c)

Learning Strategies

1A: Use what they know about ___ to predict the meaning of ...

1B: Check how well they are able to say ...

1C: Use ___ to learn new vocabulary about...

1D: Use strategies such as ___ to discuss...

1E: Use and reuse the words/phrases ___ in a discussion/writing activity about...

1F: Use the phrase ___ to learn the meaning of ...

1G: Use formal/informal English to describe...

1H: Use strategies such as ___ to learn the meaning of...

Listening

2A: Recognize correct pronunciation of ....

2B: Recognize sounds used in the words ...

2C: Identify words and phrases heard in a discussion about ...

2D: Check for understanding by ..../Seek help by ...

2E: Use __ (media source) to learn/review ....

2G: Describe general meaning, main points, and details heard in ...

2H: Identify implicit ideas and information heard in ...

2I: Demonstrate listening comprehension by...

Speaking

3A: Pronounce the words ___ correctly.

3B: Use new vocabulary about ___ in stories, pictures, descriptions, and/or classroom communication ...

3C: Speak using a variety of types of sentence stems about ...

3D: Speak using the words___ about...

3E: Share in cooperative groups about ...

3F: Ask and give information using the words...

3G: Express opinions, ideas and feelings about ___ using the words/phrases...

3H: Narrate, describe and explain ....

3I: Use formal/informal English to say ...

3J: Respond orally to information from a variety of media sources about...

Reading

4A: Identify relationships between sounds and letters by...

4B: Recognize directionality of English text.

4C: Recognize the words/phrases....

4D: Use prereading supports such as___ to understand ...

4E: Read materials about ___ with support of simplified text/visuals/word banks as needed.

4F: Use visual and contextual supports to read ...

4G: Show comprehension of English text about ...

4H: Demonstrate comprehension of text read silently by...

4I: Show comprehension of text about ___ through basic reading skills such as ...

4J: Show comprehension of text/graphic sources about ___ through inferential skills such as ...

4K: Show comprehension of text about ___ through analytical skills such as ...

Writing

5A: Learn relationships between sounds and letters when writing about ...

5B: Write using newly acquired vocabulary about...

5C: Spell English words such as ...

5D: Edit writing about ...

5E: Use simple and complex sentences to write about ...

5F: Write using a variety of sentence frames and selected vocabulary about ...

5G: Narrate, describe, and explain in writing about ...

Differentiating by Language Level Instructional Planning Guide

Beginners	Intermediate	Advanced/ Advanced High
• Visuals for classroom vocabulary and academic concepts • Native language and adapted grade level text • Short, simple sentence stems • Preteaching social and academic vocabulary • Peer interaction (same language peer as needed) • Extensive verbal scaffolding • Adapted writing tasks with drawing and scaffolding • Gestures (basic and academic concepts) • Modeling • Graphic organizers • Manipulatives • Preteaching functional language (stems for social interaction) • Pronunciation of social/ academic language • Slower, simplified speech • Instruction in high frequency concrete social vocabulary • Use of native language for key concepts • Verbal cues • Chunking use of information in print • Word bank	• Visuals for academic vocabulary and concepts • Adapted grade level text • Sentence stems • Preteaching academic Vocabulary • Peer Interaction • Verbal scaffolding • Adapted writing tasks with scaffolding • Gestures for memorization of academic concepts • Modeling • Graphic organizers • Manipulatives	• Visuals for academic vocabulary and concepts • Grade-level text • Complex sentence stems • Preteaching low-frequency academic vocabulary • Peer interaction • Verbal scaffolding as needed • Grade level writing tasks • Gestures for memorization of academic concepts • Modeling • Graphic organizers • Manipulatives

Texas Education Agency References

Names of useful webpages on the TEA website

Accommodation Resources

Accountability Monitoring Intervention Guidance and Resources

Annual Measurable Achievement Objectives (AMAOs)

Best Practices Clearinghouse

Bilingual/ESL Education

Currently Approved Innovative Courses

Districts with Campuses Required to Engage in the Texas Accountability Interventions

Division of Program Monitoring and Interventions

Dyslexia Requirements for Educator Preparation Programs

Dropout Prevention and Recovery Resources

Educator Certification

ELL Solutions Forum, Best Practices Clearinghouse

Equity in Gifted/Talented (G/T) Education

Gifted/Talented Education

Grants Administration and Federal Program Compliance

Information on State Assessments for English Language Learners

Integrated Intervention Guidance and Resources

Language Proficiency Assessment Committee (LPAC) Assessment Resources

Mailing List Administrator (LISTSERV)

PBMAS Manuals

Performance-Based Monitoring

Program Monitoring and Intervention

Project Share

Response to Intervention

Services for Texas Students with Disabilities, Ages 3-5

Standards and Programs Rider Funded Projects

State Board for Educator Certification – Administrative Rules

Student Assessment

TEA Long Range Plan for Technology

Texas Accountability and Intervention System (TAIS)

Texas Center for District and School Support (TCDSS)

Texas Educational Agency – Administrative Rules

Texas English Language Learners Portal

Texas Essential Knowledge and Skills

Texas Project First

Texas Prekindergarten Guidelines

Title I, Part C - Texas Migrant Education Program

Title III, Part A – ENGLISH Language Acquisition, Language Enhancement, and Academic Achievement Act

To the Administrator Addressed

Texas Education Agency References

Names of useful manuals and guidance documents published by TEA

2012-2014 Fall ELL Assessment Update (TEA presentation PPT)

2013 Guide to Annual Measurable Achievement Objectives

Accountability Interventions System (TAIS) Guidance

Best Practices Clearinghouse Newsletter

Dyslexia Handbook

District and Campus Coordinator Manual (DCCM)

Early Childhood Outcomes and Prekindergarten Guidelines Alignment Document

Educator Guide to TELPAS

ELPS Academy Linguistic Instructional Alignment Guide

Guidance Related to ARD Committee and LPAC Collaboration

House Bill 5

LPAC Additional Resources

LPAC Decision-Making Resources (guides and PPTs)

LPAC Framework Manual

Performance-Based Monitoring Manual

Process for Exiting Students Receiving Special Education Services from Bilingual/ESL Programs

Response to Intervention Guidance Document

Student Attendance Accounting Handbook (2013-2014) – Section 6

TEA School Transportation Allotment Handbook

Texas Prekindergarten Guidelines

Texas State Plan for the Education of Gifted/Talented Students

TELPAS Rater Manual

TELPAS Reading Test Administrator Manual

Title III Guidance Document

Names of useful websites outside of TEA

Advancing Improvement in Education (AIE)

Center for Applied Linguistics

Center for Research on the Educational Achievement and Teaching of English Language Learners (CREATE)

Center on Instruction

Colorín Colorado

Cultural Orientation Resource Center

Intercultural Development Research Association (IDRA)

National Clearinghouse for English Language Acquisition

Pearson Education

Project GLAD

Seidlitz Education

Quality Teaching for English Learners (QTEL)

Sheltered Instruction Observation Protocol (SIOP)

Texas Training Center

The National Center for Culturally Responsive Educational Systems – website

TPRS Publishing

USDE Office of Migrant Education

Establishment of Programs

Program Models

Program Goals

Program Monitoring and Evaluation

Enrollment and Registration

Funding

Language Proficiency Assessment Committee (LPAC)

Summer School

Accommodations for ELLs

Beginning/Intermediate ELLs

Community Engagement/Parental Involvement

Facilities for ELLs

Required Training & Professional Development

Staffing and Certification

Required Curriculum & Best Practices

English Language Proficiency Standards (ELPS)/ Proficiency Level Descriptors (PLDs)

Sheltered Instruction

ELLs Served by Other Programs

ELLs with Unique Characteristics

State of Texas Assessment of Academic Readiness (STAAR)/End-Of-Course (EOC) Testing

Texas English Language Proficiency Assessment System (TELPAS)

Federal Accountability

State Accountability

Dropout/Personal Graduation Plans (PGP)/Graduation

School Improvement

References

Alford, B., & Niño, M.C. (2011). *Leading academic achievement for English language learners.* Thousand Oaks: CA. Corwin.

Castillo, M. (2012). Guiding educators to Praxis: Moving teachers beyond theory to practice. ProQuest, LLC., Ed. D. Dissertation, Arizona State University.

Cummins, J. (1991). *Interdependence of first -and second- language proficiency in bilingual children. Language processing in bilingual children*, 70-89.

Echevarria, J., & Hasbrouck, J. (2009). Response to Intervention and English learners. Houston, TX: Center for Research on the Educational Achievement and Teaching of English Language Learners (CREATE). Retrieved June, 22, 2011.

Escamilla, K., Hopewell, S., Butvilofsky, S., Sparrow, W., Soltero-González, L., Ruiz-Figueroa, O., & Escamilla, M. (2013). *Biliteracy from the start; Literacy Squared© in action.* Philadelphia: PA. Caslon Publishing.

Gay, G. (2002). Preparing for culturally responsive teaching. *Journal of Teacher Education.* Washington DC, 53(2), 106-116.

Goldenberg, C., & Coleman, R. (2010). *Promoting academic achievement among English learners: A guide to the research.* Thousand Oaks, CA: Corwin.

Gómez, R. (2006). Promising practices: Dual language enrichment for ELL students K-12. *TABE Journal*, 9(1), 46-63.

Hamayan, E., & Field, R. (2012). *English language learners at school: A guide for administrators.* Philadelphia: PA. Caslon Publishing.

Krashen, S. D. (1985). *The input hypothesis: Issues and implications* (Vol. 1, p. 985). London: Longman.

Krashen, S. D., & Terrell, T. D. (1983). *The natural approach: Language acquisition in the classroom.* San Francisco: CA. The Alemany Press.

Krashen, S. (2011). *Free voluntary reading.* Santa Barbara: Libraries Unlimited, ABC-CLIO, LLC.

Lara, M. (2011). *Siete pasos para crear un aula interactiva y rica en lenguaje: Estrategias para un aprendizaje significativo en aulas bilingües.* San Clemente: CA. Canter Press.

Ong, F. (Ed.), (2010). *Improving education for English learners: Research-based approaches.* Sacramento: California Department of Education.

Saunders, W., Goldenberg, C., & Marcelletti, D. (2013). English language development: Guidelines for instruction. *American Educator,* Summer 2013.

Saunders, W., Goldenberg, C., & Marcelletti, D. (2013). English language development: Guidelines for instruction. *American Educator,* Summer 2013.

Seidlitz, J., & Castillo, M. (2010). *Language & literacy for ELLs: Creating systematic change for academic achievement.* San Clemente: CA. Canter Press.

Seidlitz, J., & Jones, C. (2010). *RtI for ELLs: Considerations for success with diverse learners.* Second Edition. San Clemente: CA. Canter Press.

Seidlitz, J., & Kenfield, K. (2011) *38 great academic language builders.* San Clemente: CA. Canter Press.

Seidlitz, J., & Perryman, B. (2011). *Seven steps to a language-rich interactive classroom.* San Clemente: CA. Canter Press.

Seidlitz, J. (2010). *ELPS flip book: A user-friendly guide for academic language instruction.* San Clemente: CA. Canter Press.

Seidlitz, J. (2008a). *Navigating the ELPS: Using the new standards to improve instruction for English learners.* San Clemente: CA. Canter Press.

Seidlitz, J. (2008b). *Sheltered Instruction Plus: A comprehensive plan for successfully teaching English language learners.* San Clemente: CA. Canter Press.

Secretaría de Educación Pública (2008). *El enfoque intercultural en educación: Orientación para maestros de primaria.* Coordinación General de Educación Intercultural y Bilingüe. Secretaría de Educación Pública. México, D.F.

Short, D., & Echevarria, J. (1999). *The Sheltered Instruction Observation Protocol: A tool for teacher-researcher collaboration and professional development.* UC Berkeley: CA. Center for Research on Education, Diversity and Excellence.

Thomas, W. P. & Collier, V. P. (2012). *Dual language education for a transformed world.* Albuquerque, NM: Fuente Press.

Walqui, A., & Van Lier, L. (2010). *Scaffolding the academic success of adolescent English language learners.* San Francisco, CA: WestEd.

Wright, W. (2010). *Foundations for teaching English language learners: Research, theory, policy, and practice.* Philadelphia, PA. Caslon Publishing.

JOHN SEIDLITZ ★

John Seidlitz is an Independent Educational Consultant and the author of *Sheltered Instruction Plus: A Guide for Texas Teachers of English Learners, Seven Steps to a Language-Rich Interactive Classroom, Navigating the ELPS: Using the New Standards to Improve Instruction for English Learners,* and a contributing author for *The SIOP® Model for Teaching History-Social Studies for English Learners.*

He taught social studies and ESL in Floresville, Texas where he served as a secondary ESL program coordinator. Because of his interest in working with teachers, he decided to work at the regional level and became a social studies and ELL Specialist at ESC, Region 20 in San Antonio, Texas. He served 51 districts and 13 charter schools in implementing research-based approaches to working with ELLs.

In 2002, he left ESC, Region 20 to become a member of the SIOP National Faculty where he had the opportunity to work with teachers throughout the country implementing a researched-based model for instructing ELLs.

In 2007, the state of Texas published the English Language Proficiency Standards (ELPS) as part of the Texas Essential Knowledge and Skills (TEKS). The standards required that teachers in all content areas implement linguistically accommodated instruction for ELLs. Mr. Seidlitz collaborated with the Texas Education Agency to create ELPS Academies (trainer of trainers) for Texas' 20 regional service centers.

In 2008, he co-developed the *Seven Steps to Developing a Language-Rich Interactive Classroom*™ instructional delivery model. In 2011, this delivery model became an essential component of the Institute for Teachers of English Language Learners (ITELL) project, an institute for teachers of ELLs developed by Arizona State University through a Department of Education research grant.

In 2012, he began to work with refugee populations throughout the country and co-authored *The Texas Refugee Framework: A Collaborative Approach* with Feyi Obamehinti in 2013. The framework outlines specific approaches districts can use when meeting the needs of their refugee students.

Mr. Seidlitz founded Seidlitz Education, which is dedicated to the mission of G*iving Kids the Gift of Academic Language*™.

MELINDA BASE ★

Melinda Base's work as an educator has as its foundation a deep love for teaching, a desire to nurture developing educators, a desire to support district and campus leaders in their work, and a commitment to serve ELLs throughout the state of Texas.

Her first teaching position, as an English as a Second Language (ESL) and Reading teacher in Alamo Heights ISD in San Antonio, introduced her to working with ELLs. During her thirteen-year tenure with AHISD, she earned a M.A. in Reading Education and began doctoral coursework in School Improvement at Texas State University-San Marcos. As part of her studies, Melinda was a co-author on articles related to educational administration in Mexico and the US, and spiritual leadership. During her doctoral studies, she served on faculty at Texas State University in the Department of Curriculum and Instruction.

Melinda then moved to San Marcos High School to serve as the Newcomer Academy teacher. While at SMHS, Melinda was honored as Teacher of the Year. She then moved into an administrative position with Del Valle ISD. She served as a campus Instructional Facilitator, campus Instructional Administrator, and district Language Coordinator.

Melinda's K-16 experience supported her transition into her work as a Bilingual/ESL Education Specialist at Education Service Center, Region 13. Her areas of expertise included accountability, assessment, and compliance in second language programs. She was also a successful presenter both at the center facility and in districts across central Texas.

In addition, Melinda served on the TEA committee for the annually published *List of Approved Tests for Assessment of Limited English Proficient Students.* She also provided required state trainings for many educators in central Texas, including the LPAC, TELPAS, and ELPS Academies.

Summer 2013 marked a significant transition for Melinda as she retired from ESC, Region 13. She moved from Texas to Washington State and has founded Halcyon Stone, LLC – an education consultancy. She also contracts with Seidlitz Education to author and produce books and resources to support teachers and leaders of ELL programs.

MÓNICA LARA ★

Dr. Mónica Lara's enthusiastic approach to teaching and learning in English and Spanish is the trademark of her over 20 years in education. She is an experienced teacher, bilingual reading specialist, assistant principal, and educational specialist in the areas of dyslexia and bilingual/ESL education at ESC, Region 20 in San Antonio, TX. Dr. Lara's biliterate and bicultural belief system is engaging, invigorating, and refreshing when she delivers her signature message: Enseñanza para todos (teaching for all). Dr. Lara holds a Bachelor's degree in elementary and secondary education, a Master of Arts degree in reading, and a Ph.D. in Culture, Literacy, and Language – a testament to her commitment to and belief in teaching English language learners. Her research interests include early reading assessment and biliteracy education. She is an author and co-author to many publications. Currently, she serves as a reviewer for The Southwest Teaching and Learning Journal. Dr. Lara is a Language and Literacy Consultant with Seidlitz Education.

MARIELA A. RODRÍGUEZ ★

Dr. Mariela A. Rodríguez is an Associate Professor in the Department of Educational Leadership and Policy Studies at the University of Texas at San Antonio. She was raised in Brownsville, TX where she was an elementary bilingual educator. Mariela received her Ph.D. in 2003 from New Mexico State University in Educational Administration where she was a W.K. Kellogg Doctoral Fellow.

Her scholarly research focuses on the role of school principals supporting English Language Learners in dual language education programs. Her work has been published in the *International Journal of Leadership and Education*, and the *Journal of Latinos and Education*. Mariela currently serves as a mentor for a local elementary school that belongs to the Roche Center's Two-Way Immersion Network for Catholic Schools. She is also a member of the Executive Committee of the University Council for Educational Administration, a national consortium of higher education institutions committed to advancing the preparation and practice of school leaders to benefit schools and children.